LOOKING BACK, MOVING F

Transformation and Ethical Practice in
the Ghanaian Church of Pentecost

How do Ghanaian Pentecostals resolve the contradictions of their own
faith while remaining faithful to their religious identity? Bringing together the anthropology of Christianity and the anthropology of ethics,
Girish Daswani's *Looking Back, Moving Forward* investigates the compromises with the past that members of Ghana's Church of Pentecost
make in order to remain committed Christians.

Even as church members embrace the break with the past that comes
from being "born-again," many are less concerned with the boundaries
of Christian practice than with interpersonal questions – the continuity
of suffering after conversion, the causes of unhealthy relationships, the
changes brought about by migration – and how to deal with them. By
paying ethnographic attention to the embodied practices, interpersonal
relationships, and moments of self-reflection in the lives of members of
the Church of Pentecost in Ghana and among the Ghanaian diaspora in
London, *Looking Back, Moving Forward* explores ethical practice as it
emerges out of the questions that church members and other Ghanaian
Pentecostals ask themselves.

(Anthropological Horizons)

GIRISH DASWANI is an associate professor in the Department of
Anthropology at the University of Toronto.

Anthropological Horizons

Editor: Michael Lambek, University of Toronto

This series, begun in 1991, focuses on theoretically informed ethnographic works addressing issues of mind and body, knowledge and power, equality and inequality, the individual and the collective. Interdisciplinary in its perspective, the series makes a unique contribution in several other academic disciplines: women's studies, history, philosophy, psychology, political science, and sociology.

For a list of the books published in this series, see pages 257–9.

Looking Back, Moving Forward

Transformation and Ethical Practice in the Ghanaian Church of Pentecost

GIRISH DASWANI

UNIVERSITY OF TORONTO PRESS
Toronto Buffalo London

University of Toronto Press 2015
Toronto Buffalo London
www.utppublishing.com
Printed in the U.S.A.

ISBN 978-1-4426-4916-3 (cloth)
ISBN 978-1-4426-2658-4 (paper)

Library and Archives Canada Cataloguing in Publication

Daswani, Girish, author
Looking back, moving forward : tranformation and ethical practice in the Ghanaian
Church of Pentecost / Girish Daswani.

(Anthropological horizons)
Includes bibliographical references and index.
ISBN 978-1-4426-4916-3 (bound). – ISBN 978-1-4426-2658-4 (pbk.)

1. Church of Pentecost.   2. Church of Pentecost – Membership.   3. Pentecostal converts –
Ghana.   4. Pentecostal converts – England – London.   5. Religion and ethics.   I. Title.
II. Series: Anthropological horizons

BX8762.A45G44 2015   289.9'409667   C2014-907220-1

This book has been published with the help of a grant from the Federation for
the Humanities and Social Sciences, through the Awards to Scholarly Publications
Program, using funds provided by the Social Sciences and Humanities Research
Council of Canada.

University of Toronto Press acknowledges the financial assistance to its publishing
program of the Canada Council for the Arts and the Ontario Arts Council, an agency
of the Government of Ontario.

 Canada Council   Conseil des Arts
for the Arts   du Canada

 ONTARIO ARTS COUNCIL
CONSEIL DES ARTS DE L'ONTARIO
an Ontario government agency
un organisme du gouvernement de l'Ontario

University of Toronto Press acknowledges the financial support of the Government
of Canada through the Canada Book Fund for its publishing activities.

This book is dedicated to the memory of my grandfather,
Vassiamal Daswani (aka Victor Baboo) of Kumasi, Ghana.

Baabi a yëfa ko na yëfa ba

The place we pass through in going, we pass through in returning.

Akan proverb

Contents

Figures

Acknowledgments

I want to thank the serendipitous convergences that led to this book's eventual fruition. It started in 1999, when my father, who lives in Australia, called me in Singapore to ask me to join him on a trip to Ghana. He wanted to visit his family, from whom he had been estranged for many years. That journey affected both our lives, and was the beginning of my ongoing fascination and love for the country where I came to locate my research and to which I still return. The following year, I started my graduate studies in social anthropology at the London School of Economics and Political Science (LSE). The time I spent there helped shape the ways in which I value the significance of ethnography as a wonderful tool to explore the diversity of the human condition. It is also where I developed an appreciation of ethnography's contribution to social scientific theory, not as its mere accessory or as a single story colonized by Western theory, but rather as a method rooted in grounded theory that allows us to substantiate ideas and stories located in actions and cultures. Initially I was torn between different research projects but once I had decided on Ghanaian Pentecostalism, The Church of Pentecost (CoP) presented itself, and, since 2002, has provided me with a rich site of research both in Ghana and in London. Its leaders and members warmly welcomed me into the church and allowed me to fully participate in its activities. My journey of exploring the significance of ethnographic theory and its engagement with my research did not end with the completion of my doctorate in 2007, but continued to develop with my interactions with students and colleagues at the University of Toronto, where I have worked since. I wish to express my gratitude to the many interlocutors, teachers, colleagues, and friends who have helped me along the way.

The LSE was my intellectual home for several years and a source of inspiration as well as a training ground of academic vigour. To my peers, teachers, and supervisors, thank you for providing me with knowledge and guidance, encouragement and friendship, and sometimes a place to rest my head, during the best and the worst of times. This appreciation specifically includes my doctorate supervisors, Matthew Engelke and Henrietta Moore. To my friends – you know who you are: you made my life in London so much more rich and alive.

In London, CoP UK missionary Apostle N.A. Ofoe-Amegatcher was central to providing my initial entry into the church, and his letter of introduction helped to open many doors and arms in CoP Ghana. Other CoP leaders in Ghana, who generously shared with me their time as well as gave me access to church documents and library resources, included Apostle Alfred Koduah, Apostle Michael Ntumy, and Apostle Opoku Onyinah, among others. My sincere gratitude also goes to the pastors and members of the Pentecost International Worship Centres in London, Accra, and Kumasi, many of whom allowed me into their lives for a short but significant period of time. Other church members include the prophets I met in Ghana and those who worshipped in the Dansoman area of Accra, who provided a welcoming space for me to spend many weekday afternoons and evenings. I am also grateful to the Religious Studies Department at the University of Ghana, Legon, for allowing me to use their departmental library and for the kind assistance and friendship of Reverend Dr. Cephas Omenyo. To all of you: *Meda wase paa. Onyame nhyira wo.*

The vibrant environment at the University of Toronto (UofT) has also contributed significantly to my work's continuing development and deserves credit for positively shaping the intellectual ideas within this book. More specifically, I want to thank my colleagues and the administrative staff from the UofT Scarborough and the UofT St. George graduate Department of Anthropology, as well as those from the Department for the Study of Religion and the Centre for Diaspora and Transnational Studies. They have provided a supportive community where wonderful conversations are shared and through which ideas are freely exchanged. I am also grateful to my students, past and present, for being positive forces in my own thinking and sharing with me their vivacious curiosity and passion for learning. Awards from the UofT Scarborough and the Jackman Humanities Institute at UofT have provided me with several opportunities to return to Ghana between 2008 and 2013.

I also wish to thank several people for having read, commented upon, and helped me with the technical aspects of my work: Francis Cody, Simon Coleman, Maggie Cummings, Florent Giehmann, Frederick Klaits, Lena Mortensen, Sangeeta Mulchand, Valentina Napolitano, Alejandro Paz, Peter Williams, and Carolyn Zapf. My appreciation also extends to Sandra Bamford and Ato Quayson, who have encouraged and supported me in Toronto. The same goes for Michael Lambek, whose scholarship has provided me with intellectual nourishment, and whose influence on my work is evident throughout this book. His ability to convey the highest standards of excellence, not only on an academic but also on a human level, is a continuing source of inspiration to me. Another person I am indebted to is Naisargi Dave, who carefully read the entire manuscript and whose insightful questions inspired me to reconsider some earlier aspects of my argument. Joel Robbins has been a significant intellectual interlocutor, but more importantly, he very generously read an earlier draft of my manuscript and provided me with comments that served to improve its overall structure. Richard Werbner gave me wonderful advice and has been a source of intellectual support. My gratitude goes to the two reviewers of my manuscript, as well as to Doug Hildebrand, for his understanding, patience, and support throughout the process of turning my manuscript into a book. Parts of Chapter Two were previously published in 2013 as "On Christianity and Ethics: Rupture as Ethical Practice in Ghanaian Pentecostalism," *American Ethnologist* 40 (3): 467–79, and a portion of Chapter Three appeared in 2010 as "Ghanaian Pentecostal Prophets: Travel and (Im)-Mobility," in *Traveling Spirits: Migrants, Markets, and Moralities*, edited by Kristine Krausse and Gertrud Huewelmeier (Routledge Press). Portions of Chapter Four appeared in 2011 as "(In-)Dividual Pentecostals in Ghana," *Journal of Religion in Africa* 41 (3): 256–79, while part of Chapter Five appeared in 2010 as "Transformation and Migration among Members of a Pentecostal Church in Ghana and London," *Journal of Religion in Africa* 40 (4): 424–74.

To my families in their varied forms, extensions, and locations: you have been pillars of strength during the book's completion. When in Ghana, members of my family provided me with a place of solitude and refuge. I thank them for the conversations and laughter that made me feel more at home in Ghana. My family in Singapore has also been a great source of support, and my mother's continued love and encouragement has always been important in dispelling any doubts I may have had along the way. To my father, who led me to Ghana, and to my family in Australia: I will always look forward to the fufu times and to dancing Azonto with masks on. My family in Quebec has helped me to celebrate every small accomplishment and to enjoy the long winters in Canada: *Je vous remercie pour votre amour et votre soutien*. Finally, to Katherine Blouin who has read this book with care and patience several times over and who continues to be an endless source of love and encouragement: *Tu es mon rocher*.

Abbreviations

ATR	African Traditional Religion
CAC	Christ Apostolic Church
CoP	The Church of Pentecost
CPP	Convention People's Party
C&S	Cherubim and Seraphin
NDC	National Democratic Congress
NLC	National Liberation Council
NPP	National Patriotic Party
PENSA	Pentecostal Students Association
PIWC	Pentecost International Worship Centre
PNDC	Provisional National Defence Council
PWM	Prayer Warriors Ministry
SU	Scripture Union
UCCF	Universities and Colleges Christian Fellowship

LOOKING BACK, MOVING FORWARD

Transformation and Ethical Practice in
the Ghanaian Church of Pentecost

Introduction

It was a hot Wednesday afternoon in March 2004, in a suburb of Accra, Ghana's capital. The dry season, accompanied by the *harmattan*, a desert wind that blows in from the Sahara, was about to give way to the rainy season. Albert Successful, a young man in his early twenties, stood patiently in front of several rows of white plastic chairs neatly arranged under the shade of two mango trees. The chairs slowly filled with men and women arriving for that day's prayer service; they had come from different parts of Accra in search of relief from a host of personal problems to which Jesus was the solution. A banner bearing the words *Jesus Anaa Wontumi Taake* (You Cannot Compete with Jesus) was loosely stretched between two trees at the entrance to a dirt trail that led to this small opening in the bush. The meeting was not a regular church service but an informal prayer meeting led by a prophetess from The Church of Pentecost (CoP). According to Albert, the prophetess could see into the future as well as uncover the root of problems. As a dedicated churchgoer, Albert had been tasked with preparing the attendees by saying a few encouraging words before the arrival of the prophetess and the many hours of prayer that would follow.

On that day, Albert shared his thoughts about what Pentecostal transformation meant to him, the difficulties he faced, and the legacy he wanted to leave behind. Accepting Jesus as his Saviour had not only transformed him, he said, but had also saved his life. "Our God is larger than the local gods and will deliver us from our enemies," he told his audience. He explained how he had been the victim of witchcraft attacks and was excluded from a family inheritance. In order to escape these destructive relationships and in search of better opportunities, he had migrated to Accra from his village in the Brong-Ahafo region.

Figure 0.1 Banner at the entrance to the prayer centre. (Photo by the author.)

Being born again allowed him to make a break with his past. Albert also took the surname "Successful" after converting to Pentecostalism. This name reflected the promise of future success and prosperity that his new religious identity suggested. Yet, over time, he had come to realize that his non-Christian past continued to haunt his Christian life and that success was not as easily achieved as he had believed. Albert struggled with the social relations that continued to connect him to the world he was trying to leave behind and to those who held him back from achieving his dreams. "So how do I still live and carry on with such confidence?" he asked the prayer centre attendees as he reached the end of his sermon. "Because I know the God I am worshipping, and that my time is coming. A time is coming when the Lord you are serving will arise and come to your door. Christianity in Ghana is not a religion. It is about relationships. Don't expect God to come down from heaven. He will touch someone's heart to help you in your need."

Figure 0.2 Albert preaching. (Photo by the author.)

I first met Albert at a small CoP assembly in Dansoman, one of Accra's many growing suburbs. An involved and integral member of CoP, he spent most of his days praying alongside his fellow converts and assisting them in prayer. Albert eventually became one of my main interlocutors in Ghana; he was instrumental in introducing me to other key members of the community, as well as to the diversity of Pentecostalism in the country. Over the course of my research, we would spend many hours chatting on long *tro-tro* (minivan) journeys around Accra to prayer services such as the one just described, in local *chop bars* (restaurants), and on the front porch of my house after church services. A recurring theme in our conversations was relationships. Through his relationships with Jesus, Pentecostal pastors, church members, and prophets, Albert came to see CoP as his spiritual home and acquired a new confidence to bravely face the difficulties that he associated with an increasingly precarious economy, witchcraft, and traditional authority. Another theme

was his absolute conviction that his conversion would bring about a
brighter future. In one of our first conversations, Albert shared with me
the prophecies that confirmed his ambitions of success and future travel
outside of Ghana. A CoP prophetess had told him that he would become
a famous evangelist and travel abroad. "Until I fulfil that destiny, until I
fulfil that purpose, I cannot die or be killed. Not until God's purpose for
my life is fulfilled," he told me.

This book examines the shared expectations and concomitant limitations of Pentecostal Christianity in Ghana and among the Ghanaian diaspora in London. If Christianity in Ghana is about relationships and
having confidence in the future-to-come, as Albert suggested, the question of "how to carry on as Christians" simultaneously pervades the
lives of converts in Ghana and abroad. My interlocutors were also assessing and critiquing how the past comes into play in Pentecostal
Christianity, as well as how they relate to each other, to the Holy Spirit,
to other spirits, and to their changing socio-economic environment.
They were evaluating their responses and responsibilities to these human and divine others. By looking at the tensions inherent in Pentecostal transformation and the uncertainties of a Christian life, this book
provides an ethnographic understanding of the different ways in which
religious transformation and continuity converge in the lives of my
Ghanaian Pentecostal interlocutors.

During my fieldwork with CoP in Ghana and London between 2002
and 2004, I came to realize that my interlocutors shared ethical concerns
regarding what Pentecostal transformation should look like and how it
could be achieved in their own lives and in the lives of others. These
concerns materialized as questions, which varied from "what" ("What
are the acceptable forms of Christian practice?") to "why" ("Why do we
continue to suffer from witchcraft and attacks from spirits?") and
"how" ("How do we lead good Christian lives in a changing cultural
environment?" and "How do we maintain a personal relationship with
Jesus alongside our responsibilities to others?"). While prayer services
such as the one I described earlier were popular in that they allowed
Ghanaians to regain control over a host of current problems, these services were also potentially controversial for CoP leaders and other
members of the church. They raised questions and doubts concerning
the finality of conversion and how Pentecostal change should be expressed and embodied once a convert was born again.

Drawing on the complexities of such questions, this book examines
the intersections of religious change and continuity, and shows how

they exist as ethical problems for my Ghanaian Pentecostal interlocutors in CoP. For Albert, as for many others in CoP, religious change is accompanied by the question "How do I carry on with confidence?" As I shall propose, this question reveals the ways in which Pentecostal transformation, often viewed as a rupture from a non-Christian past, is also seen as a "problem of continuity" that various groups within the church try to resolve differently. The ethical tensions that church members routinely face in the resolution of such problems often unfold in the space created between the contradictory assertions of the church leaders and the work of the prophets. The diverse ways in which the prosperity gospel of health and wealth is adopted in CoP and in other churches is another source of tension. Prophets, like prosperity preachers, often draw the line between acceptable and unacceptable continuities in social life and religious practice in a different place than do the church leaders, setting up a field of tension that church members find themselves traversing. Church members face another set of contradictions when they migrate to London, where, in addition to being evangelists whose duty it is to spread the Gospel, they are migrants who have to negotiate an unfamiliar society and work economy.

These multiple tensions, and the attempts to resolve them, provide opportunities for reflection on the different relationships that church members value and on the central role played by ethical practice in negotiating their Pentecostal identity. I argue that Pentecostal transformation as ethical practice involves three interconnected issues: (1) processes of church discipline and regularization aimed at maintaining continuity with a Christian future; (2) moments of uncertainty and indeterminacy, which destabilize and question the conventional parameters of what is acceptable in the present; and (3) acts of philosophical labour and critical reflection whose goals are either to alleviate moral ambiguities or to create innovative positions around which new norms eventually develop (Moore 1975; Dave 2012).

In furthering my argument, I draw on a combination of epistemological tools stemming from the anthropology of Christianity and the anthropology of ethics. Such an approach allows me to reach a renewed understanding of the processes whereby Ghanaian Pentecostals resolve the contradictions within the personal interruptions and interpretations of their own faith regarding what constitutes good or right religious observance, while remaining faithful to their religious identity. I suggest that approaching Pentecostal transformation as ethical practice allows for a better understanding of the religious subject's response to an incommensurability of values and practices internal to Pentecostalism. As I go on to describe, my research experience, as well as the recent anthropological literature on Christianity and ethics, has played an important role in shaping 'my analysis of Pentecostal transformation as ethical practice.

Unfolding a Question

Landing on the shores of my field site in London in 2002 was a process of negotiation. Indeed, my explicit research intentions were complicated by implicit circumstances. I had initially planned to study the religious lives of the Ghanaian diaspora in London, but I found it difficult to locate a potentially welcoming communal space where Ghanaians met regularly. Realizing that churches play a prominent role in the social lives of Ghanaian migrants in London, I attended the meetings of different Ghanaian Christian associations. While still deciding on where to locate my research, I met a CoP member who introduced me to his church. The church had just acquired an abandoned cinema hall in Dagenham, east London, and was presented to me as the fastest growing church in Ghana, with a significant number of its members living in London. I eventually shifted my attention to CoP and conducted my London-based fieldwork in the Pentecost International Worship Centre (PIWC), which is also located at the headquarters of the church in the United Kingdom.

I was warmly welcomed and introduced to others as a research student and potential convert. It did not take long before I was an active participant in weekend church services, Friday prayer meetings, Bible study classes, men's group meetings, youth group meetings, and other social activities that the church organized. While a small group of church members came from the Caribbean or other African countries, southern Ghanaians made up the sizeable majority of the church's membership. PIWC services were in English, but informal conversations shifted easily between Twi and English. Most of my interlocutors held several part-time jobs, alongside family obligations or participation in diploma and degree courses. My initial study of the community thus focused on the intersections of their spiritual and material worlds, and treated their religious identity as central to how they negotiated their busy schedules and the everyday realities of their lives as migrants.

Early on in my fieldwork, however, I realized that I could not claim to understand what a Pentecostal identity meant for church members unless I spent time in Ghana. After carrying out research for several months in London, I travelled to Ghana in May 2003, where I spent a year with CoP. My research in Accra and Kumasi, Ghana's two largest cities, revealed to me the diversity of Pentecostal Christianity and alerted me to the differences within CoP that were not so apparent in London – differences in the ways that its church leaders, prophets, and ordinary members interpreted Pentecostalism. With its headquarters in Accra, Ghana, CoP provided diverse social locations where church members actively engaged with the history of ideas surrounding the Christian church and its beliefs. It provided a stable social form through which individuals and groups experienced Pentecostal knowledge and reflected on their opinions and expectations regarding personal and social transformation.

In Ghana, I quickly realized that Pentecostalism is not simply an individual message of salvation separate from the secular work economy and people's worldly ambitions. Its message, images, sounds, and practices can be perceived in its members' day-to-day activities, actively mediating between their marginal economic positions and their aspirations for a better life. Amidst daily economic activities, a cacophony of Pentecostal songs of worship and voices of prayer can be heard through church amplifiers and car stereos, spilling out onto the streets and enveloping the cityscape, filling the work day with the inescapable sounds of Christian gospel music and its themes of salvation, hope, and liberation from suffering. Signboards, posters, and banners line busy roads, advertising Pentecostal prayer events and prophetic services that promise solutions to problems and a transformation from a "nobody" into a "somebody."

My return from Ghana to London in 2004 coincided with a growing anthropological literature on Christianity. In just over a decade, much has been written about the anthropology of Christianity, including an ongoing discussion concerning the Christian ghosts of anthropological writing.[1] This literature helped reveal that the foundations of anthropological thought have been inhabited by a Christian philosophy and showed that anthropologists and their methods were sometimes influenced by their Judeo-Christian background. As I became better acquainted with these works, I came to realize that my own upbringing has helped me to understand this literature differently. While I do not believe there is such a thing as a "secular reality," I also did not grow up in the Christian "West." Instead, my early education in Singapore, from the mid-1970s through the late 1990s, put me in contact with diverse groups of people with varying

Figure 0.3 Map of Ghana. (Courtesy of Peter Williams.)

religious backgrounds, including Muslim, Hindu, Taoist, Buddhist, and Christian. It provided me with some insight into the heterogeneous nature of what many consider "God" (or "not God"). I have visited astrologers and diverse sites of religious worship with my mother, searched for ghosts in abandoned buildings with schoolmates, and listened to friends and family tell stories of having been possessed by, or having seen, spirits and other unearthly creatures. While serving in the Singapore army as part of my national service, I was instructed, along with other recruits, not to urinate under trees or disturb graves when training at night without first acknowledging the spirits that possibly inhabited these spaces, in case they became annoyed and returned to the camp with us. Such personal experiences led me to firmly believe that one does not have to experience the supernatural in order for it to become part of one's life and to have an influence in ways that others might call superstitious.

I took this same openness to the force of the invisible in shaping people's lives through stories and life experiences into my research on Ghanaian Pentecostals. While I am not a Christian myself, I cannot deny that there were times during my research when I shared experiences that my interlocutors would call the "Holy Spirit." These experiences, and the ones that my interlocutors shared with me, should not be considered as manifestations of false consciousness. This view would be unhealthy scepticism, unproductive to any research on religious-like phenomenon. Also, while a comparative framework for studying Christianity is helpful, comparing expressions of Christianity with other religious and non-religious frameworks is equally important. Maintaining a healthy scepticism has helped me to see Christianity not simply as a cultural other, separate from other religious forms, but also as a distinct way of expressing the inexpressible in one's life. Christianity simultaneously brings decisions, doubts, and dilemmas into the lives of the same believers who are trying to make sense of what is happening around them and who wrestle with questions such as "What happens next?" and "How should we live as Pentecostals?"

A burgeoning anthropology of Christianity provided the conceptual tools that led me to identify rupture as central to the lives of the people I worked with. Through accepting that they are sinners and that Jesus died to save them from their sins, Pentecostals emphasize a radical break with the past (Meyer 1998b; Robbins 2007b).[2] This focus on discontinuity is important to how Pentecostals reconsider cultural practices constituting persons, places, and community. Yet rupture is only part of a larger process of change and acquired intimacy associated with Pentecostal conversion. For example, my interlocutors often used the word "transformation" when speaking about their experience of conversion. Transformation was indicative of more than just a discontinuity from a non-Christian past and the undoing of traditional moralities. It simultaneously invoked a new, intimate sociality through which the convert identifies with God and the church. A conversation I had with a church member helps illustrates this dual purpose of transformation.

After an Easter Sunday service, which had been preceded by several days of fasting and prayer, a church member in Ghana described his conversion experience to me. He described it as an encounter with God that changed his life completely. He began by telling me about his school years, during which he had to study "religious knowledge."

> We were taught certain things to recite, to pray at certain times, taught the Bible. But unfortunately this did not lead me to Christ. This was just informative knowledge of the Lord. There was no intimacy, just a teaching about God that did not change my life.

He then went on to describe a special moment, when he spontaneously went into a trance.

> I felt myself going up to Heaven … [I]t was a very beautiful place filled with light. Three times I tried to enter, but could not and fell back down to earth. After the third time, I woke up in bed crying real tears. It was on that same day that I walked to The Church of Pentecost and accepted Christ without anyone preaching to me. There was a total transformation in my life. I started fellowshipping with the church … [T]he places I used to go, I couldn't because of the relationship, the love, the caring, the sharing. That brought me closer to the people of God. So I remained with them and gradually was also growing in the things of the Lord … This transformation I am talking about has to do with my mind. The way I used to think, the way my perceptions and conceptions were, were totally changed. I came to realize that God is real. I came to realize that God controls my life … I want to conform to that will which God has for my life.

This conversion narrative importantly addresses an altering of consciousness, and shows how the mind and body converge in Pentecostal transformation. For this church member, religious conformity is also personal freedom: freedom to be different, to live differently. Becoming part of a Christian community is important, and is not simply obligatory but also desirable. The authority in his words came not from himself but from the God of the Bible. Here, "belief" and "disbelief" appear to be questions for the unbeliever, but not for the believer who comes to realize that God is real (Pouillon 1982). The same person told me, "After my transformation experience, I became God's hands and feet." This erasure of the line between absence and presence shifts the attention from what belief "is" to what it "does." His testimony highlights how his transformation from information about God to intimacy with God filled an existing gap and simultaneously invoked the "new" in his life.

A key question for this book is not whether transformation is central to understanding Pentecostalism in Ghana, but how Pentecostals experience and describe their transformation through their relationships with others, both human and non-human. Over time, I realized that Pentecostal transformation presented a new problem in the lives of believers, partly caused by the expectation that life is supposed to be better after conversion ("how things ought to be") coming into conflict with the often shared experience that life is not always better ("how things are"). As a result, church members had conflicting visions about how transformation should be applied in practice. They struggled with questions regarding their Christian future and how to make sense of change while maintaining continuity in their lives. As determined in their terms, Pentecostal transformation is an ethical practice that creates a commitment to specific disciplinary practices and standards concerning how a virtuous and prosperous life ought to be achieved, while simultaneously presenting new dilemmas and questions.

My central research question thus became "When does Christianity become a question that needs a resolution?" An anthropology of ethics helped provide a framework for understanding how Pentecostal transformation is ethically situated, bound by the criteria for what is promised and acceptable after conversion, but also necessarily unpredictable and inconsistent due to the presence of others, including the Holy Spirit, ancestral spirits, witches, and Ghanaian and British culture. With this new question, I was able to explore the relational quality of ethical practice, which foregrounds the multiple ways in which CoP actors evaluate Pentecostal transformation. I was also able to investigate the questions these actors ask themselves concerning which aspects of the past have to be left behind and which carried forward, and to examine the compromises that have to be made in order for them to remain committed.

These questions and the attempts at their resolution provide opportunities for reflecting on traditional culture and old and new Pentecostal practices. They also highlight the different sets of relationships that church leaders and members value and the central role played by these valued relationships in their Pentecostal identity. In order to understand where these tensions arise from, it is useful to examine CoP within the larger context of the rise of Pentecostalism in Ghana.

The Church of Pentecost (CoP)

Whenever I told other Ghanaians that I was doing my research on CoP, three pieces of information would typically be shared with me. I was told that CoP was one of the oldest and most established Pentecostal churches in Ghana, that the church knew how to pray, and that it was very strict and focused on church discipline. These characteristics were commonly used to distinguish CoP from the hundreds of other Pentecostal and charismatic churches in Ghana. Although Ghanaians more often than not label themselves as simply "Christian," there are several recognizably different types of Christians in the country.[3] These include historic churches, African independent churches, classical Pentecostal churches, neo-evangelical churches, and neo-Pentecostal/charismatic churches (Omenyo 2002, 34). While CoP is usually assigned to the category of classical Pentecostal churches, its popularity comes from its ability to selectively incorporate aspects of the different Christian movements. The church is therefore well situated in the conversation concerning "What has changed?" and "How do we deal with religious change?" in Ghana.

Differentiation between types of Pentecostalism has gained importance since the 1980s, when this religious movement exploded onto Ghana's religious scene. It arrived precisely at a time when failed structural adjustment programs and economic reforms left little hope for the future. By the 1990s, Ghana's turn to neoliberalism had led to unfettered foreign investment and the shrinkage of state services (Rothchild 1991). Development projects and political promises that brought specific expectations of economic growth but failed to improve the majority of people's lives helped produce a crisis of legitimacy (Aryeetey, Harrigan, and Nissanke 2000), expressed through a growing informality in the political economy as well as an increasing public obsession with the occult or supernatural. The fragility of institutional structures that provide social continuity and hope has allowed Pentecostal churches to play an important role in the exercise of "governance without government" (Hardt and Negri 2001, 14). The rising popularity of Pentecostal Christianity in Ghana also overlapped with Ghana's turn to democracy in 1992, the appearance of a more recent wave of Pentecostalism known as charismatic Christianity, as well as the proliferation of Christian television and radio shows, Christian books, and audio and video cassettes (Meyer 2004b). In what follows, I find it useful to distinguish "Pentecostal" from "charismatic." According to Rosalind Hackett, "the term 'pentecostal' refers to the older churches (dating from the 1930s and often of Western provenance), while 'charismatic' is applied to the newer (post 1970, referred to by some Western scholars as 'neo-pentecostal'), locally generated movements and ministries whose focus is healing, prosperity, and experience" (1998, 259; see also Synan 1997, 215–33). While CoP is commonly assigned to the category of classical Pentecostal churches, it also sees itself as a Protestant church and simultaneously shares certain similarities with the charismatic movement. It is also of no small significance that many leaders of the charismatic movement in Ghana were once members of CoP.

CoP is one of the oldest Pentecostal churches in Ghana, coming into existence through the missionary involvement of the British Apostolic Church in 1937.[4] It was known for the longest time as "McKeown's Church." James McKeown, the founder of CoP, was one of the first British Pentecostal missionaries to arrive in the Gold Coast. For McKeown, simply claiming a Christian identity or acquiring knowledge of salvation through missionary education and reading the Bible was not enough. He wanted the people of the Gold Coast to engage with Christianity in a more meaningful way, through "Jesus first." Pentecostal transformation had to be demonstrated by a personal relationship with Jesus that emphasized the role of the Holy Spirit in religious experiences.[5] The church has since become an independent global church, with eighty-eight branches located outside of Ghana and a worldwide membership of over two million (CoP 2008). It has grown from a religious movement with mainly poor and uneducated members into an international institution whose members include educated youth and a rising middle class of English-speaking Ghanaians. The specifics of CoP, especially its organizational structure, are particularly important in explaining why it has become so successful in Ghana and abroad. Unlike many charismatic churches located in urban areas, CoP has an effective rural base that serves as the first point of contact for Ghanaian converts before they migrate to urban city centres such as Kumasi and Accra. Another important contributing factor to CoP's success is its strong clerical and bureaucratic structure that controls the organization and operations of church officers, pastors, and prophets.

CoP has both a strongly hierarchical and a charismatically open structure. The church emphasizes the Four-Square Gospel: holiness, salvation in heaven, the gifts of the Holy Spirit such as speaking in tongues, prophecy, healing and deliverance, and a belief in Jesus, the sooncoming king. If the hierarchical structure of the church is tightly controlled, whereby church leaders work hard to enforce their own views about how matters of continuity and discontinuity should be handled, at the same time the church makes an official, structural place for prophets. Prophets battle with witchcraft and other spirits, are able to see into the future, and can help heal people from illnesses. Their prayers are effective in helping Ghanaians with more mundane problems, such as marriage and fertility, entrepreneurial opportunities, obtaining jobs and overseas visas, and realizing their ambition to travel overseas. Inspired by the Holy Spirit, prophets attract many new members to the church, but often act in ways that escape the church leaders' control.

Many Ghanaians often seek the help of prophets in times of personal suffering and illness, when they need direction in life and believe their destiny to be blocked by witchcraft or ancestral spirits. While the work of prophets is grudgingly accepted within the church, it is also vigorously contested. Prophets become a cause for concern, as they are reminiscent of a traditional African world view or a reminder of a modern charismatic presence in Ghanaian Pentecostalism. Church leaders as well as ordinary members raise questions about where to draw the line between "good" and "bad" or "true" and "false" practices. Church leaders worry that prophets and charismatic teachings sometimes mislead "naive" converts into believing that ancestral spirits and witchcraft continue to possess the lives of believers once they are born again. They also worry that too much emphasis and dependence on prophets distract converts from achieving a personal relationship with Jesus and his second coming, wherein charismatic authority becomes a form of re-enchantment or fetishization of the world. As a result, the actions and prayer performances of prophets are subject to the scrutiny of church leaders, who actively debate whether prophets are following biblical principles and whether they obtain their spiritual power from the Holy Spirit (*Sunsum Kronkron*) or from a traditional spirit (*Sunsum Abosom*). These debates and conflicts deal with the felicity conditions surrounding the maintenance of a shared Pentecostal faith and not with the sanctity of the born-again experience.

The church also takes a strong theological stance against the more worldly prosperity gospel churches that are currently hugely popular in many parts of the world, including Ghana. These charismatic churches, also known as Ghana's "new Christianity," emphasize the promise of health, wealth, and prosperity, and claim that demons and ancestral curses continue to affect believers' lives even after they have come to Christ (Gifford 2004).[6] Charismatic churches preach and promote what is commonly known as the prosperity gospel. It stresses that an individual achieves success and prosperity ("health and wealth") once he or she is born again and accepts Jesus as his or her Lord and Saviour (Coleman 2000, 2011b; Gifford 2004). Accordingly, once born again, Christians are free from the sins of poverty and sickness. All they need to do is simply "name and claim" the "health and wealth" that is rightfully theirs. Seen to be responding to new soteriological needs created by the advance of capitalism in Ghana, the expansive presence of these charismatic churches is cause for worry for CoP leaders and other mainline Christian churches. If the Protestant-Calvinist spirit helped put in place the underlying set of values that led to the modern capitalistic work ethic in the Western world (Weber 1958), the recent capitalism of the Protestant-Pentecostal spirit in Ghana is seen to be promoting a set of neoliberal values that poses a threat to CoP's Pentecostal tradition.

Church leaders are concerned that certain distinctions – which CoP holds to be important – between what are acceptable and unacceptable Christian practices are in danger of being eroded. They worry that the charismatic churches promote a message of salvation that neglects the importance of certain Christian virtues such as patience and holiness, focusing instead on individual aggrandizement and the promise of immediate returns; that conversion is becoming merely an instrumental response to the personal desires of Christians; and that Ghanaians are turning to Pentecostalism simply for the promise of financial success and the expectation of miracles. They also fear that the charismatic churches place undue focus on the continuing presence and power of traditional and ancestral spirits in the lives of the converted. For CoP leaders, Christian salvation is complete and a convert is fully transformed once he or she is born again. While CoP leaders share the belief that witchcraft and ancestral spirits do exist, they are also convinced that once a convert is committed to Jesus Christ and baptized in the Holy Spirit, the traditional past and the spirits of the past no longer have a hold over him or her.

In engaging with premises and arguments for understanding personal and social change, CoP leaders today are concerned with, and critical of, matters that involve the changing public sphere, globalization, and cultural change. They strive to maintain and manage the boundaries of religious change, educating church members on how to perceive Pentecostal conversion as real change rather than as an addition to past cultural formations. They focus their attention on the cultivation of a virtuous Christian subject through an education of specific disciplinary practices that emphasizes holiness, patience, and submission to church authority. Through the transmission of radio and television programs, public sermons, the publication of religious books, and the exercise of institutional authority, they provide moral guidelines for Ghanaians on how to regulate their personal conduct and to lead virtuous lives. In this book, I treat church values and institutional authority as important frames of social interaction. However, I also see them as subject to ethical disputes in contexts involving a variety of issues: how to make a complete break with the past, the inconsistencies of being able to do so, the constancy of Pentecostal practice in different situations, and the rigidness of boundaries between what is acceptable and unacceptable Christian practice.

As this book shows, several key aspects of Pentecostal transformation are contested within the church, within Ghana, and in London. A constant question in the lives of my interlocutors was "How do we make sense of our transformation?" During my research, I realized that this question was as paramount as it was problematic, especially since it could not easily find a space to be interpreted or debated within a single field of anthropology. In its further elaboration, this book makes two points. First, taking relationships as central to understanding Pentecostal change and continuity has broader, theoretical implications. Indeed, such an approach shifts our focus from the Christian debates on the appropriate role of materiality within a transcendental religion to the ethical questions Christian believers ask themselves while seeking to maintain a meaningful balance between religious transformation and continuity. Second, I bring the anthropology of Christianity and the anthropology of ethics into one analytical framework. This integrated focus allows us to acknowledge the reality that despite church members' attempts to create a universal Christian identity, this new identity is inseparable from the situational, contradictory, and innovative ways in which it is articulated and experienced. As I go on to demonstrate, the combined anthropologies of Christianity and ethics provide a better understanding of the particular ways through which Christian transformation is contested and challenged, appropriated and adopted, explicitly pronounced and implicitly practised.

Anthropologies of Christianity and Ethics

My analysis of Pentecostal change has benefitted from the anthropology of Christianity "for itself" and not merely "in itself" (Robbins 2003b, 191). It has been accepted that early anthropological studies on Christianity did not go far enough in considering Christianity as a site of action in itself, in asking the question "What is characteristic about the ways Christianity shapes those societies in which it is adopted?" (Peel 1989, 424). This approach offers a number of major benefits. First, religious motives are of primary importance. The literature does not try to fit empirical information into explanatory schemas, but allows the social actions of believers to guide the theories employed (Cannell 2006a; Robbins 2007b). Second, the material and the ideological worlds of Christians are taken as part of the same sign system, creating a semiotic ideology that includes both linguistic and non-linguistic signifiers, in which particular moral interests are endowed (Keane 2007; Engelke 2007).[7] Third, this approach acknowledges that Christianity is concerned with how the past dissolves into the present through a distinctive, meaningful arrangement of cultural categories (Meyer 1999; Robbins 2004a). Such an approach also recognizes that Christianity possesses a transformative and political force and that the relationship between the political and the religious is intrinsically a historical one (Marshall 2009).

Taking a historical perspective, scholars of Christianity have paid increasing attention to how a Christian narrative can be differently appropriated by local parties over time (Meyer 1999; Peel 2003; Maxwell 2006; Cannell 2006a; O. Harris 2006; Gow 2006).[8] Scholars have also demonstrated how conceptual oppositions such as rupture and continuity are historically co-constructed.[9] In studying the indigenous interpretations of the Christian messages among the Ewe in southeastern Ghana, for example, Birgit Meyer (1999) demonstrates that Pentecostalism is the outcome of an active, self-conscious engagement with the problems of the present rather than a continuity of Ewe culture. She shows how, through the image of the devil, the spiritual beings of the old religion became part of Ewe Protestantism. Translation of the Christian message into the vernacular did not merely replace the local tradition, nor did it simply create continuities with the indigenous past.[10] Instead, it created something of a new quality, where continuity and rupture coexist within a single interpretive framework and the debates about a practical or lived Christianity have an uneasy relationship with official versions of the religion.

While rupture is central to Protestant ideology, it may not matter as much for those who convert to Protestantism. Many of my Ghanaian Pentecostal interlocutors share more in common with Fenella Cannell's Filipino Catholics, who have "a muted and ambiguous interest in the economy of salvation" (2006a, 26), than with other Protestants whose main goal is to patiently await the eventual return of Jesus, or the rapture. Even if the presence of a transcendent deity is acknowledged, Christians may have little concern for the heavenly afterlife. Maintaining clear boundaries between what is and what is not Christian is not always a straightforward process. Thus, when writing about a practical Christianity, anthropologists often "face a conundrum" regarding "[w]hat to include and what to exclude" (O. Harris 2006, 62). To what extent do objects of worship, sources of power, and ritual practices resemble pre-Christian ones, and how do we make such distinctions (O. Harris 2006; Kirsch 2008)? These questions point to the uncertainty that all Christians face when pondering what counts as real change, and who is and who is not a true Christian.

For many members of CoP, questions about religious change and relationships with human and non-human others may give rise to moments of uncertainty, which lead them to ask questions about how to discern the genuine from the counterfeit. The uncertainty concerning relationships is, in part, caused by the Christian "problem of presence" (Engelke 2007), of not knowing the exact material form that a transcendental God takes in a given situation. For example, church members may question whether certain objects used in prayer are appropriate channels for divine blessings, or whether the spiritual advice of a prophet comes from a traditional spirit or the Holy Spirit. While Christian uncertainty looks at the issue of determining God's presence in the lives of religious subjects, it is through the affective immediacy of relationships that ethical practice becomes an important consideration and that the question of "how to carry on" becomes embodied and expressed. By only considering the Christian "problem of presence," we potentially exclude the affective possibilities that relationships bring and ignore the quality of experience or intensity that later becomes qualified and expressed as emotions or beliefs (Massumi 2002, 27–8). Emphasizing the ethical nature of relationships provides a subtle yet important shift of attention, moving from the theological problem that Christians share and resolve in different ways to the ethical problem of how a Christian life is experienced and actively expressed in the presence of others and in the face of challenges and difficulties.

In arguing for a better integration of ethics within the anthropology of Christianity, I build on Joel Robbins's (2004a) premise, according to which religious change is registered in moral terms, and Christian actors consciously consider the challenges and changes involved in conversion while evaluating how to respond to such change. Robbins's work on the adoption of Christianity by the Urapmin of Papua New Guinea (ibid.) examines the ways in which the Urapmin negotiate between traditional and Christian world views, as represented by two paramount values of relationalism and individualism. Their conversion to Christianity leads the Urapmin to approach much of life as a process of moral decision-making. They wrestle with questions of how to live as good people through further questions of how Christian rupture should be demonstrated and what traditional forms of social life are acceptable. Building on his theoretical model regarding rupture, Robbins (2010a) has also suggested bringing anthropologists and Pauline philosophers into dialogue with each other in order to achieve a better understanding of change as "eventual." On this matter, Alain Badiou's idea of "event" as situated universality acknowledges the connection between the subject and the transformative event (Badiou 2001, 2006) and, as such, can be constructively applied to my understanding of Pentecostal transformation. According to this concept, while a shared set of criteria defines religious transformation as an event that demands an ethical response, the way in which one is transformed (as well as the circumstances surrounding the transformation) has a unique effect on the convert.[11]

My focus on ethical practice complements a cultural analysis of Christian conversion through a closer examination of the circumstances around the event of born-again conversion, carried out over an extended period of time. Situational analysis, a method that originated in the Manchester School of Social Anthropology, is useful to my understanding of ethics since it does not consider culture as a system of bounded symbolic categories.[12] Instead, culture, whether "Pentecostal," "Ghanaian," or "British," never comes together as a whole, but only in a partial way through the action of particular agents (Kapferer 2010, 14). This approach takes into account situations or events in which different belief systems may coexist, and examines the relationship between religious ideology and action from a situational point of view (Long 1968). It also analyses events as the outcome of rigorous questioning and debates, which ultimately become narrow interpretations of the more complex arrangement in which they are situated (see Evens 2005; Kapferer 2010). The recent turn to ethics in anthropology is important

to the development of my argument, as it places more attention on the
means (the journey) than on the ends (the results) of religious transformation (Laidlaw 2002). It allows me to understand how social worlds
are always multiply partially (dis)organized (Povinelli 2011, 8) and
how different groups in CoP evaluate the event of transformative
change through their relationships and encounters with others, including invisible beings such as the Holy Spirit, other spirits, Christian ancestors, and the divine.

As I discovered over time, Pentecostal transformation borders on the
explicit contestations and implicit tensions between linear and non-
linear trajectories, reversible and non-reversible paths, and continuous
and disruptive ideas of change. Pentecostal Christianity offers Ghanaian believers an inhabitable ideology of transformation that is in negotiation with the place of the past in the present and the role of personal
freedom amidst social and communal obligations, and is motivated by
questions about the locus and an appropriate expression of real change.
In moving towards a better understanding of Pentecostal transformation, as more than ritual practice and as more than a set of shared
beliefs about the presence of God, I proceed to an elaboration of transformation as ethical practice.

Pentecostal Transformation as Ethical Practice

The opening account of the informal prayer meeting illustrates the importance of ethical practice in understanding Pentecostal transformation. The potentially controversial nature of such prayer meetings allows for the crystallization of multiplicities inherent to Pentecostal life
in Ghana and for the object of Christianity to emerge as a topic central
to ethical practice. Mama Alice, the prophetess of the prayer service,
was known to be both spiritually powerful and dangerous. She helped
break people's connections to ancestral spirits and loosen their ties to
witchcraft, and also protected many from the impending collapse of
their businesses and possible death. "Our enemies set traps for us," she
told the attendees, "but because of the blood of Jesus, we are still alive."
According to her, the gifts of the Holy Spirit, which allowed her to be
the conduit for powerful prayers and prophecy, were also subject to the
criticism and envy of others, including church elders and pastors. These
church representatives warned her not to make references to witchcraft
and to stop prayer practices that were not sanctioned by church leaders. She was eventually told to stop her prophetic work. The church

Figure 0.4 Mama Alice, dressed in white, sitting with her prayer assistants. (Photo by the author.)

leaders wanted her to align with a specific idea of Pentecostal transformation that was in accordance with church doctrine. Instead, Mama Alice decided to leave the church and, in turn, church members were told to stop associating with her. Rather than discontinue their patronage, however, many continued attending her prayer meetings. Albert and other CoP members saw no contradiction in attending these banned prayer services while also identifying as good Christians and dedicated CoP members. They relied on their own practical judgment to decide on what Christian path to follow or how to move between these possibilities. The anthropology of ethics can thus help us to better understand how Christians deal with the tension between the application of specific criteria, the recognition of their limits, and the management of questions such as "What next?"

The study of ethics in anthropology draws inspiration from several sources within philosophy and the social sciences. The philosopher

Immanuel Kant wrote that morality consisted of following rules and doing one's duty (*deos*), irrespective of the consequences for oneself or others and of the social context in which one lives. This rationalist definition lends itself to debates over the role of experience and agency in the development of a moral person. Émile Durkheim, drawing on Kant while challenging his idea of duty, argued that individuals want to commit themselves to one or more moral communities. People demonstrate obedience through self-discipline by entering into relationships of moral obligation. A sense of autonomy is possible when these same individuals also become morally reflective subjects within a secular and rational society. Anthropologists have also drawn on other philosophers, including Aristotle and Michel Foucault, in pointing our attention to the possible ways in which virtues and values become internalized, enforced, and challenged within diverse social and cultural contexts.

The Greek philosopher Aristotle has helped anthropologists of religion contemplate how virtue is acquired habitually by way of embodied dispositions, as well as by the performance of acts that are deemed "good" through the lens of virtue ethics (Lambek 2000; Mahmood 2005).[13] As my interlocutors explained to me, attending church regularly and knowing how to pray and live a good Christian life are important, whether in Ghana or in London. Learning and successfully incorporating biblical narratives into one's personal narrative is also essential to any successful conversion and for a proper understanding of the "good" in social relations. This point was clearly conveyed to me by a church pastor, who lamented about the confusion some Ghanaians experience between traditional moral codes of practice and the Christian notion of biblical sin. The CoP pastor explained that traditional believers are not immoral, since they have social rules and sanctions against inappropriate behaviour. Instead, he described them as lacking a morality grounded in a narrative of Christian retribution:

> They [non-believers] had to learn that sin was something they already had due to their biblical genealogy to Adam and Eve, the first man and woman. They inherited the sins of Adam and Eve and therefore had to be saved through accepting Jesus Christ. "But how?" some people would ask. "These are the sins of a man who lived long ago. It has nothing to do with me now." They had to learn that according to the Bible and biblical genealogy they were all sinners, born into sin since Adam, and that unless they repented and accepted God's only son and saviour, they would go to this place called Hell after they died.

The Christian past shapes the present, just as the present changed my interlocutors' understanding of the past. Pentecostalism gave church members a new relationship to Christian history and its biblical characters, and simultaneously provided them with a sense of a shared past and a common futurity. This collapsing of different space-times relies heavily on narratives of virtuous Christian ancestors, heroic biblical characters, their battles against their enemies, as well as promises from God. A Christian narrative becomes integral to the making of the born-again self, allowing church members like Albert to transform from someone "without a future" to someone "with a future." When speaking of his migration to Accra, Albert often compared himself to Joseph from the Old Testament. Like Joseph, who had to face many trials and betrayals from his own family before becoming successful, Albert left home in order to escape the dangers of his stepmother's witchcraft and to seek a better future. He said to me, "My destiny is in my own hands. I am no longer afraid of my stepmother. I now know that she can do me no harm. I am now someone who has a future." This temporal reorganization of one's past and future happens in hindsight. It requires the recognition of a new genealogy – not merely following customary laws but also altering one's perception of origins – in order to become a virtuous Christian subject.

According to French philosopher Michel Foucault, ethics refers to a set of practices different from those pertaining to Durkheim's morality: it is an "exercise of the self on the self by which one attempts to develop and transform oneself, and to attain to a certain mode of being" (Foucault 1997a, 282). It allows a better understanding of how power, implicit to any cultural understanding of freedom, is a relational exercise involved in complex struggles over the control of people's conduct. Similarly, born-again conversion is commonly expressed as a complete change in the convert's life, which needs to be maintained through practices, such as prayer and fasting, and new codes of conduct, such as righteous living, modest dressing, abstinence from alcohol, and the strict avoidance of sex before marriage. Through the subsequent control of personal conduct, CoP converts are able to demonstrate the "character of God" and become a particular kind of virtuous subject, in which the convert is both an empowered subject of this new prescriptive practice regime and actively involved in its reproduction (Foucault 1997c; see also Marshall 2009; O'Neill 2010). As CoP members regulate themselves and their own transformation, church leaders spend a significant amount of time policing the boundaries of Pentecostal transformation and helping church members to do what is right and become good Christians.

However, what happens when different ideas around what is ethically good cannot be adequately resolved? As the everyday lives of church members are filled with contradictions and complications, a commitment to religious change does not always resolve the more situational questions such as "What should I do next?" The discrepancy between many of these questions and the answers provided by the church have further implications for the role of ethics in understanding the reflective aspects of religious transformation.

Drawing on both Aristotle and Foucault, I want to explore how believers make themselves and are made into virtuous subjects, but also how they critically reflect on church norms and on disciplinary practices. For Foucault (1997a, 284), while morality is built around codes and rules of conduct, "ethics is the considered form that freedom takes when it is informed by reflection." Church members also participate in what Aristotle has called practical judgment (*phronēsis*), where they evaluate specific circumstances and exercise their judgment in order to do what they believe is best. The concept of reflection or practical judgment contributes to a renewed understanding of the ways in which people sometimes come to hold incommensurable values and shifting obligations (Lambek 2000). For many of my interlocutors, Christianity's role is not simply to help them discover the "truth" in oneself, but also to help them arrive at a multiplicity of healthy and happy relationships (Foucault 1997b, 135).[14]

My use of the term "ethics" is multidimensional.[15] It references the interdependence and mutual implications of an embodied and norm-based morality as well as more specific, deliberative moments of reflection and judgment, which are part of the same ethical practice my interlocutors are involved in. Yet a focus on ethics also entails paying attention to the varied understandings of a transformation as lived in moments where comprehension and certainty may never be achieved, or may arrive only later in an unexpected form. In addition to taking Aristotle and Foucault as starting points for the analysis of the ethical lives of CoP members, my sustained ethnographic attention to the emotive anxieties and moral judgments around positions of uncertainty regarding Pentecostal transformation also departs from them by pointing to the moments when transformation is formed by different degrees of potential openness and closure, of alienability or integrity, and of proximity or distance to human and non-human forces. Foucault's ideas on subjectivation illuminate the ways in which a micro-politics of power operates and, in Pentecostal contexts, show how believers both transform and regulate themselves through practices of the self. Yet this approach does not adequately address the unique biographies of individuals or the importance of the intersubjective experiences of the human and non-human other(s) in and on the self. The Aristotelian perspective on virtue importantly addresses shared ideas of the "good" and the practical judgments that people make in order to lead a good life, but it does not always consider the ambiguities of action or the views that are not consistently in line with the dominant ideology.

While CoP members are committed to a set of shared Christian values and its virtuous practices, the study of ethics poses the problem of uncertainty among values. If my interlocutors adhere to shared codes of practice aimed at making them good and virtuous Christians, they also face situations in which doing the right thing is not clear, and the correct answers are not straightforward. As such, ethics also acknowledges the problems and pitfalls that, in certain circumstances, come with doing what is right or good. In order to understand how Ghanaian Pentecostals perceive their own transformation, this book inserts ethics into a wider network of entangled relationships and meanings. It takes into account what Avery Gordon (1997, 4) calls a "complex personhood," which recognizes "that people suffer graciously and selfishly too, get stuck in the symptoms of their troubles and also transform themselves."

Agreement on the rules and boundaries of Christian practice or on what constitutes "freedom" and "happiness" does not always provide a sufficient reconciliation between two or more opposed, yet coexisting, ideological systems. While CoP members embrace a born-again Christian rupture with the past, many become less concerned with "what" the boundaries of Christian rupture are than with seeking answers to the more personal "why" questions – questions concerning the reasons for the continuity of suffering after conversion, the cause of unhealthy relationships, and the changes brought about by migration – and "how" to deal with them.[16]

In this book, I am less concerned with the question of how Christianity is mediated than with the problem of the in-between itself, and with the different ways church members and other Ghanaian Pentecostals live in and make sense of states of being more or less Christian. A focus on the simultaneous and affective relationships CoP members have with God, Jesus Christ, and the Devil, with the Holy Spirit and traditional spirits, as well as with Christians and non-Christians, brings forward the productive complexities and contradictions of religious life that inevitably proceed from any shared notion of religious change.

While they strive to be virtuous subjects who work hard to cultivate their inner selves, many CoP members also question the shared dimensions of their religious identity in reaction to changing personal and social circumstances. It is precisely through the incommensurability of practices internal to Pentecostalism, as well as through dilemmas over how internal and external practices interact, that Ghanaian Pentecostals rediscover what type of Christians they are and how they can remain committed.

Ethical practice plays a central role in the lives of committed Pentecostal Christians – a role it could not play in the lives of those who merely follow rules and obey laws – in that it deals with the sometimes piecemeal ways in which ideology is invoked. This practice, alongside their own analysis of ideas about social and cultural change, allows for a closer examination of the micro-transformations of ordinary Pentecostal Christian actors. By paying more attention to the moments of ethical deliberation that emerge from the negotiation of self–other relationships, the anthropology of ethics can help us better assess multiple considerations and ambiguities that a Christian identity holds for Ghanaian Pentecostals, as well as the processes through which they come to evaluate the contradictions and pitfalls of their own faith. Apart from linking the micro-social and the macro-social, a focus on ethical practice also allows us to articulate the relationships between the local and the global that are key to the very essence of CoP.

A Global African Church

This book on Pentecostal transformation focuses on an African church that is located in more than eighty-eight countries worldwide. The setting matters, because Africa often signifies what is materially deprived and religiously possible in a globalized world. Books on the "occult" and the extreme religiosity of Africans in reaction to changing forms of capitalistic production and new forms of economic marginalization have been widely published.[17] While they help us to understand how modernity is not a singular phenomenon but rather a historically produced and plural one, these books sometimes convey the assumption that African religiosity is solely a response to socio-economic changes (Marshall 2009, 29). The example of CoP demonstrates that religion is not merely a response to economic events, but constitutes in itself a mode of transformation. Its growth coincides with earlier prophecies within the church, according to which CoP would become international

(CoP 2000). This promise of overseas expansion comes with the commitment to preach the Gospel to other nations.

The global expansion of CoP has coincided with the rising popularity of Pentecostal-charismatic Christianity in Ghana and the growing migration of its members to cities around the world. One of the first Pentecostal churches in Ghana, CoP originally drew the majority of its membership from labour migrants and the urban poor, who helped the church expand into neighbouring African countries. From the 1980s, the church began a reverse mission to the West, when many of its members migrated to Europe and America as economic migrants and students.[18] These overseas members started prayer fellowships in their host countries and later requested missionaries from CoP headquarters in Accra.

Many Ghanaians share the dream of travelling or migrating to the "West." When church members migrate from Ghana to London, they encounter contradictions between their lives as immigrants and their status as citizens of heaven. The experience of economic migration, the attempts to evangelize within new host countries, and the many demands and disappointments from family and friends in Ghana are all factors that challenge the notion of Pentecostal transformation as a unidirectional or evenly global process. CoP expatriates struggle and work hard to redefine what Christianity means in their new cultural environment. Religious affiliation becomes an important way for African Christian immigrants to legitimately make demands otherwise denied them, to claim a sense of place and belonging in the city, and to intervene as Christian citizens who believe they have been brought to London for a purpose other than economic security (H. Harris 2006; Fumanti 2010).

While Pentecostalism can be described as both global in its reach and local in its orientation (Robbins 2004b; Coleman 2010a), I have attempted to understand my interlocutors' own involvement with the "global" through their church's expanding networks and the simultaneous tensions and limits that arose from their engagement with "culture." However, problems and questions specific to their Christian identity continue to follow them wherever they go. Whether in Ghana or London, CoP members experience inconsistencies between what they are told to do (by church leaders and their elders) and what they feel is the best course of action under certain circumstances (as responsible Christians and as social beings with other responsibilities). It is because of these inconsistencies that CoP leaders and members reflect on the ways through which religious change ought to take place, on how social relationships are made and unmade, and on how they become connected and disconnected.

The church's own global transformation raises doubts about when and how these changes should take place. In the process of migration and attempts at evangelism, CoP members ask themselves whether certain relationships and their outcome are positive or negative, healthy or unhealthy, successful or unsuccessful. Ghanaian and British "culture" become objectified problems that need to be frequently addressed by church members and leaders alike. The discourse of culture, like that of tradition, is not opposed to modernity, but it becomes a means by which an intergenerational and intercontextual conversation on Pentecostal values is reconfigured. For example, according to some church leaders, aspects of a "postmodern" culture threaten to disrupt the conceptual order of transcendental certainty through which Pentecostalism thrives. In London, references to British culture become a way of describing and criticizing the indiscipline of the youth and the potentially immoral landscape that threatens to destroy family life. I show that this disorder also provides for important sites of creativity, allowing for the development of new ways and measures susceptible to bringing order back into perspective for both church leaders and members. To that end, this book offers a theoretical framework for understanding how Pentecostal transformation is bound by the moral criteria regarding what is promised and acceptable. It also shows how such transformational processes are seen as necessarily unpredictable and inconsistent because of the presence of others as interrupting forces.

As such, this book aims to convey the different voices simultaneously deployed in relation to, and in construction of, a Ghanaian Pentecostal self. Debates on how a Pentecostal life should be lived include questions regarding church identity, a changing Ghanaian public that is becoming infected by liberalization policies, and issues pertaining to migration and globalization. By exploring the ambivalence and emotive anxieties of Ghanaian Pentecostals in southern Ghana and London, this ethnographic account focuses on transformation through conflicting voices and multiple aims regarding personal and social change, and the consequences that their decisions bring as fundamental constituents of the convert's identity. Allowing for moments of doubt and the weighing of multiple considerations can illuminate the multiplicity and heterodoxies of Christian experience and practice, as well as the ways in which Pentecostal actors shift between different roles and conflicting self-representations. In bridging discourses of Pentecostalism in Ghana and London, I connect the lives of church members in Kumasi, Accra, and London through a shared discourse of transformation and uncertainties.

In the Field

Most of my interlocutors in London led very busy lives. As a result, I had to employ methods of gathering data that required some flexibility on my part. This meant that, apart from weekly church services and prayer meetings, I sometimes accompanied church members on their daily activities, met up with them at times that suited their busy schedules, or joined them when they visited other church members, friends, and family. Since I was also interested in the other aspects of their lives, including work, family, their life histories, and stories of personal relationships, I deemed that I would get more relevant information by engaging in conversations over an extended period of time. I spent several months, from October 2002 to April 2003, conducting research at PIWC in London before leaving for Ghana.

This was not my first time in Ghana. Many of my father's immediate family are naturalized Ghanaians and, since my grandfather's generation, have made Ghana their home. While I did not grow up in Ghana and knew little about Pentecostalism before my research, the experience of having lived there for several months between 1999 and 2000 helped familiarize me with my research environment and allowed me to acquire a basic knowledge of Twi. In Ghana, I divided my time between different church settings, continuing to attend PIWC in Accra while attending the prayer services of a local Twi assembly close to where I lived. I also visited several prayer camps in southern Ghana and other CoP assemblies, including PIWC Kumasi. By spending more time with and subsequently interviewing church leaders, church members, and prophets from May 2003 to May 2004, I was better able to discern the institutional diversity of CoP.

At no point did I pretend that I was Christian. As I was introduced to the church through the resident missionary in the United Kingdom and knew other church officers, many church members assumed that I was born again or that I had a Christian background. They saw me praying with them, regularly attending church services, and taking a strong interest in the history and activities of the church. There were some occasions when my non–born-again status generated tense and difficult situations. I would be confronted by church members and asked if I had "given my life to Jesus." When I replied in the negative, the response was "Why?" and "What was I waiting for?" In one instance in London, after having observed me pray with them, a church deacon found out from someone else that I was not born again. He turned to me and said loudly, "I know who my God is. Do you?" On those occasions, my resolve to remain calm while listening patiently to their views provided opportunities for learning and new forms of social acceptance. In addition, many appreciated my active participation and attempts to pray and understand the Bible with them. Some friends were genuinely upset that I was not born again, while others offered suggestions on how to pray to Jesus, handing me certain texts from the Bible to read and sharing their personal testimonies with me. Many proselytized to me in church as well as during my interviews and conversations with them.

In Ghana, my non-Christian background usually took a back seat. It was more often than not assumed that I was Christian. When it was discovered that this was not so, more of an effort was made, especially by prophets and prophetesses, to place me within a Pentecostal Christian framework. Some even told me that the Holy Spirit had informed them that I was born again, and prophesied to me regarding my ancestral past and my personal destiny. Even when I denied being born again, one prophet remained convinced that I had accepted Jesus secretly and had been baptized by the Holy Spirit. Another prophetess proclaimed to a group of church members that I would become a great evangelist, while another prophet symbolically and publicly "washed" me in the blood of Jesus to demonstrate to the congregation that I was baptized and spiritually clean. Many prophets and ordinary church members who attend local assemblies and prayer camps have little formal education and do not speak much English. Most of my interviews and conversations with them were conducted in Twi with the help of a translator.

Apart from ordinary members like Albert, who hold no official position within CoP, the global church community includes apostles, pastors, evangelists, prophets, elders, deacons, and deaconesses. Men hold all the important offices within the church hierarchy and are the decision-makers. Church leaders are members of the Executive Committee and the General Church Committee, holding ordained offices in the church. They make decisions to ensure the smooth running of CoP and enforce the social rules and values of the church. The General Council is CoP's highest policy-making body; it includes the overseas resident missionaries, the regional heads of the church in Ghana, and other apostles who hold positions within the administrative structure. Members of the Executive

Committee, who also usually hold the position of apostle, include the chairman, the general secretary, the international missions director, and six other apostles and prophets who hold administrative responsibilities within the church. Many church leaders have recently become theologically educated in Ghana and overseas, or have a university degree. All of my conversations with church leaders and PIWC members were in English. In Ghana, I got to know a diverse range of people, including leaders and members of other charismatic and Pentecostal churches, independent prophets, and traditional priests. I met with several leaders of the charismatic churches who were once members of CoP, including Charles Agyin Asare of Perez Chapel International, Nicholas Duncan-Williams of Christian Action Faith Chapel, and Paul Owusu Tabiri of Bethel Prayer Ministry International. My interactions with them provided a more nuanced picture of Ghanaian Pentecostalism.

A Map of the Book

This study is divided into seven chapters. Chapter One provides the historical and social context for the rise of Pentecostalism in Ghana. It examines the ethical dilemmas arising from Pentecostalism's growth and looks at how CoP forms an important part of that history. The differential nature of a Christian declaration of transformation for the self-identity of Pentecostals becomes apparent; I also explore how Pentecostals traverse Christian integrity and social flexibility. Chapter Two turns to an ethnographic analysis of the use of sand in church prayer in Ghana, a practice that became a catalyst for controversy within CoP. By contrasting the institutional approach to transformation with the ways in which it is practically negotiated by a church pastor in Kumasi, this chapter focuses on the ethical concerns CoP leaders have regarding the return of the past in the present and the introduction of new Pentecostal teachings in Ghana's changing market economy. Chapter Three introduces the reader to the work of prophets and prayer in Ghana. I show how a prophet's prayer is believed to increase one's chances of success and lead to migration in the future. While prophets are highly valued for their spiritual power, they are also scrutinized by church leaders for their resemblance to traditional priests. Moreover, although prophets help others to obtain visas and realize travel dreams, they may paradoxically never leave Ghana themselves. This chapter explores the dilemmas that such contradictions create in the lives of church members and prophets, and how they work to resolve them.

In Chapter Four, I focus on two Pentecostal Christian women in Accra who sought healing and spiritual help in times of sickness and personal suffering, one from a traditional priest and the other from a CoP prophetess. The chapter addresses the question of Christian personhood through the contingencies involved in balancing individual aspirations for personal change against one's moral obligations to others, both human and non-human. Chapter Five introduces the story of Eben, who has migrated to London, and compares it with Albert's story, which brought him from the countryside to Accra. Differently placed, these two men similarly balance family relationships and witchcraft attacks with their commitment to a Pentecostal identity in their respective homes. If Albert's relationships with prophets are central to negotiating his Pentecostal identity and the dangers of a Ghanaian sociality, Eben sidelines the role of prophets in his quest for a personal relationship with God in London. Turning away from Ghana in Chapters Six and Seven, I focus on London's PIWC community, where a wider circuit of evangelism is challenged by new work economies and migrant identities. I explore how "culture" becomes a discourse about selective incorporation and exclusion, a negotiation of everything that falls outside of and on the boundaries of a transcendental Christian God. Ethical practice becomes important for how Ghanaian Pentecostals in London deal with the contradictions between their special status as citizens of heaven and their reality as economic migrants. The Epilogue revisits the central propositions of the book, paying particular attention to the process of looking backward and forward in time, a negotiation mechanism that Ghanaian Pentecostals use when assessing and critiquing their past and when making a commitment to move forward into the future.

Chapter One

Rupture and Continuity

Religious ethics penetrate into social institutions in very different ways.

Max Weber (1922)

A historical property has morals and ethics of the society that created it and can be revived. What I mean is that we can discover new possibilities from the process of dismantling, transforming and creating.

Ai Weiwei (2013)[1]

This chapter provides a historical overview of Pentecostal networks in Ghana. The exercise of tracing these networks backwards aims not at establishing the "origin" of Pentecostalism in Ghana, but at understanding how CoP maintains both a historical continuity and a discontinuity with a time before.[2] In the first half of the chapter, I examine the historical spread of Pentecostalism in Ghana; in the second half, I describe the role of Christian narratives in diagnosing the present and reimagining the future. In order to comprehend how CoP is part of a changing history of synchronous networks, I first provide a backdrop of Pentecostalism across space and show its shifting patterns over time. As I go on to demonstrate, transatlantic networks involved not only the hierarchical mingling of the colonial and the native, but also the synchronous interdependencies of multiple Christian others in helping change the configuration of these respective groups. In the next section, I explore how the phenomenon of the Holy Spirit widens out from issues of personal transformation and healing into issues of intra-denominational conflict and competing values. The various attempts of Christians to emplace the Holy Spirit into a personal, historical, and social narrative are what I call the politics of the Spirit.

Transatlantic Politics of the Spirit: Earlier Origins of Ghanaian Pentecostalism

Pentecostalism's point of entry in Ghana can be explained by a series of historical factors: the seeking of alternative sources of healing and spiritual power, missionary education, access to missionary print media, and ongoing transnational and missionary links between West Africans (as well as within West Africa) and the West (Europe and America). While the ideal of being born again in the Holy Spirit has been present in West African evangelism since 1817 (Peel 2004, 25), some of the first Pentecostal missionaries in West Africa were a group of African Americans connected with the Azusa Street Revival in Los Angeles who went to Liberia in 1907 (Anderson 2004, 115).[3] The journeys of the famous Liberian prophet William Wade Harris, who travelled throughout the Ivory Coast and on to Western Ghana in 1914, provide examples of how the work of the Holy Spirit supposedly resulted in tens of thousands of conversions to Christianity (Hastings 1979; Debrunner 1967, 269–77). Casely Hayford, a leading barrister and Methodist layman in the Gold Coast who was converted by this "Black Elijah," is quoted to have said, "This is not a revival. It is a Pentecost" (Debrunner 1967, 271). Following Harris, other prophets emerged, some carrying wooden crosses and dressed in long white gowns as they drove out evil spirits and led their own evangelistic activities (Larbi 2001, 63–8). These prophets demonstrated the power of the Holy Spirit by alleviating suffering and told converts to give their lives to Jesus, while disposing of any traditional idols, medicines, and fetishes.[4]

These African preachers and prophets travelled far and wide, helping create revivals in the mainline churches and paving the way for indigenous Pentecostalism in Ghana. Their rise in numbers coincided with a serious economic depression caused by the sharp fall in the price of cocoa and "the revivals in cult life, or imported cultic practices" between 1930 and 1940 (Assimeng 1995, 12). A good example was the Tigare cult, an anti-witchcraft shrine, which was probably imported from Côte d'Ivoire in the wake of the dramatic economic changes of the 1930s. As Max Assimeng observes, "barring the twentieth century revival in the activities of the fetish shrines, religious 'newness' in Ghana should more appropriately be deemed to refer to the constantly-emerging sectarian and revivalist phenomenon within the Christian persuasion" (ibid., 15).[5]

An early incarnation of Pentecostalism, formed around the phenomena of spiritual churches (*Sunsum Sorè*), became a new source of spiritual power that helped people reap material benefits and protected them from the effects of witchcraft and suffering. It also allowed for traditional concepts of power, healing, and spiritual protection to converge in the person of the Christian prophet (Baëta 1962; Wyllie 1980).[6] While there may have been certain perceived continuities in religious practices and expressions of spiritual power, the Christian prophets were not the same as the anti-witchcraft shrines. The prophets distanced themselves from traditional religious practices and insisted that converts burn any medicines or fetishes upon conversion. They generally helped draw a large number of converts into the Roman Catholic and Anglican churches. One notable exception to this characterization that must be mentioned is Peter Anim.

Peter Anim (1890–1984), who is known as the "Father of classic Pentecostalism in Ghana," left his orthodox Christian background to seek a more spiritual life and form his own church (Hanson 2002, 57). As far back as 1917, Anim, who had been educated by the Basel Mission in the Gold Coast and was a member of the Presbyterian church, took an interest in a religious periodical edited by the Faith Tabernacle ministry in Philadelphia, Pennsylvania, called *The Sword of the Spirit*.[7] Anim found these teachings attractive because they differed from anything the Presbyterian church had taught him, and because his own life was punctuated by sickness. In 1920, after the death of his wife and his own miraculous recovery from chronic stomach troubles, he converted "into the faith" and decided to put these teachings into practice (Larbi 2001, 100). By means of correspondence with Pastor Clarke, the leader of this religious organization, Anim formed his own Faith Tabernacle church in Ghana in 1922, and in 1923 his certificate of ordination was issued by Clarke. Although not a Pentecostal organization, the teaching of this ministry that resonated most immediately in Anim's Ghanaian ministry was faith healing.

Around that same time, Anim had also been receiving copies of another religious magazine, *The Apostolic Faith*, published by a Pentecostal movement based in Portland, Oregon. It was the first print publication that came out of the American Azusa Street Revival of 1906 and proved crucial to the rise and spread of the Pentecostal message in places as far away as India and China (Maxwell 2006, 29). The rise in cost-efficient practices of print technologies allowed the easy consumption and spread of Pentecostal broadsheets, tracts, and short booklets. These and other Pentecostal publications were not profit driven and served to inform others around the globe of Pentecostal revivals and their shared message. These texts became important instruments of proselytism and helped create an imagined community of Pentecostals around the world (ibid.). It was in this publication that Anim first read about the Holy Spirit.

When Clarke was excommunicated in 1926 for alleged adultery, Anim faced a moment of uncertainty regarding his association with the Faith Tabernacle. Clarke's American-based group was supposedly unemotional and regarded speaking in tongues and the gifts of the spirit as satanic. The lack of attention to certain spiritual aspects of conversion demonstrated through ecstatic forms of worship and the infilling of the Holy Spirit in prayer did not provide Anim with what he called a "deeper faith and greater spiritual power" (Larbi 2001, 103). He gave these new teachings about the Holy Spirit more serious consideration. In 1930, Anim separated from the Faith Tabernacle and adopted the name "Apostolic Faith."

This search for the Pentecostal experience and power was closely tied to another affiliation with Pentecostal missionaries from the United Kingdom. Close relationships with the Faith Congregation in Nigeria and its leader, Pastor David Odubanjo, led to contact with the Apostolic Church, UK, and its representatives, who were visiting Nigeria in 1931.[8] Emmanuel Larbi (2001) notes that Anim was seeking a Pentecostal experience that emphasized an emotive connection to God through divine healing, prophecies, and miracles. This narrative builds upon apostolic and biblical roots in claiming the restoration of God's presence in the world through events Larbi describes as the "Holy Ghost Outpouring" (ibid., 104); these events include the baptism of the Holy Spirit, speaking in tongues, healing, and prophesy.[9] One such event is said to have occurred in 1931 through a unique encounter with the Holy Spirit, by means of prayers in the bush, close to a small town in eastern Ghana called Asamankese. This and subsequent events have been described as the first spontaneous and unregulated outburst of the Holy Spirit in the history of the Gold Coast. They happened around the same time that transatlantic connections were being forged between Anim and the Apostolic Church, UK.

While Pentecostal identity is partly constituted in relation to the circulation of texts and the ability of these texts to address certain types of people through an imagined community, placing relative strangers on a minimally shared footing, the ways in which these various networks orientated themselves to the texts is an important consideration (Kirsch 2008). In other words, while Anim received magazines and pamphlets from overseas Christian networks, he did not adopt them wholly but interpreted them selectively in establishing his Pentecostal identity. Christian texts and mass-mediated global registers continued to undergo a process of decontextualization and subsequent recontextualization, leaving them open to interpretation and moral evaluation. As a recipient of this international distribution of texts and a participant in religious networks outside of Ghana, Anim was able to help establish an African independent church that had international affiliation but was forged with a distinctively personal religious identity. This became obvious when the Apostolic Church, UK, sent its first missionary to the Gold Coast.[10]

Not long after the Apostolic Church, UK, missionary James McKeown (1900–1989) started working with Anim in 1937, a dispute between them arose over the practice of divine healing, whereby believers need only rely on prayer for healing without the help of doctors or the use of biomedicine. This difference came to the fore when McKeown fell ill with malaria and had to be taken to hospital. While in hospital, he received medical treatment and eventually recovered.[11] This event created an ethical dilemma for McKeown and Anim, as well as for their respective supporters within the church, concerning the relative strength and limits of their Pentecostal faith. For Anim, the very materiality of medicine and doctors threatened to relegate Jesus to second place. While the use of Western biomedicine was not an issue of theological concern for McKeown in that it did not diminish his faith in the Holy Spirit and its tangible presence in his life, for Anim, the use of medicines became a measure of McKeown's lack of faith. They did not share the same ethical rationalization for Pentecostal transformation, which led to an intradenominational struggle for control of the religious community (Weber 1958).[12]

McKeown and Anim could not work together. Their attempt to embody the Holy Spirit in their own lives turned into a conflict of interests. While McKeown and Anim shared a belief in the mediating presence of the Holy Spirit, they held a different politics of the Spirit. McKeown's use of medicine clashed with one of Anim's other key values, divine healing, which helped frame how Anim came to hold his Pentecostal identity. How religious values come to have an influence over people is also based on the ethical practices through which these values become implicitly shared. As a result, McKeown and Anim had competing visions of a Pentecostal identity and how Pentecostal transformation should be applied in practice. The conflict between McKeown and Anim was over the felicity conditions surrounding the maintenance of a shared

Pentecostal faith and not the sanctity of the born-again experience. It dealt with the question of how the Holy Spirit should be emplaced and embedded in their own lives and those of their followers. In these instances, where situational adjustments are made in reaction and in relation to moments of uncertainty and doubt, new communities of practice emerge. And this is exactly what happened. The inability of McKeown and Anim to resolve their differences led to a split between them in 1939, with McKeown going on to lead the Apostolic Church of Gold Coast and Anim calling his group the Christ Apostolic Church.

Internal contestation over the appropriate boundaries of Pentecostal transformation caused another division in the church further down the road. By allowing certain evangelical Christian groups from North America to lead a revival in the church, McKeown created problems between himself and his missionary headquarters in the United Kingdom. Church leaders point to the period between 1953 and 1969 as the time that "prophetism" became prominent in CoP. A team led by Thomas Wyatt from the Latter Rain Movement in North America visited CoP, the then Apostolic Church of Gold Coast, in the early part of 1953 (Onyinah 2002, 192–3). The work of this movement, which included personal prophecy and the belief in divine healing and other miracles, left a strong impression with local church members. According to CoP leader Opoku Onyinah, this visit "demonstrated to them faith in the immediacy of God in practical terms" (ibid., 194–5). After these visits, certain members, men and women who felt that they had the calling of a prophet, began holding prayer meetings in their various areas, praying and exorcising demons. These earlier prophets and their activities provided McKeown and other church leaders opportunities to see continuities between Pentecostal Christianity and a this-worldly focus found in a Ghanaian, mainly Akan, theosophy (Atiemo 1995; Larbi 2001; Asamoah-Gyadu 2005a).[13]

The matter of the Latter Rain revival in the Gold Coast was raised in the General Council of the Apostolic Church at their Quadrennial Conference held in Bradford, United Kingdom, a meeting attended by McKeown.[14] When participants at this meeting were asked to recommit to the doctrines and practices of the Apostolic Church, McKeown and another pastor refused. This event led to McKeown's dismissal. In 1953, McKeown's organization in the Gold Coast split from the parent body, the Apostolic Church, UK. Afterwards, McKeown's church developed an urge to belong to a global movement. The different relationships that helped build CoP highlight the role of ethical practice in determining how rupture with the traditional past, and continuity with a Christian past, were put into practice, and how far-away places in the world map became key resources that provided a dynamic context for religious interaction. However, this urge to become global was also influenced and directed by other vectors of change in Ghana between the 1950s and 1990s.

Transnational Christian Networks and Pentecostal Change (1950s–1990s)

Upon independence in 1957, Kwame Nkrumah, Ghana's first prime minister (1957–1966), adapting a verse from Matthew (6:33), is quoted as saying, "Seek ye first the political kingdom and all other things shall be added to you" (Pobee 1991, 8). Nkrumah, who founded the Convention People's Party (CPP) in 1949 after breaking away from an elite-dominated party called the United Gold Coast Convention, was a pan-Africanist and a self-identified Marxist. Nkrumah, who claimed to be "a non-denominational Christian," instrumentally employed a Christian rhetoric in building his mass appeal (ibid., 117–18). In comparing himself to Jesus and employing "martyr motifs," Nkrumah was promoted as the "African Messiah after the order of Jesus" (118–20).

Nkrumah's focus on rapid industrial growth and expansion in university and higher-level educational facilities led to an urbanization process, through which people from the outlying rural areas poured into cities – especially Accra, Tema, and Kumasi – in search of employment and better economic fortunes. This development was accompanied by an increased attention and higher numbers of conversion to Pentecostal Christianity. From the late 1950s onwards, the popularity of Christian student fellowships at the pre-university (Scripture Union) and university (university Christian fellowships) levels helped spread a new brand of evangelical and Pentecostal Christianity. These parachurch groups created a renewal that was predominantly school based. The Scripture Union (SU) and the evangelical fellowships in the universities were pioneered by British expatriates in Ghana, who stood for the conservative evangelical position of graduates of the then Inter-Varsity Fellowships of Evangelical Unions, now Universities and Colleges Christian Fellowship (UCCF) (Adubufuor 1994, 3–5). Over time, these Christian fellowships, which included house, town, work, and student fellowships, expanded in size and number, consequently influencing a whole new generation of CoP members.

The SU and the university Christian fellowships contributed to the building of the religiously disciplined Christians, who were trained to be holy and honest. The SU was an influential force for students from different church denominations who went on to become teachers and political leaders as well as important religious figures in Ghana (Barker and Boadi-Siaw 2003). This holiness movement focused on evangelism, Bible studies, becoming born again, receiving the baptism of the Holy Spirit, speaking in tongues, and leading holy lives through fasting and prayer – all the components of Weber's Puritan personality, which are intrinsic to Ghanaian Pentecostalism. As these Christian fellowships did not have any church affiliation, they provided an alternative to members of the mainline orthodox churches, who desired a spiritual revival but were not ready to leave their "mother churches" (Hanson 2002, 122).

The SU and other Christian fellowships taught Ghanaians what it really meant to be Christian and how to have a personal relationship with God. Chris, an elder with PIWC London, described to me how his childhood membership in the SU during secondary school and a prayer fellowship in his later teenage years played important roles in the early formation and development of his Pentecostal identity. His personal religious trajectory is one that many church members growing up in Ghana in the 1960s and 1970s share.

> I have to trace it back to primary school. I attended the Presbyterian school and one of the good things about the Presbyterian school was that they encouraged children to learn Bible passages by heart … this was going back as far as 1966 … but I didn't understand what it meant to have a personal relationship with God. I enjoyed reading the Scripture in the same way that one enjoys reading poetry or one enjoys reading a storybook, as you know the Bible is full of stories … It was only when I went to secondary school was when I joined Scripture Union. I was about thirteen years old, and they explained what it means to be a Christian, that one had to formally and publicly accept Jesus Christ as his or her personal Lord and Saviour in order to become a Christian. So I did that … That has affected my life throughout – [t]he choices I've made in life, my career choices, the places I've been, the woman I married, and generally my life as a teenager … That was the way I spent my youth … So very, very early on I was the secretary of the Christian fellowship, and later on I became the president of the Christian fellowship.

In 1966, Nkrumah was overthrown in a military coup led by Colonel Kwasi Kotoko and Major Akwasi Amankwa Afrifa from the Second

Infantry Brigade. This military government, which called itself the National Liberation Council (NLC), returned power in 1969 to a civilian government run by the elected Progress Party under the leadership of Dr Kofi Abrefa Busia. However, even this did not last long. Another *coup d'état* followed in 1972, led by military Colonel I.K. Acheampong, whose military regime lasted until 1978. Political instability and economic hardship followed Ghana throughout the period of Acheampong's rule. The earlier holiness movement was starting to make way for a new dominant force in Ghana's Pentecostal scene: the charismatic teachings of power and deliverance, and the prosperity doctrine.

By the 1970s, becoming born again became a symbol of prestige and power in Ghana. It was a sought-after status that many young people wanted for themselves. Becoming born again was considered analogous to joining the ranks of an elite Christian group. For example, many school-going youth attended summer camps and prayer retreats organized by the SU, aimed at introducing students to the Holy Spirit.[15] It was during these spiritual retreats that many young Ghanaians learned about and first experienced the baptism of the Holy Spirit. The Holy Spirit baptism and the power that came with it served to distinguish the strong in the Spirit from the ordinary Christian. As Chris, the PIWC elder, went on to say, "They were the super spiritual people, and we were the dry, ordinary, powerless who saw these guys as powerful and anointed. So we went to these guys and asked them, 'How do you get this Holy Spirit?'" Younger Ghanaians were emulating many of the older youths whom they admired and looked up to. Chris, however, had to wait several years before experiencing the Holy Spirit baptism himself.

In the late 1970s, the crusades of American Morris Cerullo and the missions of Nigerians Benson Idahosa and W.F. Kumuyi introduced new charismatic teachings. From the late 1970s until the early 1980s, Oral Roberts, who put forward the concept of "seed faith" as a means of having one's needs met, was featured prominently on GBC-TV every Sunday evening from 6 pm to 7 pm. Kenneth Hagin's emphasis on his positive confession "You can have what you say," Morris Cerullo's popular slogan "Have the experience," and Yonggi Cho's guide to applying "home cell dynamics" all helped influence the changing form of Pentecostalism in Ghana. These travelling evangelists and television shows helped normalize the expectation that all born-again Christians ought to experience the power of the Holy Spirit in their lives. Chris worked to prepare himself for his eventual experience of the Holy Spirit baptism by attending the evangelical rallies and the prayer group meetings of neo-Pentecostals in Ghana. He narrated its importance to me in this way:

You have to remember that this was the 70s, and at that time the issue of the Holy Spirit and baptism of the Holy Spirit and so on, that issue was new to people. The Holy Spirit is not new because he has always been around. But in the 1970s … people like Gordon Lindsey, Morris Cerullo, and T.L. Osborne started to talk about the power of God and how believers should not just walk around holding the Bible and attending church but they must experience the power of God in their lives. And this experience of power in Christian's lives became very important.

Around this same time, a good number of Ghanaian students had more free time to spend gaining knowledge and experience in the changing Pentecostal scene. Many of these neo-Pentecostals were awaiting entry into universities or were without jobs and members of prayer fellowships. The reconstitution of these fellowships into churches provided an avenue for employment and income, allowing these young people the opportunity to engage in freelance evangelism.[16] The phenomenon of freelance evangelism in Ghana was further influenced by international contacts and conferences between local evangelists and big American organizations. Chris, however, was disappointed by the popular methods that many of these evangelists used to invoke the power of the Holy Spirit in the lives of others. He saw many of their methods as purely instrumental. They did not acknowledge the personal intimacy that he was after. However, after several attempts at receiving the Holy Spirit during public prayer events, he decided to stay home and pray every night until he received the baptism of the Holy Spirit. He eventually succeeded and spoke about it as experiencing the "presence of Jesus" standing next to him, which made him break down into tears.

> Towards the end of the 1970s, I received the baptism of the Holy Spirit … If you like, in the first part of my Christian life I was just building knowledge of God but when I received the Holy Spirit, then everything simply exploded. I almost became something like God's hand and God's feet. I felt like an instrument in God's hands to do something … Whereas before I felt like I was a member of a group or a member of a club. That was a dramatic transformation.

In the following decade, other American-based para-church organizations and interdenominational fellowships – for instance, the Full Gospel Business Men's Fellowship and Women Aglow International

– helped pave the way for Pentecostal spirituality to enter the mainline churches (Larbi 2001, 296). Others, including Derek Prince as well as Reinhard Bonnke and his Christ for All Nations team based in Frankfurt, Germany, were also influential in Ghana's changing Pentecostal scene. Prince's book *How to Pass from Curse to Blessing* (1986) is said to have been one of the most influential texts at the time. It taught that demons had the power to cause illness and psychological problems, and that curses held converts back from receiving God's blessings. Such teachings were popular in Ghana and other parts of Africa, as they confirmed the volitional nature of ancestral curses and witchcraft spirits. God's name and power were regularly invoked in prayers as sanctification of success and well-being in life. Christian theologies, such as the "faith gospel," also known as the health and wealth gospel, emphasized that the Christian is already healthy and wealthy, and that the believer has only to have faith and take possession of this reality.

On 31 December 1981, Flight Lieutenant J.J. Rawlings took over in another military coup (also known as his "second coming"), following which he set up the Provisional National Defence Council (PNDC). Rawlings took charge at a time when Pentecostalism's presence in Ghana was visibly increasing, and African traditional religion (ATR) presented itself as a public challenge to Christianity. The political and economic circumstances that would follow led many Ghanaians, including Chris, to leave Ghana and seek their future elsewhere. Rawlings consciously set out to promote ATR (for example, by giving its representatives airtime on public radio) in order to teach Ghanaians about their African traditional religious past that they had since forgotten. In 1989, Rawlings tried to introduce the Religious Bodies Registration Law (PNDC Law 221), calling for all religious institutions in Ghana to register with the National Commission on Culture. This policy was intended to curb the increase of new churches, but was quickly shot down when the Christian Council of Ghana and the Catholic Bishops' Conference publicly objected to it. These and other government interventions were seen as a threat to Christianity because they were aimed at curtailing the rising Christian activity in the country. However, with the increasing popularity of Pentecostalism, it was not long before Rawlings was attending church services and rubbing shoulders with many of its leaders.

By the early 1990s, "deliverance theology," which is linked to the "faith gospel," had a firm foothold in Ghana's Christian scene. It claimed to help individuals remove demonic obstacles preventing them from

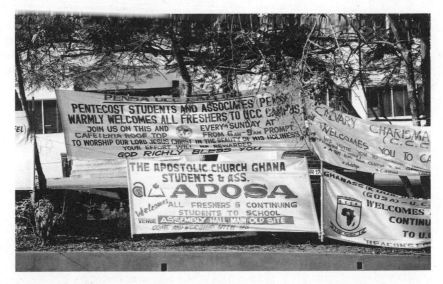

Figure 1.1 Banners advertising Pentecostal-charismatic university fellowships. (Photo by the author.)

Figure 1.2 Banner advertising the 10th Anniversary of PIWC Accra. (Photo by the author.)

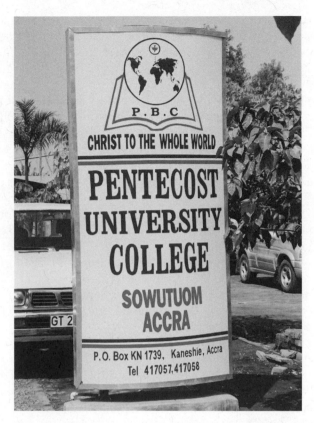

Figure 1.3 Sign for CoP's Pentecost University College. (Photo by the author.)

receiving their promises of wealth and health.[17] The continued emphasis on "success," "prosperity," and "deliverance" that these churches promoted allowed the charismatic contingent to mobilize and attract large numbers of people. Among them, a new generation of university-educated Ghanaians emerged, and their participation in these charismatic movements created new challenges for CoP leadership. This new generation was more comfortable reading, praying, and worshipping in English than in Twi or any other local language. Due to the teachings of numerous charismatic pastors, many church members became more interested in the "spiritual power" that Pentecostalism had to offer through healing and deliverance ministries. When these graduates returned to, or joined, the church, their presence increasingly posed a threat to the

Influences and seniority of the "uneducated" CoP pastors and elders who had not been to university and who did not agree with these new teachings. Many younger and educated members in CoP were disgruntled with the church leadership and many church "traditions," and joined the new charismatic churches.

Church leaders eventually responded to the rising educational level and changing expectations of their members as well as to changes in Ghana's Christian scene. They argued that these new Pentecostal teachings rendered Ghanaian Pentecostals self- absorbed in problems associated with negative aspects of African culture, preventing Christians from realizing that they already had the necessary tools for salvation upon conversion. CoP introduced English and international assemblies, initiated the Pentecost Students Association (PENSA) on university campuses, started a Pentecost University College, helped create the Ghana Pentecostal Council, and emphasized church history. These strategies were in part an attempt by the church to distinguish CoP from the mainline and other charismatic Christian churches in Ghana, which also adopted the Holy Spirit baptism and speaking in tongues, and incorporated them into their religious practices.[18] These measures included introducing theological education for CoP's pastors – a topic I shall return to in the next chapter.

Rawlings's party later became the National Democratic Congress (NDC), on the eve of Ghana's return to multiparty politics. The turn to democracy in 1992 greatly increased the presence of Christianity in the public space and turned the tide in favour of Pentecostal and charismatic Christianity. The 1990s in general saw the gradual but increasing privatization and liberalization of radio stations and television channels, as well as newspapers. By 2000, the National Patriotic Party (NPP), under the leadership of J.A. Kufuor, defeated the NDC. Many Pentecostals celebrated, because they saw this political shift as an opportunity to open up the country for a Christian renewal that would save Ghana's future.

The Future of the Church, the Future of the Nation (2000–2004)

In his book *Is Ghana under a Curse?* (2000) – a compilation of several articles written for the Christian newspaper *The Watchman* – Divine Kumah asks "why" are Ghanaians experiencing God's wrath if Ghana is a Christian country.[19] The answer he develops is that Ghana's past is filled with idolatry: traditional religious practices and self-interested and corrupt politicians who act like gods. Protestant reformers like

Kumah and Pentecostal church leaders engage with their country's history and changing political situation through a Christian narrative of salvation and redemption from an idolatrous past. The universalizing implications of a transcendental faith that promises freedom and radical rupture is available to anyone who is willing to take it up, simultaneously challenged by a non-Christian and pagan past that constantly returns to haunt it.

The Pentecostal modernist discourse is observable in two rhetorical themes: moving forward into the future and bringing people back to God. These ideas share a theoretical legacy of "moral progress," which assumes that modernity would "eliminate local traditions and irrational convictions" (Sanders and West 2003, 8). Variants of a theory of modernity hold the assumption that people can and eventually will become modern, breaking the shackles of tradition and ignorance.[20] Pentecostal Christians participate in a discourse of religious progress and rupture from the traditional past, imagining the historical changes in Ghana's political scene in continuity with a divine master plan. They also feel they have an obligation to intercede on behalf of their nation through prayer. This editorial statement of *Pentecostal Voice*, published by the Ghana Pentecostal Council (GPC), was released just before the Ghanaian elections in 2000:

> Ghana, as a nation, has come a very long way in social, political and economic experience since its independence from British rule in 1957. The sad fact is that rather than revere and draw closer to God who delivered the country from colonial domination and exploitation, most Ghanaians have, by their character and behaviour, consistently drifted further away from this gracious God. The net result of this state of godlessness is a pervasive atmosphere of lawlessness, dishonesty, national insecurity, idolatry and immorality, corruption and utter disregard for human life, which has drawn the judgment of a just God. By organising the all-night prayer meetings, the GPC and the Christian Council of Ghana have led Ghanaian Christians to fulfill their obligation to intercede for themselves and their nation. (GPC 2000)

Prior to the elections, John Atta Mills, who had become the presidential candidate for the NDC after Rawlings stepped down, went to the headquarters of the Ghana Pentecostal Council (also CoP headquarters) and asked its leaders to pray for his successful victory. They obliged by praying for him. However, "God had the final say," a CoP leader told me, as Mills did not win that year's elections, Ghana's political independence and liberation from an oppressive colonial past and an ungodly present are commonly accredited to the salvation of a transcendent Judeo-Christian God. At the same time, according to this same logic, Ghanaians are moving backward into a previous state of godlessness. Such a trajectory of progression and regression assume that Ghanaians will eventually join the advance of modernity once they return to God. These were promises of a new moral order that would take Ghanaians out of a backward state of traditional religion, poverty, national insecurity, and towards a widespread adherence to Christianity, equal opportunities, and a more centralized state under a just Judeo-Christian God.

CoP leaders offer a narrative mediation and structural response to existential questions such as "Where do we come from?" and "Where are we going?" They work hard at providing and commemorating a church history that is simultaneously a story about origins and Christian continuity. In May 2003, I attended CoP's fiftieth anniversary lectures, at which General Secretary Apostle Koduah spoke about the future of the church in what he called a "postmodern era." The anniversary lectures were held in the church auditorium of the Pentecost University College in Sowutuom, Accra. Koduah's ideas on the matter of postmodernity were closely associated with the recent era of political and economic liberalization in Ghana, described as a period of cultural change based on a model that prioritized satisfying the immediate needs of the individual, with the assumption that this path would bring social and economic benefits for all. Church leaders worried that the logic of purely interested exchange had penetrated Pentecostalism in Ghana and that changes in the market economy promoted a message that neglected the second coming of Jesus Christ, focusing instead on the immediate satisfaction of worldly needs and desires. Koduah described this new model of postmodernity as built from relations between parties that are, and whose perspectives are, by definition, seen to be equal. This ideology of individual autonomy and equality without deference to a universal God was problematic for church leaders, just as an ideology of commitment to a traditional past that does not defer personal authority to Jesus had been.

If the modern era posed the problem of not believing in anything in particular, the postmodern era, Koduah said, posed the larger and more dangerous problem of a "belief in one's self." In his lecture, he said that while "modernity" rejected religion altogether, "postmodernity" claims that no one has a monopoly on truth. The more recent postmodern concern to develop "a multicultural awareness" celebrates "differences at the expense of the universal." In Apostle Koduah's speech, he said that the world had become a "global village," affected by the philosophy of "existentialism," which caused people to believe in themselves without submission to the authority of the Word of God. This model of the autonomous individual subject, which prioritized personal freedom and unfettered consumption, created a growing anxiety concerning the boundaries of the Pentecostal subject. According to Koduah, this postmodern subject was "non-committal" and involved in a lifestyle that "makes gays and lesbians come out openly and shamelessly, makes people do things with their bodies, such as tattoos, earrings, body piercing, sex changes [and] allows sexual promiscuity." Such postmodern practices were in tension with a church ethics of bodily integrity, self-discipline, and sexual self-control. The human and sexual rights discourse in Ghana had its universalist assumptions challenged by the competing universal claims of a global faith whose morality is sustained by the Scriptures. In other words, this universal rights-based discourse is seen as not grounded in an appropriate Christian ethics of social relatedness and self-restraint. Instead, the idea of personal freedom and accompanying rights-based discourses depends on an understanding of a specific "self-owning subject" that enjoys free expression and choice regarding belief and practice (Asad 2003, 150).

"Can the Church stand the test of time?" Apostle Koduah went on to ask. "Will the next generation of church leaders be able to defend the faith in this society of permissiveness? Can we pass on the baton to succeeding generations?" The Apostle was staging a nostalgic return to a universal Christian God that should have relevance within the broader Ghanaian public sphere. He advocated that the church "go back to the Bible and engage in power evangelism to convince even the die-hard postmodernists that Jesus is still alive and the Bible is still the power of God for those who believe." This return to "origins" re-invoked an imagery of rupture, but was equally concerned with negotiating between what part of the convert's Christian present was to be retained and what left behind. The church was also attempting to mediate between a neoliberal representation of an autonomous individualist self and an interdependent Christian self. In doing so, the Apostle wanted to help the church determine the "negotiables" (church tradition) from the "non-negotiables" (what is biblical). These concerns reflected an earlier conversation I had with the Apostle in which he said:

Dynamic as the world has become, there is a need to change. Of course we don't change for the sake of changing. And there are certain things in the church that must never change. And that is the Word of God. But certain practices may have to change from time to time.

"Change" was a way for CoP to retain their younger members and to attract a postmodern generation. According to CoP leaders, many of the charismatic churches were corrupting the minds of the younger generation with harmful aspects of a new global culture. CoP had already lost a considerable number of young people to the charismatic churches. Koduah's list of "non-negotiables" included (1) strong emphasis on prayer, (2) emphasis on spontaneous worship, (3) holiness and discipline, (4) aggressive evangelism, (5) truth of the Word of God, and (6) reliance on the Holy Spirit. The "negotiables" included cultural attributes of the church, such as the segregation of the sexes, women's head coverings, and the non-flexible seating arrangement that sometimes saw the pastors and elders of the church sit on stage on big cushioned chairs in front of the congregation. This internal discussion and contestation was less often about a clash of world views than a shared reflection on what was acceptable church tradition and what should be discarded as unwarranted traditional culture.

In his closing address to the fiftieth anniversary lectures, CoP Chairman Apostle Ntumy summarized the two nights' discussions: "We have been exposed to the history of the church, to the man McKeown, the church in a postmodern world, and the way forward ... We have been reminded of our roots, our spiritual genesis." While a complete break with the past is inherent to Pentecostal ideology, another important theme is a return to one's roots. A remembrance of church history simultaneously drew upon memories of the church's founding fathers, referred to as "ancestors" and role models to be emulated and commemorated. In their remembrance, church leaders also spoke about the continuity of the church and the changing direction that the church had to take if it intended to maintain its significant growth.[21]

Writing about Nigerian Pentecostalism, Ruth Marshall describes how born-again discourse simultaneously reviews its own history and "finds its conditions of plausibility as a form of response to the ordeal of everyday life in postcolonial Nigeria" (2009, 53). According to Marshall, apart from "a linear, teleological notion of time," Pentecostalism also involves "the representation of the present as an ordeal fraught with dangers" (ibid., 65). The second advent of Christ, or the *parousia*, was one of the themes for that year's General Council meeting in Accra. This "time *before* the end," or messianic time, is a part of historical chronological time that "presents itself as the *only time we have*" (Marshall 2010, 205). In considering such messianic time, the remaking of CoP identity was not a complete rejection of the past but a way to repeatedly address the dangers of this "time *within* the present time" (ibid., 206). Such repetition, even as it acts as a return, brings forward new possibilities, while simultaneously allowing church authorities to selectively make changes that will respond to the urgency of the end times. It also contributes to the construction of a collective identity. These combined practices of past-making and future-building are a way to bind members vertically to the Christian God, to the ancestors of the church, and, simultaneously, to their leaders, helping create an origin myth about the benevolence of the early church and its fulfilment of an earlier promise.

CoP leaders were engaged in a search for authenticity, a shared identity that had to be protected from an onslaught of external threats, including the dangers of liberalization, globalization, and the practices of the charismatic churches. This search was a selective search for church "culture" that would be productive in terms of CoP's Pentecostal identity, as opposed to a dangerous worldly "culture" that promoted individualist and materialist concerns. In creating these boundaries, leaders were simultaneously constructing an essence of who they were, while defining others as anachronisms in Ghanaian society.

Conclusion

As this chapter demonstrates, the movement of missionaries, local charismatic leaders, their transregional and transatlantic connections and communications, as well as the Christian literature that formed part of these flows were important contributing factors to the changing Ghanaian Pentecostal scene. The earlier disputes between personalities such as McKeown and Anim are indicative of the questions that Pentecostal Christians in Ghana and elsewhere in the world continue to ask: "If Jesus is the answer, what are the criteria for bringing the divine into presence, and what are its limits?" This debate involves re-problematizing how the past features in the present through a process of reflection and ethical contestations. While it is important to understand the authoritative and specific techniques required to make God present, Pentecostals are also encountering dilemmas, asking questions, and making personal decisions regarding how to locate the appropriate balance between rupture and continuity in order to determine what elements pass, according to what criteria, at what scale, and to what effect.

Inherent to sharing Protestant religious values is another assumption: not everyone has the same access to the divine. Even as Protestant Christianity claims to provide believers with equal access to the divine, and even if converts share the same religious values, there is always the looming question that the other person might not be truly transformed or that some are more transformed than others. If rupture is an essential theme in Pentecostal conversion, it is also important to understand how born-again Christians ethically reflect on the potential ways in which the past features in the making and unmaking of the present and on the question of where to place their faith.

Where Christians place their faith in God is a key question, and this chapter has paid attention to the limits of rupture as well as to the role that discernment and judgment play in such processes to help maintain a continuity and community of practice. These contestations provide a rolling context for the tensions inherent to a project whose history is still unfolding, a history that values the transcendental-social over the political-mundane. Yet the political and mundane bring us back to the problems of the present, to the ethical dilemmas Ghanaian Pentecostals face in staying faithful to their commitments. Christianity as discontinuity and messianic time is not opposed to processes of integrity and historical continuity. The problems of the present are part of a politics of the Spirit – determining how to emplace and contextualize a transcendental other in the world and within a time before the end of time.

From Anim to McKeown to the present day, Ghanaian Pentecostals have actively sought to distinguish between a non-Christian past or an un-Christian present and a Christian present in order to build a common future. McKeown and Anim had competing visions of a Pentecostal community and of the ways through which rupture should be applied in practice. Such a tension concerning values is a common feature in the history of Pentecostalism in Ghana. This difference in values also applies to CoP today, and to what is described as the problems of a postmodern generation. If access to Pentecostal knowledge is represented as unmediated, free, and open to anyone who becomes born again, ethical practice allows a critical space for the ongoing, strategic negotiation of transcendental Christian values with cultural values. An attention to the dangers of the "present" entails balancing different values that might seem incompatible with each other, as well as demonstrating discernment with respect to a hierarchy of values (see Lambek 2008; Robbins 2004a).

The next chapter takes a closer look at the personal difficulties a pastor faces when striving to maintain the church position that religious transformation is complete once a convert is born again. It examines how church values become relativized through the uncertainty of self–other relationships, and how Pentecostal practice is critically evaluated and reflected upon differently by church leaders and others in the church. If the relationship between rupture and continuity is partly a strategic one, ethical practice can take many immanent forms as church members discover new possibilities arising from the process of dismantling, transforming, and creating Christian values. By attending to the uncertainties faced by Christians about what is good or right, we come closer to understanding that the relationship between rupture and continuity is intrinsically an ethical one.

Chapter Two

Uncertainties and Dilemmas

Ewiase aya basaa

The world has gone sour.   Akan proverb

"Why," says Serenus, "should I not confess to you
the truth, as to a good doctor? ... I do not feel altogether
ill but nor do I feel entirely in good health."   Michel Foucault (1993)

I was in Kumasi to visit Pastor "Kofi" (not his real name). As I sat waiting in his church office, I could not help but reflect on a prayer service
that he had organized some months before. At this service, a visiting
Nigerian charismatic minister spoke about witchcraft's continuing
presence in the lives of converts and introduced sand into people's
prayers to help break this connection. The prayer event, which I had
attended in November 2003, had the feel of a charismatic-style service
and included elements that were antithetical to what I had come to see
as CoP practice. My curiosity about the appropriateness of this service
led me to have conversations with church leaders and members about
how rupture ought to be expressed once a convert is born again. These
conversations presented different sides of a debate about the uncertainties and dilemmas that accompany any claim of Pentecostal transformation. My curiosity inadvertently also alerted CoP leaders in Accra to
the details of the church service that Kofi had organized in Kumasi.
This did not bode well for Kofi, since the leaders disapproved of the
actions of the Nigerian minister and of Kofi's invitation. I was in Kumasi to get Kofi's side of things.

Kofi looked contemplative as he sat in front of me. He had recently returned from Accra, where he had met with members of CoP's Executive Committee and been questioned by the church leaders about his views on salvation. The Nigerian minister's use of sand in prayer and his sermons on witchcraft posed several theological problems. Kofi was warned not to repeat such prayer in church, but yet he seemed comfortable with the outcome of the prayer service. I asked him what he thought about the church doctrine on salvation, which maintained that witchcraft and ancestral spirits no longer have an effect on the lives of believers once they are born again. Kofi replied, "There is truth to those who believe that there is no post-salvation deliverance. By that one sacrifice we agree that all that one has to do with our salvation is complete and total, no doubt about that." Then he paused, before saying, "However, the question to ask now is, if that is the truth, do we actually see it in the lives of people? If not, why?" From a "personal point of view," he continued, "we still find people who have problems. The reality is, even though salvation is complete, we are still human beings and are still committing sin. We open ourselves up to the devil to work in our lives for which we need the hand of God to come in." Kofi's response confirmed the church criteria for salvation, while allowing for the possibility that other methods of alleviating suffering were also possible and admissible, and that traditional spirits do not simply go away after conversion.

This chapter provides an ethnographic window into how a Christian rupture with the past is subject to personal struggles and interpersonal disputes. If ethical practice includes forms of regularization that provide church members with a sense of continuity with the Christian future, it also allows for the consideration of moments of uncertainty and indeterminacy through which alternative practices can coexist and become institutional irritants. While church leaders promote a radical rupture with the traditional past and an un-Christian present, others in CoP are more interested in a practical salvation that addresses the continued presence of traditional others in their lives. Rather than a single truth, ethical practice allows for multiple positions around how transformation can take place. By neglecting the diverse ways in which transformation is expressed and rupture is experienced, we potentially obscure the interpersonal contingencies involved in remaining faithful, contingencies that can only be partially acknowledged in born-again language and ritual. If Pentecostal subjects rhetorically claim to make a complete break with the past, they also struggle at remaining committed. This problem of continuity presents other possibilities for Christian action that may not always align with what church members are supposed to believe.

While CoP leaders and Kofi shared an ideological position regarding "what" salvation is, this stance did not resolve the more personal and situational "why" questions that persisted. These questions include "Why do my loved ones continue to suffer after conversion?" and "Why do witchcraft spirits continue to haunt the believer?" The incommensurability and incompatibility of these "what" and "why" questions have further implications for the role of ethical practice in understanding the interpersonal dimensions of rupture as radical change. Another consideration for ethical practice is the question of "when" a specific Christian doctrine becomes more or less applicable. In taking a closer look at the contexts in which rupture is claimed and put into practice, we come closer to understanding how Pentecostals maintain a sense of continuity with their religious identity, albeit differently. A description of the prayer service that Kofi organized, which got him into some trouble, seems a good place to begin.

The Thanksgiving Service

At a week-long annual thanksgiving event in 2003, a large banner with the words "An Encounter with the Supernatural" was prominently displayed across the wall behind the festively decorated pulpit in an English CoP assembly in Kumasi. Every evening, the two-storey church building was packed with hundreds of people. Those attending clapped their hands and danced to the music, sang songs of worship, and, at times, were taken over by an uncontrollable urge to pray in an unintelligible language – all signs of being filled with the Holy Spirit. Reverend Abraham Chigbundu, a visiting Nigerian pastor invited by Pastor Kofi to lead the week's prayers, asked attendees to bring handfuls of sand into church. The sand represented their ongoing connection to their ancestral lands. They were told to hold the sand in the palms of their hands and to pray over it. According to Reverend Chigbundu, these prayers helped to sever all ties to their ancestral hometowns and to the witchcraft spirits preventing them from fulfilling their destinies. He told the congregation that a Christian's blessings of wealth, health, and prosperity could be stolen by ancestral spirits and witches, and asked them to pray to be set free from any spiritual connection to their past. Their "old altars" would be replaced by "new altars," he said. At the end of each day's service, many of those attending made financial offer-ings and shared testimonies of having been set free from life's obstacles and personal suffering. Through their participation in these prayers, church members were aligning themselves with a more positive Chris-tian future in which they no longer saw themselves as victims of cir-cumstances beyond their control. They were making a break with what they considered to be lingering attachments to a negative non-Christian and traditional past (Maxwell 1998; Meyer 1998b, 1999; Engelke 2004).

This event threw into relief the social and personal tensions at the heart of Pentecostalism in Ghana and, more specifically, within CoP. Reverend Chigbundu was a charismatic minister from Benin City, Nige-ria, famous for his teachings on demon possession and on the lingering continuity of witchcraft in the lives of born-again believers. According to him, the continuing effects of witchcraft required special deliverance prayers for their removal. The belief in the continuing presence of witch-craft spirits and the use of sand, however, reminded CoP leaders of problematic continuities with traditional religion and of a charismatic Christianity that had entered the religious market since the 1980s. Many of the leaders of the charismatic churches emphasize that born-again Christians have immediate access to health, wealth, and success, and claim that demons and ancestral curses continue to affect believers' lives after they have come to Christ (Gifford 2004, 85–6). According to CoP leaders, charismatic churches have introduced a "new Gospel," whose emphasis on sensationalist prayer performances and the expectation of miracles and immediate results goes against the leaders' own focus on the Christian virtues of holiness, moral discipline, patience, and evange-lism in anticipation of the second coming of Jesus. CoP leaders also see cultural continuities between these charismatic teachings and tradition-al beliefs, and face challenges in controlling such teachings and prayer activities within the church. This problem arises partly because tradi-tional religious healers and charismatic pastors often use the same ob-jects in their healing, and both preach that witchcraft and ancestral curses still have a part to play in an individual's present suffering.

In the next section, I focus on the shared values within the church regarding what must be done about the new charismatic teachings, and on the church leaders' attempts to police the boundaries of Pentecostal rupture. I describe how establishing continuities in church practice is one important way to resolve the church leaders' "why" questions con-cerning the dangers of Ghana's "new Gospel."

Church Leaders In Ghana

> The power of Jesus Christ takes care of the individual once born again. However, now people are still preaching that these demons still have an impact on your life … [T]hese are false teachings. The fears of the unknown and malevolent spirits are bringing Ghanaians back to where they have been delivered. The problem is that many Christians do not know their position in the Lord Jesus Christ.
>
> Apostle Koduah (2004)

In my conversation with Apostle Koduah, he spoke about the changing world and the speed at which the church has been growing over the last fifteen years. He was visibly upset about the state of Christianity in Ghana. Ghana had increasingly become a "Christian country," he said, and its airwaves were saturated with Christian themes, songs, and programs. Yet, why was it still filled with problems of corruption and other moral and social dilemmas? Apostle Koduah was referring to the significant changes that had taken place in Ghana since the 1980s, specifically to Ghana's increasing neoliberal reforms and its turn to democracy beginning in 1992, which have helped promote the spread of Pentecostal Christianity. Since the early 1990s, Christianity has become the most popular religion in Ghana, he told me. The political defeat of Jerry Rawlings and his National Democratic Congress in the 2000 elections provided Ghanaians with additional hope and optimism for positive change.[1]

Apostle Koduah was upset that Ghana had not truly become a Christian country. Because of the recent political and economic developments, he asserted, Ghana and its people were once again returning to traditional religious beliefs and practices, and losing sight of the true prize – Jesus. The concerns he expressed regarding the dangers of the present are linked to the "why" questions church leaders ask themselves about the continuity of non-Christian beliefs and practices in Ghana's changing Pentecostal scene. The "present" in Ghanaian Pentecostalism has been transformed by what Birgit Meyer calls a "pentecostalite public culture," in which "pentecostalite expressive forms" such as "music, popular theater, call-in radio programs, and video-films" (2004b, 92) converge with popular culture in the public realm to feature the work of the devil in the everyday lives of Africans. The liberalization of the media in 1995 has since transferred state control of radio, television, the press, and other forms of media into the hands of private companies, giving independent prophets and charismatic Christian churches more influence in the public sphere and allowing individual church leaders to become famous (de Witte 2012; Gifford 2004; Hackett 1998). With the increasing number of FM radio stations and more television channels like GTV, Metro, and TV3 featuring Christian programs, Christian freedom came clothed in the form of new Pentecostal-charismatic teachings that were incommensurable with CoP doctrines on salvation.

This new Pentecostalism and its public presence are seen as dangerous to CoP values and the idea of rupture as complete. Apostle Koduah said that the recent charismatic Christian media explosion and the proliferation of charismatic fellowships and ministries helped spread a "skewed Gospel." He pointed to the charismatic churches' undue emphasis on the material aspects of salvation: wealth, prosperity, and health. He noted that many charismatic books had flooded the Ghanaian market from outside, coming mainly from North America and Nigeria, and that they presented an image of Pentecostalism which church leaders did not agree with. These new texts and their charismatic preacher-writers introduced teachings that emphasized prosperity, get-rich-quick schemes, instant miracles, and deliverance from witchcraft and demon possession, which encouraged Ghanaian Pentecostals to become more absorbed in problems associated with what Koduah considered negative aspects of African culture. He told me:

> It is because of our traditional beliefs. The African, and the Ghanaian for that matter, almost always fears the unknown. We feel surrounded by so many malevolent spirits, all over the place, ready to attack us. That has been our traditional belief ... Unfortunately these new preachers, people who are propagating this new Gospel, seem to be bringing the African, or the Ghanaian for that matter, back to where they have been delivered from. To say that you still have all these things hanging around you, to destroy your life ... because this is already built up in us, it easily finds a fertile ground in the minds of the average African.

Something had to be done, Koduah told me. In reaction, many church leaders took it upon themselves to publish their own books and moral manuals on the topics of ancestral curses and deliverance. Their aim was to educate their members on how to distinguish between the Holy Spirit and other spirits, between genuine rupture and dangerous cultural continuities. They wanted their church members to learn to cultivate Christian virtues such as personal discipline, patience, and individual responsibility based on a Christian character, and to avoid "cultural extremes." Apostle Opoku Onyinah, a CoP senior leader, wrote two books, *Ancestral Curses* (1994) and *Overcoming Demons* (1995), to help counter the popularity of ideas and practices concerning ancestral curses and deliverance prayer in Ghana. In his first book, Onyinah wrote that while those "not grounded in the Word of God" can still suffer attacks by demons because of weaknesses such as sin and human nature, what is called for is not deliverance but "perseverance in the Christian life" (1994, 54). In his second book, he distinguished between the work of the Holy Spirit in Christianity and the extremes of "culture," manifested in the work of charismatic prophets and the belief that "traditional" spiritual powers have a hold over an individual who has been born again.[2]

The church leaders' anxiety over the use of sand in church stemmed from their fear of the increasing penetration of charismatic practices into CoP, and their subsequent disciplining of Kofi was aimed at charging him to cultivate his faith with more vigilance. In their view, the use of sand as a medium of prayer was not acceptable, even if Jesus used sand in healing. While Jesus and his disciples used certain material objects such as sand and cloth in prayer, these practices were not intended to become paradigms or entrepreneurial models for making a profit. For CoP leaders like Onyinah, church members need to be taught the "right thing." The Bible cannot be freely interpreted; it has to be properly discerned by those who are theologically trained in order to bring the focus back to "Jesus first." According to Apostle Ntumy, CoP chairman at the time:

> If we were to leave everybody to do what they felt God was leading them to do, then eventually, there would be no control … Jesus spat on the ground and mixed his saliva with the soil, pasted it [on] somebody's eye and asked that person to go and wash. Did Jesus establish that as a parting, as a paradigm? So should you only heal people by spitting on the ground? There was a time when the apostles … you know [used] aprons and handkerchiefs from Peter and the others were sent to the people. That is true. But did Peter ever have to go to the shop, buy a whole piece of cloth, cut them into pieces, pray over them, and distribute them? … Although this has a biblical precedent, if you discern it rightly you realize that these people's orientations are not correct. You also realize that, ultimately, it is not leading people to Christ. Their faith will be in those things more than in Christ.

Church leaders' concerns are in line with continued efforts to arrest what was termed by the early leaders as "unscriptural practices" in the church through authoritative discernment. These unscriptural practices included the overdependence on the power of prophets to solve problems and the repeated use of objects in prayer, such that it becomes "formulaic" or ritualistic. According to CoP leaders, dependence on such methods or on "a powerful man of God" relegates Jesus to a secondary status. For the virtuous Ghanaian Pentecostal, experience of miracles, in itself, is not enough. The chairman of the church described to me how he eventually cured himself of a childhood stammer by seeking God's help through many days of fasting and prayer. He described a scene in his bedroom, where he had a vision of an angel touching his lips. When he awoke, his stammer had disappeared. The chairman knew that miracles happened, as he had first-hand experience of one, but without the help of a prophet and with the knowledge that God works in his own time. In this model of transformation, Pentecostal Christian virtues and good conduct are determined by the demonstration of qualities such as perseverance and patience – the act of placing one's faith in the final work of Jesus and not in the power of multiple others.

The charismatic churches and their teachings have provoked reactions of concern among CoP leaders regarding the "fear of fakery" in Pentecostal practice. Jesse Shipley has commented that a "fear of fakery" in Ghanaian public life more broadly points to the shared social anxieties about moral and religious belief. The "fake" is not a negation of value but a critical comment on it – "a deliberative space for talking about the threat and promise of individuated desires" (2009, 547). These struggles to discern the "real" and the "fake" are also important aspects of locating the appropriate boundaries of Pentecostal practice and for criticizing the individuated desires that charismatic churches promote. It is their ability to stand apart from the "fake" that gives CoP leaders their authority in circumscribing how freedom should be imagined and in illustrating how to select one particular alternative or set of alternatives out of many, while rejecting competing ones and ignoring those deemed incommensurable. In doing so, church leaders are involved in maintaining continuity with a specific Christian future, while dealing with problems of a counterfeit Christianity.

As I have shown, CoP leaders struggle with what they consider to be an increasing inability of their own members, and Pentecostal Christians in general, to distinguish between the real and the fake in Ghana's changing religious scene. Increasing numbers of senior pastors and church leaders have been theologically trained, either in Ghana or overseas, notably at the Regents Theological College in the United Kingdom, where they have earned Master's and PhD degrees in theology. Church leaders have also expanded the CoP Bible School in Accra into a theological university education centre. As a church leader told me, "If you don't have your own scholars competent enough to articulate what you believe, then you eventually keep feeding yourself with what others think is the right stuff ... If you don't know the genuine, it is very hard to determine the counterfeit."

Theological knowledge, which helped one discern between the "genuine" and the "counterfeit," was not only determined by knowing the Bible well or by receiving theological training. True discernment also had to be accompanied by a submission to church hierarchy and authority, which demonstrated what Apostle Koduah called the "character of God." According to him:

> We are more concerned about character ... Some of them might be very charismatic, but may not be submissive to authority. You can know theology from Genesis to Revelation, you can memorize the whole Bible, you can speak in all tongues, all languages of this world and be so charismatic. If you do not have the character of God, you are only making noise.

The theological and institutional agreement over what Pentecostal rupture is and how to demonstrate Christian character also allowed for a shared understanding of what it is not. The underlying assumption of such systematization and purification projects is that once people realize they are simply misguided, they can abandon false practices, places, and objects for the real thing: the transcendental (Keane 1998, 17). It is dicta such as this that lead to the confinement of Pentecostal doctrine and its practice to a certain space, a realm protected through the vigilant regulation of its boundaries, which are being threatened by cultural, charismatic, and even capitalistic penetration.

In recalling Kofi to church headquarters, leaders expected him to do more than simply explain why he did not seek permission before inviting the Nigerian pastor or why he allowed the use of sand in church prayer; they also expected him to confess and reveal the "truth" about his beliefs on salvation (Foucault 1993). Kofi's response was a measured one that did not depend on an exclusive acceptance or an outright rejection of the church leaders' views on Pentecostal rupture. Instead, it captured a component of ethical practice, which emerges out of a personal responsibility to others, set apart from church authority. It was his momentary remove from institutional power that day which allowed Kofi to envision a new form of relationality and care. For Kofi, if deliverance prayers were "wrong," in that they were a theologically unacceptable form of Pentecostal practice for CoP leaders, they also became that very potential for change, an emergent state that allowed church members to meet their personal objectives and helped them move past the spiritual obstacles in their path. Kofi's personal happiness had been interrupted by the intrusion of witchcraft spirits in his wife's life. His Christian perspective only makes sense against the situational and lived tensions within his own life and with his wife's illness. Through this experience of his wife's illness and his inability to do much to help her, Kofi came to recognize the limits of his own Pentecostal identity, its assumptions of rupture, and the difficulties of remaining consistent.

Kofi's Perspective

Kofi did not regret what had happened at the thanksgiving service. He acknowledged his mistakes – forgetting to inform the church area head and not asking permission from the church leaders when he invited Reverend Chigbundu to preach. Personally, however, Kofi had not felt anything was off when Chigbundu preached on witchcraft and deliverance. At the time, as he watched people bring handfuls of sand into church to use them to break their associations to witchcraft, it had not seemed wrong. For many of the people participating in the prayer service, himself included, the sand instantiated God's presence in their lives and did not challenge or diminish their faith in Jesus. God, in the form of the Holy Spirit, is considered a social actor whose presence allows for the element of surprise in any situation and who introduces the miraculous into the mundane. Kofi was less concerned with what he and other church members had done than with the quality of their thoughts and the substance of their actions. While he acknowledged that the church leaders were correct in their theological assessment that what he did was "wrong," why he did it and the consequences of what he did were more important questions that needed to be asked.

Kofi spoke to me about how the problems of a life lived in sin continued to haunt the world of a committed Pentecostal Christian. Kofi never made any reference to sin in a traditional context. Yet CoP leaders worry that church members continue to see sin traditionally or through the charismatic fells, as always returning and not completely washed away by the experience of being born again. In traditional Ghanaian (Akan) epistemology, sin, or *mmusu* (evil), takes the form of a mystical or spiritual force, a strong spirit that acts negatively on the spirit of a human, that "comes upon" or "follows" a person "as a result of the activity of witches, or other spiritual powers" (Atiemo 1995, 21–2).[3] This contact can lead to physical suffering and other negative experiences in life. While the concept of biblical sin in Christianity sets out to replace the traditional moral concept of *mmusu*, the idea of sin as a returning evil continues to have valence in Ghana and in people's everyday lives through more recent charismatic teachings – especially for explaining sickness, poverty, and witchcraft attacks. This way of thinking was certainly Reverend Chigbundu's political theology. His first book, *Loose Him & Let Him Go!* (1991), was extremely popular in Ghana's charismatic scene. It provided teachings on how to break free from ties of spiritual bondage to an ancestral and demonic past that continued to haunt the believer after conversion. The implicit continuity of a traditional idea of sin within charismatic teachings potentially implied that church members had not completely moved away from an African traditional world view.

Church leaders responded to such teachings through the regularization of biblical knowledge and church practice, aimed at developing a set of criteria that would serve as a basis for judging a Christian character accountable to church leadership. It also committed church members to internalizing these criteria and to evaluating both their own actions and themselves. While church values promote an unchanging liturgical order (Rappaport 1999), ethical practice entails finding the appropriate convergence between acceptable and unacceptable forms of religious practice, balancing different values that might seem incompatible with each other, as well as demonstrating discernment with respect to a hierarchy of values. For Kofi and others in the church, biblical truth becomes relative but still authoritative in times of personal difficulty, and situational judgment is prioritized over simply following the rules.

While Kofi publicly agreed that rupture with the traditional past is complete once an individual is born again, he also personally believed that prayers against witchcraft and the use of sand are necessary in cases in which ordinary prayer did not work. The sand was a practical component in Christian prayer and not a symbolic representation of a past cultural practice. "If Jesus had used sand with his saliva to recreate a blind man's eye, what was wrong with using sand to help deliver these people from connections to their ancestral past and demons?" he asked. When Kofi was still a student and a member of the Scripture Union, he had been taught about the different "stages of demon possession" as they manifested in a person's life. While he claimed he no longer theologically prescribed to this teaching, he continued to believe that demons were real and that deliverance prayers are sometimes necessary in times of suffering. He had personally benefited from the deliverance service that day, he told me. Kofi's pragmatism was also part of a personal and spiritual problem that haunted his own life.

Kofi testified to the church congregation at the end of the week's thanksgiving service, saying that the deliverance prayers had finally broken something which had been holding back the fulfilment of his prayers for many years. He told me that his wife had been living in a prayer camp outside Kumasi, in the western region of Ghana. He described her as "spiritually sick," suffering from mental health problems. A few months after their marriage, several years before, she started showing signs of insanity following a dream she had in which a woman threw a bag of snakes at her. Kofi had "tried everything to heal her," he said. All forms of church-approved prayer were used, including the laying on of hands, intercessory prayer, fasting for over forty days, rolling on the ground while praying, and crying. Nothing worked. "Things only got worse," he told me. He eventually went to seek the advice of a senior church leader whom he respected. The church leader reminded him that his wife's salvation was already complete. She was born again and had received the Holy Spirit baptism. His wife was also a prayerful Christian who was well versed in the Bible. All that was required for her to be healed was for Kofi to lay his hands on her and pray to Jesus. All Kofi needed was patience and faith that God would eventually intervene.[4]

By this time, and after having already attempted these prescribed methods without any success, he decided that he needed someone else to mediate prayer on his wife's behalf and to sever any spiritual links tying her to her past, including those exposing her to possible witchcraft attacks. Eventually, he sent his wife to a well-known CoP prayer camp that had a record of successfully healing those with mental health problems associated with witchcraft. Prayer camps are places for prayer and fasting that provide residence and are run by Pentecostal prophets or healers who serve as consultants specializing in solving or removing spiritual problems (van Dijk 1997). While CoP operates prayer camps through which prophets conduct healing and deliverance services, CoP leaders have been extremely sceptical of the popularity and special status accorded these prophets, and of their reputation for being closer to God and more spiritually powerful than other individuals. If church leaders see the sacrifice of Jesus on the cross as the "beginning" of a new life that can be realized through a continuous development forward (transitive), prophets take this "beginning" as a radical starting point that focuses on ritual praxis in the present (intransitive), where they battle demons and ancestral spirits blocking the lives and destinies of church members (Lambek 2007). Kofi's wife had spent a number of years being treated by the prophet at the camp, and her eventual healing coincided with the deliverance session during the special thanksgiving service. She had finally been delivered from the spirit that had bewitched her, and she was slowly returning to her old self. This good news had come soon after Reverend Chigbundu's visit to Kumasi, and once he received the news, Kofi publicly testified to the feeling of being freed from something that had been haunting him.

By allowing sand to be used in prayer that day, Kofi showed as much a momentary disinterest in the church leaders' definition of salvation as a display of personal responsibility in being called to act by another's suffering. Kofi's story is both intensely personal and consistent with a pattern of practicing rupture that church leaders are uncomfortable with. If salvation is complete and rupture accomplished, Kofi need not take these spirits seriously or depend on another person for deliverance, relegating Jesus to a secondary status. In this case, however, Pentecostal Christians' "belief in" statements about rupture are less important than a focus "on the possibilities for intervening in and transforming those relationships" that are unhealthy (Street 2010, 268). Kofi shared the charismatic view that traditional spirits continue to haunt the living and can possess the bodies of loved ones. He held an orientation to Pentecostal transformation that was informed by competing moral registers rather than an ideological evocation of the distinctions maintained by the church leaders in their retrospective capacity to judge his actions. His wife's illness as well as the failure of a theological position set out by those senior to him allowed him to problematize church doctrine and to make a practical judgment regarding other ways of combining a transcendental theology with the materialistic enterprise of prayer. Rather than the enactment of a set of disciplinary practices, as prescribed by CoP, Kofi's application of practical judgment was similar to the Aristotelian virtue of *phronēsis*, which consists of knowing how to exercise judgment in particular cases and circumstances (see MacIntyre 2007, 154).

Kofi's example suggests that, alongside efforts to emphasize rupture as definitive and complete through authoritative practices, importance must be given to the ethical lives of religious subjects beyond public discourse and the domain of self-cultivating practices. Kofi's Christian character was in question. Ethical practice as practical judgment, in this case, can be seen not "simply [as] an act of commission or an acceptance of obligation" but as "includ[ing] the reasoning behind choosing to [act or accept] and the reasoning that determines how to balance one's multiple and possibly conflicting commitments" (Lambek 2000, 315). Kofi had to balance being committed to church values and being a dedicated husband. His Pentecostalism was also a "practical religion, this-worldly and minimally Salvationist" (Werbner 2011, 186; see also Cannell 2006b, 144–5). While the church leaders situate "Christianity at an end-point of moral trajectories," Kofi's perspective provides ethical content to the ways human and spiritual others do both good and harm to the individual (Klaits 2011, 145; see also Graveling 2010). Placing too much emphasis on discourses of rupture can overdetermine the boundaries between selves and others. Making judgments about which path to follow depends less on what sort of regulatory rules are involved in making decisions than on how the interdependencies of our relations with others are appreciated and interpreted. Certain authoritative forms of Pentecostal rupture ceased to be a problematic for Kofi when his wife was not responding to sanctioned forms of prayer. His priority became more about finding a solution to his wife's illness and spiritually induced madness than demonstrating the Christian virtue of patience or following church rules.

Kofi assumed responsibility for his actions and the actions of the Nigerian deliverance minister, eventually submitting to church authority. When the time to re-station him in a new church assembly came, he was appointed to a small rural church in Asamankese, eastern Ghana. He knew that the church leaders had offered him another chance to prove himself and was hopeful. Their questions about his beliefs on salvation were a test of his character. Kofi compromised, submitted to church authority, and stayed within the church. However, the church leaders' disciplinary actions and negative reaction did not produce a moment of Christian uncertainty for Kofi or compromise the quality of his faith. Rather, he knew, and continued to believe, that the Holy Spirit was present that day in the sand and that witchcraft was involved in his wife's illness. In the next section, I return to the question of how ethical practice is central to understanding Protestant uncertainty.

The Limits of Protestant Uncertainty

Because rupture is registered in moral terms, ethical practice is paramount to an understanding of Pentecostal rupture. The dispute between church leaders and Pastor Kofi also fits into a larger narrative about inherent uncertainties in Protestant Christianity (Bynum 2011, 34–5; Robbins 2003b, 196). In this section, I address the uncertainty that CoP leaders face when pondering how to distinguish the "real" from the "fake." I also show how ethical practice is an important window into the lives of individual believers who are trying to negotiate among practices that are more or less Christian and between what is expected of them and what best fits the situation and circumstance at the time.

With matter posing a threat and offering salvation simultaneously, the question for CoP leaders and other Protestants is: "How do we know that this is the work of the Holy Spirit?" In a religion that emphasizes the direct relationship between God and his believers, the appropriate coming together of the transcendental and the material is a common site for evaluation and fierce contestation (Engelke 2007; Keane 2007; Robbins 2003b). In their initial anxiety about, and later reactions to, the use of sand and the invocation of witchcraft in prayer, CoP leaders were trying to make a distinction between Pentecostal rupture as real change and as an adding on to past and present cultural formations. Drawing from his research in Sumba, eastern Indonesia, and the encounter there between Dutch Calvinist missionaries, their converts, and unconverted ritual specialists, Webb Keane explains how the moral concern of identifying Protestant freedom is linked to the problem that materiality poses to this transcendental project. Indeed, the proper place of human agency, with its "possibilities and limits," plays a central role in how Protestant reformers sort out "what is ethically acceptable" from what is not (2007, 25).[5]

These questions are also closely tied to what Matthew Engelke (2007) calls the "problem of presence." According to Engelke, biblical narratives such as the Fall illustrate an inherent tension between the distance and proximity that simultaneously exist between God and human beings. In his work among the Friday Apostolics in Zimbabwe, Engelke examines the different ways in which these African Christians who do not use the Bible continue to mediate the divine. He also uses the example of the movement's founder, Johane Masowe, to emphasize the importance of considering the uncertainties that punctuate the lives of all Christians when coming to know God (ibid., 16). In Engelke's analysis, uncertainty is comparable to Victor Turner's (1967) idea of "liminality," a productive moment that eventually allows the convert to appropriately inhabit the language of conversion (see Harding 2000).[6]

"What are the limits of ethically accepted divine mediation?" CoP leaders in Ghana also ask themselves this question, regarding how a rupture with the traditional past is identified, maintained, and managed. As a result, CoP leaders educate their members about the boundaries of the limited agency that witchcraft and ancestral spirits have in the lives of born-again believers. This is done through the publication of books and moral manuals teaching them the virtues of Christian patience and perseverance, and instructing them on how to deal with dangerous spiritual entities through laying their hands on the person and praying in the name of Jesus. Uncertainty is central to Protestant Christianity, and its authoritative mediation is important in helping believers achieve moments of clarity and Christian certainty. For Kofi and many others in CoP, however, the end result of ethical practice is not necessarily one of comprehension or of the appropriation of an authoritative religious language. Agreeing upon the rules and boundaries of Christian practice does not provide a sufficient answer to questions such as "Why do some people believe in and accept Jesus Christ as their personal Lord and Savior but still continue to suffer?," a question Kofi had asked me. While recent contributions to the anthropology of Christianity have helped us understand how a moral narrative of Protestant Christianity underpins the ways in which believers work hard at distinguishing the boundaries of sincere and authoritative Christian practice, we should also acknowledge that individual believers may not always find such distinctions important. While believers are negotiating between the normative and the tacit, between incommensurable and incompatible practices, there are also times when incompatibilities between doctrine and practice matter less and living comfortably matters more.

My focus on the ethical practice of Pentecostal subjects acknowledges the importance of Christian uncertainty in the unfolding of authoritative religious speech and action. However, I also share the assumption, with other earlier scholars of Africa such as Sally F. Moore (1975, 220), that while "rules, customs, and symbolic frameworks exist … they operate in the presence of areas of indeterminacy, or ambiguity, of uncertainty and manipulability." As Moore elaborates:

> The strategies of individuals are seldom (if ever) consistently committed
> to reliance on rules and other regularities. For every occasion that a person

thinks or says, "That cannot be done, it is against the rules, or violates the categories," there is another occasion when the same individual says, "Those rules or categories do not (or should not) apply to this situation. This is a special case." (ibid., 219–20)

Such an approach, closely linked to a situational analysis associated with the Manchester School of Social Anthropology, helps in "examining the relationship of ideology to action from a situational viewpoint and not merely in terms of a set of abstract ideas which are supposed to entail certain types of behaviour" (Long 1968, 243). This situational lens fits well within a combined approach that brings together the more recent interventions of the anthropology of ethics and the anthropology of Christianity. It also serves to elaborate on the "vectoral qualities" of culture, where "[i]n real life, practices impinge on one another, and judgment must be exercised continuously" between incommensurable or competing claims and within different social roles and responsibilities (Lambek 2010, 23). This approach allows us to understand Pentecostal rupture as ethical practice, a generative process that considers the complementary dynamic between the openness, and hence indeterminacy, of any situation, the situated agent's response to that openness and indeterminacy, and the processes of subjectivation involved in generating continuity with authoritative forms of practice.

Conclusion

Protestant rupture with the traditional past is always subject to ethical disputes that have further implications for Christian practice and for the role of ethics in understanding the interpersonal dimensions of a Pentecostal Christian life. While Pentecostal conversion is usually consistent with a dominant rhetoric of rupture, this ideology is met with different opinions regarding how rupture is achieved and what is considered good or right following the born-again experience. "Rupture" and the "traditional past" are concepts commonly referred to and used by CoP leaders and scholars in discussing Pentecostal conversion. However, Kofi's case shows that when it comes to interpersonal ambiguities and conflicts of life, Pentecostal rupture is never articulated exclusively through such a dichotomy; nor does it appear as a condition to be maintained through moments of uncertainty and practices of self-cultivation. Instead, as I have argued, ethical practice helps us understand the conjunction of or movement between explicit statements about Christian rupture and implicit circumstances under which rupture does or does not take place. By focusing on ethical practices, I have placed ethnographic attention on the shared values within the church regarding what must be done, that is, orthodox practice. I have also highlighted moments of reflection in the lives of church leaders and members in Ghana regarding what ought to be done, that is, the most effective course of action in a particular situation and circumstance.

I find it useful to understand ethics as both a "morality of reproduction," whereby church values play an important role in organizing social relations, and a "morality of freedom," whereby individuals and groups within the church reflect on their opinions and make choices guided by one or more cultural domains and associated values (Robbins 2007a).[7] It was the folding back of institutional moral authority on the events of the thanksgiving service that led to Kofi's further reflection. In this case, the church and its shared values played an important role in governing the lives of its members and determining how they should conduct themselves. However, I suggest that paying attention both to the institutional deliberations that accompany a Pentecostal life and to rupture as ethical practice contributes to a better understanding of the inconsistencies that accompany a shared Pentecostal Christian identity. The consideration of ethical practice in the study of Christian rupture allows one to acknowledge multiple registers of certainty and uncertainty, between which converts move and learn how to balance various social roles, responsibilities, and commitments.

Even though church leaders and Kofi shared a public position regarding acceptable and unacceptable forms of Christian practice, this consensus did not resolve the situational necessity for Kofi of applying other Pentecostal registers in resolving the more personal questions that persisted in his life. While Kofi shared institutionally oriented church values and eventually submitted to church authority and self-discipline, his case also speaks to the ethical role of multiple others in the lives of Christians. Such a focus on ethical practice allows me to consider the role and affective presence of these others, including the Holy Spirit, family members, and other spirits, in the lives of believers, as well as to capture the personal themes of ambivalence and reflection that elude a public rhetoric of uncertainty and rupture. If the presence of the Judeo-Christian God is marked by moments of uncertainty that help the believer master the voice of religious authority, the lives of many church members also provide opportunities for creative, complex, and often ambiguous outcomes. CoP leaders' judgment of Kofi's actions did not diminish the quality of his faith or reduce the qualification of his actions during that thanksgiving service. Even if he acknowledged he had violated church canons, Kofi remained certain that God was present in that thanksgiving service, in the sand, in his own life, and in the lives of others.

It is to the role of the prophets in the lives of my Ghanaian Pentecostal interlocutors that I now turn my attention. These religious intermediaries and their prayers are seen to be efficacious in helping others to obtain overseas visas and achieve their ambition to travel abroad. Moreover, they provide healing, marriage and job opportunities, deliverance from witchcraft, and prosperity more generally. While Pentecostal prophets and their prayers foreground the increased opportunities for mobility between nations, it is equally important to understand why many do not travel themselves and, when they do, why the church plays such an important role in determining when overseas travel is successful and when it is not.

Chapter Three

Prophets and Prayer

For our purposes here, the personal call is the decisive
element distinguishing the prophet from the priest.   Max Weber (1922)

O men, how long shall my honour suffer shame?
How long will you love vain words and seek after lies?
But know that the Lord has set apart the godly for himself.
The Lord hears when I call to him.   Psalm 4:2–3

I was attending a weekly prayer centre meeting in Accra, when the resident prophet took out a crisp ten thousand cedi note from his wallet and
prayed over it. He then held the banknote up in the air, looked at his
audience, and said that whoever received the banknote would be financially prosperous in the future. The banknote was not meant to be spent
but kept safely, attracting more wealth for its new owner. Over a hun-
dred people rushed forward, falling over each other, pleading for the
money with their arms outstretched towards him. After looking around
for a while, he turned to me and said, "*Oburoni* (white man), do you
want this money?" I responded with a shrug of my shoulders, signalling
my confusion over my involvement. "You should give it to whoever
needs it most," I replied. After several minutes of walking around with
the money held over his head, looking at everyone's faces, he eventually
came back to where I was sitting and handed me the banknote. Through
what was slightly more than US$1 at the time, his performance demon-
strated more than a symbolic act of benevolence. His prayer, which invoked the Holy Spirit, converted something of known exchange value
into interest-bearing capital that could multiply exponentially, bringing
in more money and economic success. The spiritually charged banknote

demonstrated the transformative effect of the prophet's prayer, which potentially extended to everyone, including the "white man" from abroad. The significance of Pentecostal prayer lies in what it does. Every prayer service demonstrates how ritual performances make you into a new person, while at the same time transmitting a pragmatic message of material wealth, success, and migration. The ten thousand cedi banknote, which had a relatively low market value, became priceless with prayer.

This chapter examines the important part prophets play in the lives of church members by transforming the Holy Spirit into social and economic value, and discusses their role in framing and facilitating international travel to the West. I focus on the prophet's special status as someone who knows how to pray because he or she has been especially "called" by God and is seen to be "closer" to God. These religious intermediaries, who often never leave Ghana, are also regarded as efficacious in helping others achieve their ambition to travel overseas. Rather than privileging transnational mobility, I look at how the experience of immobility, or the lack of social and economic mobility, is an important way to understand the significance of prayer and the role of the prophet in mediating "the transnational," which includes but is not limited to travel between nations.

While Pentecostal prophets demonstrate the power of the Holy Spirit, they are also bound to the people they serve, as well as subject to the scrutiny of other church members and leaders in determining how the Holy Spirit is mediated. They are involved in acts of balancing between their own personal ambitions, the will of God, and communal obligations to others. The second half of this chapter provides further insight into how success and international travel are framed as "good" or "bad." While Pentecostal transnational networks foreground the increased flows and mobility of people, ideas, and practices between nations, it is equally important to understand the logic that frames transnational (im)mobility as an ethical practice. In other words, when is exclusion from international travel deemed "good," or alternatively, when is transnational mobility considered "bad"? Before providing a better understanding of the work of prophets, I shall first turn to the prayer rituals Pentecostals perform together.

Prayer Performances in CoP

CoP is known as a church that prays. "Without prayer, we cannot do anything," church members repeatedly told me. Many of my interlocutors explained to me that they did not know how to pray until they

Figure 3.1 Prophet standing on stage. (Photo by the author.)

joined CoP. Prayer also had the serious purpose of recreating church members' social and moral worlds, while allowing the individual to become part of a collective effervescence that emanates from their participation in rituals (Durkheim [1912] 1995). While Pentecostals publicly oppose ritualistic practice, Robbins (2009a, 56) has suggested that in order to comprehend the institutional success of Pentecostalism or the motives behind people's commitment to Pentecostal ideology, it is important to understand the "fundamental role of ritual in Pentecostal social life."

Anthropologists who have worked on ritual since Durkheim have argued that while rituals provide participants with a shared meaning, ritual symbols and acts are semantically underdetermined and cannot be considered intrinsically meaningful. It is necessary to take into account issues of social context, pragmatic intention, and performance when associating meaning to the ritual form or practice (Bell 1992; Humphrey and Laidlaw 1994). Each context of prayer consists of a sequence of actions and words that ushers in a state of transformation. It is thus important to make a distinction between the different types of Pentecostal prayer performances within CoP and to acknowledge how transformation is perceived differently in them. Unlike the prophet's prayers at prayer camps and prayer centres, which were directed at overcoming individual problems associated with economic precarity as well as the negative effects of witchcraft and spirits, church prayer services had a collective objective in mind: they shared themes associated with the church community and the conditions for leading a good Christian life.

During fieldwork, I participated in different types of prayer performances, which included Sunday church services, weekday prayer group services in church, and prayers held in prayer camps and prayer centres that were run by prophets. I realized over time that I had begun to adopt many of my interlocutors' speech forms and actions in prayer. I learned how to pray for several hours at a time, my palms facing upward and speaking out loud, sometimes pacing up and down, my hands motioning in gestures, with which I would attack or scold my "enemies." Such an Aristotelian model of transformation draws attention to the embodied practices that help shape and create the inner subject over time. In the Ghanaian Pentecostal context, however, this model tells only half the story. As much as actions can be replicated and help create the ethical person, according to many church members, I could not pray effectively since I had not experienced the Holy Spirit baptism.

While the cultivation of practice, articulated with motivations, emotions, and bodily capacities is important in producing transformative aspects of prayer for the individuals involved, an Aristotelian model of transformation needs to be supplemented with a Platonic one. In a model of Platonic transformation, Ghanaian Pentecostals are more concerned with the unchanging presence of God in prayer. Thus, when learning to pray, one may learn the actions of prayer but simultaneously be unable to situate these practices in "an unchanging truth" that originates "beyond human experience" (Bloch 1998, 70).

Spiritual prayer could not simply be learned or performed, but required the "presence of God." In a CoP "Know Your Mission Areas" guide, a page on "Guide for Spiritual Prayer" tells the reader what prayer should be about:

> Prayer is not just presenting God with a long list of duties we would like Him to perform … We need to take time to enter the presence of God. We need to clear our minds and focus our attention on God. We need to hear what the Holy Spirit is saying to us and let Him guide us how to pray effectively. (CoP, n.d.)

Church prayer becomes effective to the extent that the transcendental – something beyond the domain of the communicable – enters the bodies of believers. By expressing an interpersonal relationship with God, church members were not only acquiring a new language, but also using that knowledge to relate to an external force, an Other that comes to dwell inside them. Prayers act as what Birgit Meyer calls "sensational forms" (Meyer 2011, 29–30; 2006), which are irreducible to mere actions; they are what enable the practitioners to authoritatively experience the transcendent (ibid.). These same prayers are a "viscerally intimate" feeling inseparable from a relationship with a God who speaks to you (Luhrmann 2004, 526). This transcendental force has ways of "dropping into" your spirit and "speaking" to you personally as the individual who is in need of a personalized message. When I asked a church leader how God speaks to us individually, he proceeded to describe the ways God spoke to him:

> You see, whenever God wants to speak to you, He speaks to you specifically. Somebody is preaching and you get the thing in you as if the person knows you, but the person doesn't know you. You see, the Word comes to you and God deals with us as different people. What will touch me may

not touch you. He knows our needs ... You may be listening to a cassette. Somebody is preaching in the same way. Then he says something in it that is meant for you. Yesterday, I was watching a videocassette and when the woman finished, I had to pray and pray because I saw that this was my need. Or you can read the Bible and then just a verse. You read the verse and that breaks you down. That breaks you down, pushes you somewhere, and you find out that "Yes, I've reached a stage where I need to watch this very carefully." This is how God speaks to us.

Pentecostal prayer is more than the formulaic aspects of religious language. It includes a creative component, whereby the specific circumstances associated with each performative reading of the text allows for its recontextualization and reappropriation (Shoaps 2002). I shall now describe a typical Sunday church service of the sort that is regularly held in either Twi or English. While Ghanaian Pentecostals oppose ritualistic approaches to prayer, consciously rejecting inauthentic efforts such as mine, their prayers still involve ritual performances that are a very important part of their everyday social life (Robbins 2004b, 2009a). For most born-again churches, if the doctrine of holiness looks "inside" the self, a doctrine of empowerment simultaneously shifts the focus "outside" (Peel 2004, 26); yet, in both cases, ritual performance is key. What these following descriptions of prayer illustrate are the different ways in which the presence of God is achieved and the strategies of ethical self-formation through which God speaks to his people.

The CoP services I attended began with opening prayers designed to ensure the smooth delivery of the service and prepare members and pastor for the message to be delivered. The Holy Spirit was invoked to guide the church through prayer. People prayed out loud, some praying in tongues while others quietly mumbled to themselves. Opening prayers invited the Holy Spirit to take control of events, praise, and worship. Praising God was important because it "lifted" and "glorified" God's name, creating an atmosphere of worship. It allowed the Word and the Holy Spirit to inhabit believers emotively. Praising God consisted of upbeat Pentecostal songs accompanied by a band playing musical instruments, including electric and bass guitars, drums and other percussion instruments, a synthesizer, and African drums. Church members clapped their hands, while swaying their bodies to the music and dancing in a celebratory fashion.

This praise performance was usually followed by worship that consisted of slower, more emotional songs, where the Holy Spirit was invoked into the church premises and into the believers' bodies. The front doors of the church hall were usually closed at this time, and late-comers were asked to wait outside until the end of worship. The evocation of mood in ritual was an important component of the praise and worship music that preceded the sermon and the giving of tithes. Worship was especially directed towards being absorbed in the act of prayer. This expressive display of emotion could climax in inspired speeches such as prophecy, song, or more speaking in tongues. Someone inspired by the Holy Spirit would then interpret God's message for the church. Others, who had received visions during worship, would be allowed to share them with the church. The Holy Spirit would be thanked for "his" presence, and the worship would be called to a close.

The church's doors would then be opened again, allowing latecomers inside the building to join for the sermon. Announcements were made regarding church events and other community news items, and people would subsequently come forward to share testimonies of the miracles God had done for them. A sermon followed this portion of the service, delivered by a pastor or an elder of the church, who had usually prayed and fasted for days before taking the pulpit. The sermon was important because it transmitted divine messages, guided by the Holy Spirit, which the audience would personalize and make meaningful through the act of listening. Many have said to me that they felt God was speaking directly to them during a particular sermon, and that this experience had life-transforming effects on them. An inspiring sermon spoke to the listener about his or her life and problems, while also encouraging him or her to give more tithes and offerings. Delivering a sermon was more than a reliance on procedural knowledge or learned practice. Sermons also demonstrated how it is possible "to do things with words" (Austin [1962] 1975).[1] In her work on evangelical Christian conversion among members of an American Baptist church, Susan Harding makes a convincing argument for the power of rhetoric in Christian transformation. Quite literally, she shows that "speaking is believing," for the listener's mind becomes a contested terrain taken over by the fundamentalist speaker's language, inadvertently allowing the potential convert to have a conversational relationship with God (2000, 59).

In CoP services, non-believers or backsliders who were touched by the sermon usually come forward to the front of the church at the end of the sermon in order to receive Jesus Christ. On occasion, the speaker would tell the audience that God had spoken to him or her about a person or a group suffering from specific problems. These various people were asked to come to the front of the church and be prayed for. The church pastor and elders would then surround those who had come forward and lay their hands on them. These periods of more personalized prayer were generally limited to a few minutes towards the end of the service.

Other opportunities were also available for church members to attend more intense prayer sessions dedicated to spiritual warfare. These smaller prayer meetings were held during weekdays, usually made up of ten to fifteen people, and known by different names such as "Prayer Force," "Prayer Warriors," or the "Engine Room." To be part of the prayer group, one had to be a committed Christian. This meant one had to be baptized in the Holy Spirit, fast regularly, speak in tongues, and take spiritual warfare seriously. Praying in tongues was a prerequisite to an effective prayer that could battle with the demons of the world and change life's circumstances. Prayer leaders were people chosen to lead and instruct the group in prayer. They were usually senior members of the church and played the role of military officers, leading God's army into battle. Their weapons were the words and actions performed during prayer. Members who were not baptized in the Holy Spirit and did not speak in tongues were advised to refrain from engaging in such prayer; this was indeed seen as dangerous because the devil, once targeted, could retaliate. As a church elder explained:

> Spiritual warfare, call it what you want, intercession, prayer force. It is eventually warfare. We have to grow from fighting battles to fighting wars … [Y]ou cannot say that you do not know of the things of the spirit ... so if you are not born-again, you have no business in spiritual warfare ... otherwise the Devil will come after you.

As much as I learned the religious speech and actions, I lacked the religious transformation or "sincerity" that every other church member shared. One could "learn" how to pray through learning the words and actions of prayer. However, as I discovered, effective prayer was also about intuitively "knowing" how to pray, an emotive state reached when an inner relationship with Jesus has been established. This experience concurs with that of Tanya Luhrmann, who, in her own work on religious practice in an American Christian prayer fellowship, writes about conversion as a specific kind of learning process that is more than simply acquiring a new language. Through new relational practices, believers learn to associate certain physical and emotional states as signs of God's presence, but they also come to emotionally attach themselves to the premise that these signs are real (2004, 519). Becoming an agent of God is therefore not simply mastering learned techniques which help frame emotional responses averring that "God is real." It requires emotional commitment. As my interlocutors reminded me, efficacy in prayer only came after stepping "into the unknown," which meant sincerely accepting Jesus into my life and receiving the baptism of the Holy Spirit.

By experiencing an intimate interpersonal relationship with God, church members are not only ritually acquiring new knowledge or language (see Harding 2000), but they are also using that knowledge to relate to "an inner 'object'" (Luhrmann 2004, 519). As in accounts of spirit possession, the displacement of intentionality is central to the practice of being filled with the Holy Spirit, a process that entails explicit shifts in voice (see Boddy 1989; Lambek 1981). However, unlike spirit possession, an inner transformation gives agency to words and actions, an agency whose source of authority is deferred to an elsewhere, beyond a here and now. In this model of Protestant transformation, sincere religious action and speech are crucial. The measure of sincerity centres more on "truthful propositions," which come from a transcendental source that precedes and accompanies action, rather than bodily practices and trained habits (Keane 2007, 210; see also Humphrey and Laidlaw 1994, 5).

Given this context, how then does prayer become a certain kind of "technology" for self-fashioning and the creation of sincere subjects? Writing about "technology," Martin Heidegger makes a connection between technology (techne), as a set of creative activities and skills, and a mode of bringing-forth (poeisis) that he sometimes calls an "unconcealment of Being," which for him takes the place of transcendental truth (Heidegger 1997, 12–23). Looking at prayer as "technology," in Heidegger's terms, can help us to understand the different contexts of prayer as forms of active mediation, involving moments of unconcealment through which the Holy Spirit comes into presence (see also Lambek 2010; Coleman 2010b). Pentecostal Christians transform themselves to accommodate the transcendental in their self and gradually build themselves up through the cultivation of practice and the accumulation of virtue. Only then are words and actions in prayer seen to actually do something, to have meaning, as opposed to simply being representative of personal intentions that lack efficacy. It is through participating in prayer performances such as these that church members embody continuities with their born again Christian identity and aspirations of health, success, and migration to the West. However, it is the prophet who, above all, knows how to tap into the Holy Spirit's power and help others achieve their ambitions.

Prophets and New Beginnings

Much of the prophets' popularity lies in their ability to understand the suffering of ordinary Ghanaians and to mediate between God and Pentecostal believers. Their diagnosis of the spiritual root of people's problems requires empathy (see Werbner 2011, 39). For example, Prophet Mintah, the founder of CoP's Okanta Prayer Camp, said to me when I met him, "Only a person who has suffered will be able to know God through the spirit, not through the flesh." While prophets do not usually play an active role in the leadership and running of the church, many serve to demonstrate the power of the Holy Spirit more effectively than church leaders. Prophets provide guidance to the church and its members by means of prophecy and help in healing the sick, and they deliver people from demons and spiritual obstacles perceived to be holding them back. The prophets are also seen as being less removed from the ordinary people. They are both respected and feared by people, and are often contrasted with the more bureaucratic church leadership and their emphasis on formal education.

Aunty Grace, a prophetess of a famous prayer camp in Edumfa, told me she had a spiritual degree that was more important than a university degree. Her "degree" in the Holy Spirit has provided her with financial success, respect, and social status in Ghana. Many important politicians, businesspeople, and foreigners, as well as the poor and uneducated, have sought her help and spiritual advice to interpret dreams and obtain protection from witchcraft. As special agents of God, prophets may not be theologically trained or formally educated, but they have come to best represent and embody the spiritual power that Pentecostalism promises to its believers. Unlike formally organized church prayer services, which have a more collective objective in mind, prophets' prayers are directed at overcoming individual problems associated with witchcraft and ancestral spirits. Another important difference is that CoP prophets operate in prayer centres and prayer camps.[2]

Prayer camps, which are usually located in rural areas or just outside urban centres, are residential and separate from church assemblies. Prayer centres, on the other hand, are non-residential and found within the premises of local church assemblies on weekdays.[3] Visiting a prayer camp usually also involves fasting and praying over longer periods of time, and is aimed at receiving an answer from God concerning a particular request (Onyinah 2002, 252). For Ghanaian Pentecostals, prophets have the authority to will God into battle against their enemies and jealous kin who wish them harm or do not want them to succeed. The many themes constantly reiterated during these prayer services include financial problems, health, fertility, and marriage.

Rather than for a specific transformation of self, church members seek prophets for a transformation of specific circumstances. Such Christian prayers are sometimes described as serving to fill the gap left by the demise of traditional religious activities and rituals, helping individuals to achieve particular ends, such as removing evil powers and coping with difficult life conditions (Meyer 1999, 138–9, ch. 6; Robbins 2004a, ch. 7). As John D.Y. Peel has argued regarding Nigerian Aladura churches, the potency of multivocal prayer brings about transformation in people's lives while drawing on practices that are aimed at attaining this-worldly ends (1968, 296). This portrayal is also true for Ghana, where demonstrative public displays of Pentecostal prayer are culturally recognizable forms for dealing with social and economic problems in the here and now that possibly have a spiritual cause (Asamoah-Gyadu 2005b).[4]

I met Kofi at one of these prayer centre services. He had been attending these special services for a few weeks in the hope of transforming his life, and had heard that the prophet was a powerful "man of God." By this, it was meant that since the prophet was "closer" to God, when God spoke to the prophet, he in turn received God's messages through prophecies, visions, intuitions, and sometimes an audible voice in his head. This communicative relationship was the outcome of extended prayer and "gifts" of the Holy Spirit. Kofi's wife, who had been unable to conceive for many years, had been attending these prayer services for much longer than he had. Since attending, she had become pregnant. Convinced of the power of the prophet's prayers, Kofi now frequented these services himself, praying for a successful business with future opportunities for migration.

Migration was another topical concern. People were praying, or asking God, for visas to make their passage out of Ghana possible. At the same time, they were addressing the physical suffering and economic hardships in their lives. "Where do you want to go?" I asked Kofi. "Germany," he replied. He had an uncle who was living there and who would help him find a job once he managed to get his visa. "Life in

Ghana is hard. It is difficult to make enough money to pay all your bills. What more, if you have to support your whole family at the same time?" he told me. "What is stopping you from going to Germany?" I asked. He had been trying to get his visa to leave Ghana but had been unsuccessful on several occasions. Apart from the usual difficulties of getting a visa to travel to Europe, he blamed his financial difficulties on jealous relatives from his wife's side of the family. "They are witches," he claimed. This statement was quickly followed by another, "But I believe in prayer." He added:

> I used to go to a Pentecostal prayer camp, Edumfa, where the prophetess Aunty Grace prayed for my business. When I came back from there I started to make lots of money. However, she told me that I had to return to the prayer camp if I wanted to remain successful. I did not listen and never returned. My business collapsed. My wife's family has witches, and they were jealous of my success. That is why it is important that we pray continuously. There is power in prayer.

The prophets' prayers and the prophecies they provide offer a form of ethical guidance. Kofi visited prophets to protect himself from witchcraft and to make his dreams of a successful business and future migration to Germany come true. Praying continuously was important. More important was one's continued attendance at these prayer camps. Kofi had confirmed the prophet's authority by returning to seek the prophet's help. While the Holy Spirit's power is available to all born-again Pentecostals, the prophets are seen to be more successful at converting their prayer into tangible outcomes, including international travel and economic success. Their ability to see what others cannot see and to prophesy about future outcomes provides them with spiritual power and capital that others do not have. Pentecostalism in Ghana cannot be understood as merely a religious phenomenon or as a negation of secular principles. For ordinary church members, Pentecostalism brings the promise of transformation through a new global status, a promise of increased financial success and a greater chance for overseas travel.

A CoP Prayer Centre: Prosperity, Success, and Overseas Migration

Becoming "somebody" in Ghana is closely tied to aspirations of increased wealth and transnational mobility, whereby the ease or freedom of movement is closely associated with economic and social advancement. This "will to be mobile" is reflected in the popular discourse about international travel to the "West" (*aborokyere*) shared by many Ghanaians. It is in the West that the unfulfilled promise of individual prosperity and success can finally be achieved. While international travel, which has become associated with the idea of hustling or seeking out one's destiny and fortune (Akyeampong 2000, 186), is a prominent feature of Ghanaian social life and popular culture, it is also a difficult objective to achieve. Travelling to anywhere in Europe or North America is a laborious and expensive process. It involves numerous humiliating experiences for Ghanaian applicants, many of whom are rejected anyway, and includes the practical difficulties of obtaining international visas and financing such a trip. For Ghanaian Pentecostals, the Holy Spirit becomes a spiritual resource that helps them transcend "local" problems while connecting them to an ideological "West" and ideas of prosperity that follow. Throughout this process, the Pentecostal prophet stands out as an important spiritual icon, someone who is able to tap into the power of the Holy Spirit and convert desires for a better life and international travel into a real possibility.

I often attended the twice-weekly prayer services of a local church assembly in the Dansoman district of Accra. These prayer services, which started around 9:30 am and only ended around 2 pm or 3 pm, were usually packed with hundreds of people, mainly women. The services were healing and deliverance sessions, led by a church elder known as Prophet Alfred. The prophet called the prayer centre "the last stop" for people who could not find solutions to their problems. The church services opened with prayers, followed by sharing the Word of God. After passages from the Bible were read, a band would kick in as people were led in more prayer and worship. Songs accompanied by music and dance would invite the Holy Spirit to fill the bodies of the believers and take control. At the beginning of these services, the prophet, dressed in a long gown, would sit on stage, looking distant and concentrated. The prophet would then disappear into a room by the side of the church, before reappearing twenty minutes later with a sudden burst of energy, transformed by the Holy Spirit, to lead the songs of praise and worship. During these prayer services, Prophet Alfred would sometimes roll on the floor with tears in his eyes as he sang songs of worship to God. Just as quickly, he would motion the band to pick up the pace and start dancing, clapping his hands, slapping the tambourine, or twirling his handkerchief, while everyone else followed along.

Figure 3.2 Prophet Alfred singing songs of worship with the band. (Photo by the author.)

On occasion, the prophet told individuals that they had the opportunity to travel out of Ghana and asked them to bring their passports on subsequent visits so he could pray over them. He said, "In Akan, a person who stays in one place without travel is called *Okurasenii* (villager)." He went on to say that only when people travelled out of their familiar surroundings would they "learn" and "see the glory of God." According to Alfred, migration involves new forms of social coalition that represent an elevation of social status from "villager" (*okusarenii*) to "townsman" or "foreigner" (*aborokyere*), cutting across descent groups and kinship affiliations. Alongside migration, an ideology of transformative change linked travel plans with the Judeo-Christian God. Alfred specified:

> It is not good for a man to stay in one place. He needs a transformative change in his life … [W]hen the opportunity comes, we should not delay because God also regards us. In the agenda of God, he wants his people to grow, in terms of travel. And for his children to know that he is a creative God.

Figure 3.3 Prophet Alfred and followers worshipping with tambourines. (Photo by the author.)

Prophet Alfred was a CoP elder who interceded for others, giving Ghanaians the extra advantage while striving for successful visa applications and the resolution of problems related to travel. Where individual prayers were not powerful enough, prayers led by a prophet became necessary. When I first met Albert, he was helping Prophet Alfred in the prayer centre. In his journey from his hometown to Accra, Albert placed emphasis on the importance of prayers and prophecies from prophets, such as Alfred, to provide him with guidance and direction for the future. The prophet's help was necessary when Albert's own prayer became ineffective. The prophet, Albert said, "knows the procedure for effective prayer, how to approach God for people." By this he meant that the prophet received answers to prayers that did not reach God through individual prayer. Albert told me that when individual prayers were being "blocked" by one's own sins or witchcraft spirits, the prophet was then regarded as a key interlocutor.

As European countries regulate the entry of migrants from poor countries through rapidly changing immigration policies, the role of

religious intermediaries in obtaining a visa has become more important. It is often the unpredictability of successful visa applicants and the
unseen nature of bureaucratic structures in foreign embassies that make
the relationship between a prophet's prayer and visa acquisitions a significant one. The prophets' gift of "faith," which is granted to only a
privileged few, allowed them to better navigate this unseen world and
provide the extra advantage in visa applications – among other things.
The prophet "sees" into the spiritual nature of the problem. As Prophet
Alfred told me:

> If they want to go abroad, they need some prayer before the chance comes
> out. Just recently, a female wanted to travel to London. Over the last two
> years, she had received admission to one of the universities in the UK. But
> when she went to the embassy for the visa, they refused to give it to her.
> Her daddy went up and down, but they refused to give it to her. She told
> me that was what she was fighting for, a visa for over the last two years.
> So my prayer team and I entered into a period of fasting and prayers. We
> kept interceding for her for about one to two weeks. Then, I told her to go
> and submit her visa form. And one week later, she went for it. She came
> back to church that Monday afternoon during the prayer service. She was
> singing and praising God ... Personally, I haven't travelled before. But the
> people I have prayed for can tell you that if not for the prayers they re-
> ceived, their lives would have been useless.

During prayer services, Alfred would sometimes pray over passports,
asking the Holy Spirit for successful visa applications. Alfred would
also pray over items such as bank notes and handkerchiefs, and ask his
clients to hold on to them during their visa interviews. Stories of successful prayers circulated; people recounted how Alfred had helped
them to find jobs, overcome sickness, find marriage partners, and obtain
visas, while their own efforts had previously failed. I heard a story that
on one occasion Prophet Alfred gave someone a white handkerchief
that he had prayed over. He told the person to hold the handkerchief
during his interview for a UK visa. The man did as he was told and was
successful in getting his visa. These prayer items were not merely symbolic of the intention to travel, but were also, in themselves, travel facili-
tators that helped convince the stubborn and difficult embassy staff to
approve visa applications.

By taking part in these prayer performances, church members bring
into being a commitment to the future they long for. The prayers led by

the prophet are powerful in that, because of their repetitive nature, they become warlike and sacred, actions that also derive their power from the Holy Spirit. Certain phrases such as "in the name of Jesus," "blood of Jesus," "Holy Spirit" are used, accompanied by actions like stamping one's feet on the ground (stamping the head of the devil), repeatedly clapping one's hands (sometimes compared to "bullets" or "physical blows" to the enemy), and making slashing motions so as to "cut" one's enemies. These actions return from the spiritual realm and into the material world in the form of the sickness or death of those behind the believer's problems (that is, those considered their "enemies"). As David Maxwell (2006, 192) notes, the word "Jesus" in Pentecostal prayer is invested with not only a nominal, but also a verbal function, whose "incantatory power," when repeated over and over again, encourages and provokes divine action. The prayers of the Ghanaian prophets are seen to battle against enemies who wish to harm their clients, and to open up the way for future travel and financial success. Spiritual battles were a common occurrence in these prayer centres and prayer camps. Here is one example of a prophet helping a woman to remove the "spirit of death," which was holding her back from future travel.

"Look at me!" (*Hwe Mi!*), Prophet Alfred yelled to the crowd gathered in front of him. He stretched out his hands to the audience. While looking at him, some people started to react. One woman jumped out of her seat and ran amok, but was soon restrained by the prophet's assistants. As soon as the prophet stood in front of someone and looked at him or her, his assistants hurried behind the person. They knew that it was just a matter of time before the person fell backward or jumped up from his or her seat. "Receive it, receive it" (*Gye, Gye*), the prophet shouted, stretching his arms out as if sending an invisible force of energy towards the audience. One girl screamed and struggled against the assistants. "Come out!" he screamed to the spirit inside her that caused her to fight his prayers. He then called another woman forward and told her that as he was sitting down, he felt a spirit try to attack him and take some of his power. He asked her to close her eyes and stretch out her arms. He prayed over her and commanded the spirit to leave her. She started spinning around several times until she eventually collapsed on the floor. He told everyone to close his or her eyes and go into the spirit. He prayed that the Holy Spirit would pick out and bring forward all those bound by chains of bondage. He identified the woman as having a spirit of death on her, like a rope tied round her neck. He questioned the spirit of death in her and the woman started to scream.

Figure 3.4 Prophet Alfred sending spiritual power. (Photo by the author.)

"Why?" he asked the spirit in the woman, and the reply was, "If you stop praying, I will eventually leave her alone. I intended to kill her." She fell to the floor, and he put his finger on her chest and told the spirit to leave.

Pentecostal prayer and prophecies serve as more than mere signposts for transformation and migration. In these prayer performances, CoP members are not only transmitting transcendental messages encoded in the Pentecostal ideology. They are also participating in the re-enactment of new beginnings, where they are both transmitters and receivers, fused with the message (Rappaport 1999, 104–38). In addition, prophets are not simply telling Ghanaians that change is possible (Gifford 2004, 61); prophets allow believers to participate through ritual performances that provide a commitment to a transcendental God who can make the impossible possible. Another way for people to be involved in the re-mapping of a future is for them to witness and receive prophetic visions and prophecies. For example, in a recollection of the church service themed "The Hour of Crossover," another prophet from CoP compared himself to a shepherd helping his "skinny flock" cross over to greener pastures, what he called the "West End." Through his vision, he reproduced a Christian discourse of exodus that reflected the ongoing concerns of economic mobility and international travel:

> I was teaching my church congregation the reality about the dramatic event that God performed when the Israelites migrated from Egypt – the land of slavery – to the promise-land. Instantly, my spiritual eyes opened and I saw twenty skinny flocks and their frustrated shepherd. While looking at the flocks and the shepherd at the dry desert land, there was another man at most about twenty feet tall wearing a pure white garment like an Angel. He had a long rod or a shepherd staff in his right hand. He then called the shepherd and gave him the rod in his right hand and asked him to follow him with his flocks to the place he is going to show him to feed his flocks forever. They followed him to a large riverside. When they got to the riverside, I saw a very big billboard with inscription on it, "Get Ready for Crossover to a Green Land of Pastures" … and I saw a dry way in between the divided river and he [the Angel] ushered the shepherd to take his flock through it to the other side of the river, described as West End. And they did just that, as the man has told them. On the other side of the river, I saw fresh green grass fields and very nice beautiful buildings and I saw snow raining – which represented a place of rest, healthy living, riches and prosperity, peace.

The prophet was drawing on specific ideas of the "West" commonly held by many Ghanaians ("a place of rest, healthy living, riches and prosperity, peace"), signifying their aspirations for international travel and overseas wealth as well as their shared experiences of economic hardship. In such a discourse, Ghana and the "West" are mutually dependent concepts, where the plenty of the "West" is also indexical of the experience of scarcity in Ghana. The prophet, who was the "shepherd" helping his flock cross over to the other side of the river, went on to describe how God spoke to him and helped him identify twenty people who were meant to travel overseas:

> Honestly speaking, truly, we are serving a living God … I then kneeled down and prophesied that "If I be a man of God, then every single one of you would get your visa to travel." There is no way these people you see here would be denied a visa to travel again throughout their life time.

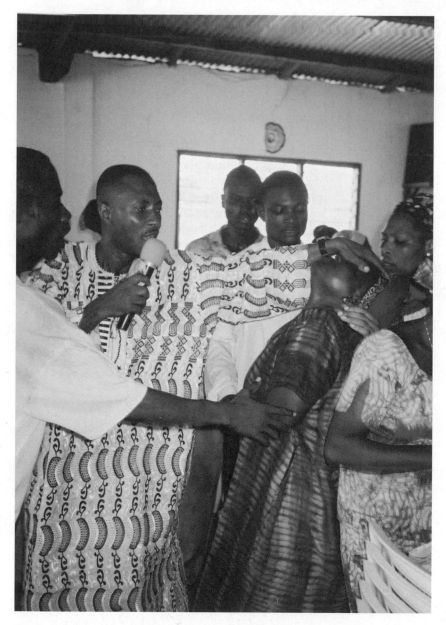

Figure 3.5 Praying for a woman with one hand on her forehead. (Photo by the author.)

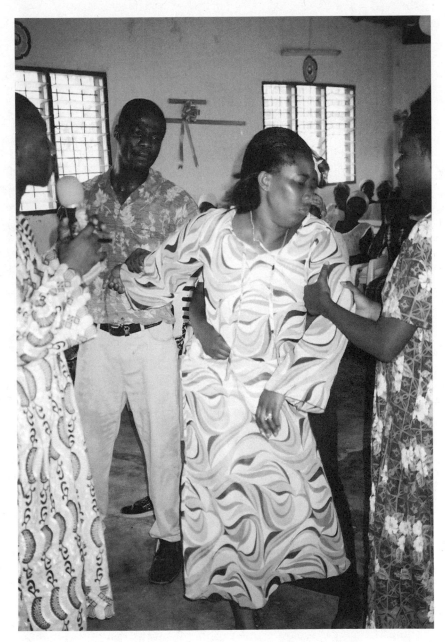

Figure 3.6 Woman becomes possessed. (Photo by the author.)

The prophet called on the authority of the Christian God and his own authority as "a man of God" to promise visas to twenty people that night. However, for all his spiritual power and authority, the prophet did not include himself in these prophecies. He was not one of those twenty people that God had spoken about. As a man with similar global ambitions himself, he had never travelled outside of Ghana. Neither can I confirm whether any of the twenty people he called out eventually received visas to travel. While many Ghanaians participate in these prayer performances, few achieve their goal of travel or financial success. The importance of such prayers, however, lies not in how many people have their wishes fulfilled or dreams materialized. Rather, these prayers ritually create a transformation of self through a personal commitment to a future, which is not limited to the constraints of the nation-state, failed economic policies, or the whims of institutional visa brokers. The prayers provide believers with hope, which emerges out of a new sociality to express their desires, while allowing them to co-suffer and co-transcend their problems. This scene raises the further questions of the specific calling of prophets, their ability to help others become more internationally mobile, and their own relative immobility in relation to the people they are serving. Before examining why some prophets do not travel themselves, it is important to understand why prophets are seen as better channels for the Holy Spirit and, concomitantly, what sets them apart from church leaders and other ordinary CoP members. While church prayers allow members to step into the unknown to pray for the church and themselves, prophets are set apart from others by their "calling" from God. It is this calling that makes their prayers more efficacious and that draws people to them.

The Prophet's Calling and "Waiting on God"

By helping others become more socially and economically mobile, prophets achieve a certain level of social and economic mobility themselves. Prophet Alfred was no stranger to travel, and had increased his level of mobility since accepting his calling as a prophet. He had earlier migrated to Accra from an area in the Asante region in search of a better education and a good job. He initially underwent vocational training to be a technician. However, he could not find work and later became a taxi driver until he finally received his calling from God. A personal "calling" from God separates the prophet from the rest of society and even from the pastors of the church. Before receiving their calling, prophets always speak about an interaction with God that comes in the form of a relational activity: instructions through dreams, visions, or an audible voice in their head. Although an intimate experience, the prophetic calling is not simply an individual message to the prophet-to-be. The message must be shared, reinforced by significant others.

When he received his calling, Alfred waited for confirmation through the dreams, visions, and prophecies of others in the church. He subsequently worked under another more experienced prophet, while keeping his job as a taxi driver. A few years later, he received another direction from God, who told him to give up his secular work completely and devote all his time to his prophetic work. He attempted to go against these instructions, being unsure as to whether what he was hearing was his own voice, the devil's, or God's. Alfred eventually suffered financial setbacks, and his business declined. He then decided to go away for a few weeks to fast and pray, in the hope of receiving a sign from God regarding his decision to leave his secular work and become a full-time prophet. Confirmation finally came from two different church members, who said they had received messages from God (one through a dream, the other through a voice in his head) confirming that Alfred was supposed to be a full-time prophet. Alfred rented his taxi out to someone else and spent his time praying for others and running the prayer centre.

While Alfred helped others pray for international visas, he had never travelled outside of Ghana. In our conversations, Alfred reiterated the importance of "waiting on God" and the need to be obedient. Listening to God was an important part of the prophet's work. It was only through listening to God first that God in turn would hear the prophet's prayers. While Rijk van Dijk (2001, 2002c) describes prayer camps in Ghana as places where "individuality" is foregrounded through deliverance prayers, "dividuality" is equally, if not more, vital to the understanding of the relational nature of prophetic activities and the continuity of long-term relationships between prophets, church members, and church leaders.

Alfred had a large following, made up of church members and non-church members alike. He was constantly in demand; people were always coming to seek his help, calling him on the phone, visiting the church or his place of residence. He had helped many people to travel overseas. When I asked him why he had not travelled overseas himself, he replied that he was "waiting on God" to speak to him first. It was important not to travel for the sake of travelling. Such a venture would not be successful. He complained that while church leaders have the opportunity to travel through overseas assignments, prophets have to wait for invitations from other church members and usually do not have enough money to finance their own trips. Alfred had hoped that church members, whom he had previously helped and were now overseas, might send him an invitation to visit them or provide money for an airline ticket. Yet he complained that once abroad people quickly forget the prophets and their help. Expatriate Ghanaians become busy earning money and making a new life for themselves.

Alfred commented that many Ghanaians who do manage to go overseas continue to suffer and lead difficult lives. While he was interested in visiting Europe and America, he did not see himself leaving Ghana for good. He said it was a misconception that all Ghanaians wanted to migrate and live in the West. International travel was an opportunity for further social mobility, a better income, and further education. However, his work as a prophet was based on the needs of Ghanaians in Ghana and on God's calling for him to help those who remained in Ghana. There were many more Ghanaians suffering in Ghana than overseas, and it was his duty to stay and help. He knew that the spiritual authority of a prophet is not simply given but achieved through ongoing moral relationships with others. Prophets depend on various sets of interpersonal relationships in order to control important communication channels and access to centres of power and influence. These relationships were central to how Alfred viewed himself as spiritually powerful and successful.

While his individual calling provides him with the spiritual legitimacy to carry out his prophetic activities, the prophet's ability to continue "working" depends on the trust and social recognition of a large network of clients, both inside and outside the church. These clients ensure the livelihood of the prophet through the provision of money, clothes, and other items of value, such as jewellery and, sometimes, property and cars. The religious legitimacy and spiritual authority of prophets in Ghana are not only achieved through the large numbers of Ghanaian Pentecostals who seek their help, but also from the social recognition and approval of other prophets and, more importantly, church leaders.

Alfred's spiritual status was also achieved through acts of negation (see Lambek 1992). He explained to me that he would not travel without receiving instructions from God first, and the approval of church authority. In denying himself the opportunity to travel, he was demonstrating Christian virtues such as obedience to God, submission to church authority, patience, as well as the validity of God's "calling," which aimed at having him serve CoP members in Ghana. By denying himself certain opportunities, he was submitting his own will to the will of God who, in turn, would reward him in the future. These acts of negation also separated him from others within the church, acting on their desires for reward and self-aggrandizement. Furthermore, his refusal to pursue his own desires allowed Alfred to achieve a domesticated agency that stemmed from a spiritual, divine authority.

Alfred knew that a prophet who seeks to pursue individual profit or personal gain outside the church would be seen to have questionable morals. A source of tension within CoP was the inconsistency with which prophets articulate the message of salvation. While church leaders accepted the importance of the prophets and the contribution of prayer camps to the growth of the church, they objected to church members' overdependence on the prophet's power and a lack of faith in their own relationship with Jesus. The prophets, many church leaders told me, interpreted biblical scripture in ways that suited their prayer practices, rather than the other way around. The prophets' attempts to align prayer practices with church doctrine were seen to be insincere since, on many occasions, the personal messages they received from the Holy Spirit went against church doctrine. "No scripture is of private interpretation," an apostle of the church said to me. "One person alone cannot claim that he or she has heard from the Holy Spirit." Prophecy in the church, according to him, was to be "tested" and "weighed" by the church and biblical doctrine. Regardless of this tension between church leaders and prophets, church members continued to seek the help of the prophet to overcome the persistent effects of demons, witchcraft, and ancestral curses in their lives – to seek new beginnings.

CoP prophets were well aware of the consequences of not following rules, disobeying church authority, or drawing too much attention onto themselves. Unlike prophets who work outside of established church structures, CoP prophets cannot operate independently or in other countries without the support of the church or church leaders. This is an important reason why CoP prophets do not simply offer their services and engage in prophetic activities in overseas branches of CoP. The church leaders wanted to limit the role of the prophet in overseas branches so as to promote a message of salvation that was not dependent on the power of prophets, deliverance prayer, or prophecies. They also did not want the prophets to operate alone, away from .the

oversight of the church. One church leader told me that CoP's hierarchical nature helped the prophets "not to be bossy, not to be that arro-
gant, not to be proud, and not to be famous":

> And once you pull a crowd, your chance of becoming famous is there and
> once you become famous you become puffed up. And sometimes, these
> people feel that because they have that demonstrative ability, they've
> made it.

I shall now discuss the example of a CoP prophet whose own individual calling and prophetic activities came into conflict with the attempts of church leaders to domesticate his spiritual agency. While
many prophets in CoP included men and women who became popular
and gathered some social and economic mobility, in many cases, it was
their immobility that made them successful in the eyes of the church.
Being a virtuous prophet in CoP proceeds from following church guidelines and knowing one's place in the church hierarchy.

Transnational Mobility and Spiritual Crisis

Owusu Tabiri served as an evangelist and prophet for many years before leaving CoP to start his own ministry. He was the first member of
the church to be ordained as an evangelist and prophet and given a
salary. In 1990, while still with CoP, he started Bethel Prayer Camp in
Sunyani, Ghana. He said that he had received his "practical training"
from the early apostles of the church, serving as an elder before being
ordained as an evangelist by the church leaders. His ambition was to be
like the earlier CoP leaders and the early apostles of the Christian
church. However, he told me, "popularity brings jealousy and when
God begins to bless you, you become enviable." From 1993, he was
frequently travelling to Europe and North America as an ordained CoP
evangelist. He said that the gifts he received from the Holy Spirit and
his calling as a prophet allowed many people to "see" the power of
Jesus Christ through his healing and deliverance services. According to
him, it was during the height of his popularity that the church leaders
"decided to eliminate [him] from the system." His wealth and popularity became subject to public scrutiny and media attention, and his practice of deliverance prayer became a source of a tension within CoP (see
van Dijk 1997; 2001, 227). He eventually resigned from CoP in October
1995 to form his own church, Bethel Prayer Ministries International.

Figure 3.7 Owusu Tabiri. (Photo a gift to the author from Owusu Tabiri)

Apart from revealing the existing tensions between prophets and church leaders and their differing views on deliverance prayer, this example demonstrates how increased international mobility, success, and fame can be framed as "bad" if not accompanied by obedience and submission to church authority.

Tabiri was subject to the scrutiny of church leaders after a video recording of one of his overseas trips came to their attention in Ghana. In a prayer service, which was recorded on video, he publicly told an old woman that he could see two pythons "sucking on her breasts" and that this "witchcraft" was the cause of her downfall. Tabiri subsequently prayed for her. He was famous for certain prayer practices linked to the deliverance of demons, commonly known as "breaking," "binding," and "bombing" (see Larbi 2001). The church leaders at the time, who later watched the video, reprimanded him for this incident and asked him to restrict his prayer practices, which they described as ritualistic and unnecessary. They also told him to stop accusing people of witchcraft. According to the church leadership, such accusations were not only against Ghanaian law, but also produced a wrong impression among overseas church members and outsiders. For while church leaders accepted the existence of witchcraft spirits, they believed that these spirits could not possess members of the church once they were born again and had accepted Jesus. Church leaders also did not want prophets to reproduce negative aspects of Ghanaian culture in the West. Tabiri was promoting a message of salvation that was not sanctioned by church leaders, and they were responsible to call him to account should he stray. He later "resigned" from the church as a result of this misunderstanding. In this example, the use of media technology in church and, more specifically, the recording of such overseas prayer events played an important role in mediating the boundaries and limits of Pentecostal transnational mobility and the work of the Holy Spirit.

According to the church leaders, Tabiri was given a choice to discontinue the practices that the church found problematic. While he had attained a level of social and international mobility within the church, CoP leaders also had the authority to arrest his movement and restrict his practices. According to Tabiri, however, witchcraft was behind people's suffering, and his work and personal calling were to help people break free from its effects. Over the course of several meetings with me, he told me that the leaders of CoP did not understand the "suffering of the ordinary people." According to him, the church leaders had come to be corrupted by this-worldly desires and ambitions, having lost touch with "the things of the spirit." He said, "Such people [the church leaders] have not faced the spirit of poverty and hardship; they have not been tormented by the devil." Tabiri explained that the church leaders "had been to good schools" and were theologically trained. While he considered himself uneducated, he said to me with pride, "[M]y ministry is not book long. I am trained in the Holy Ghost University." For him, his practices were ethical, since they were biblical and had been revealed to him by God. He was preaching a "simple message" that allowed people to come to Christ, where miracles followed. In this case, ethics was not a matter of reason or duty, as Kant would have it; neither was it an Aristotelian virtue ethics connected to embodied practices. Instead, Tabiri's choice to follow the voice of the Holy Spirit and his own convictions were described as originating from a sacred power outside himself.

Faced with a choice between submitting to church authority and continuing his prophetic and prayer activities, which had become popular with many church members, Tabiri decided to resign from CoP and start his own church. CoP leaders responded by writing letters to all their branches instructing their members not to associate with Tabiri and to discontinue relationships with him. This action caused a split in the church and also served as a warning to other prophets. Tabiri went on to claim that his calling was "from God" and not from the church. When he left, he took many CoP members with him, tapping into the diasporic networks within which he had gained popularity over the years. As a result, several church assemblies in the diaspora and many church members left CoP and became part of Tabiri's new church, Bethel Prayer Ministries International. Yet, his denial of church authority and his "resignation" continued to haunt him. He was always very emotional when recollecting the role of the church in the development of his own Christian life and the way in which church leaders had dismissed him as a problem and a threat. While one can say that his break from CoP allowed him a certain level of mobility, people in the church continued to question the wisdom of his decisions and the success of his own ministry. By turning away from the church into which he had been called, Tabiri was seen by some as also rejecting his spiritual foundation and the spiritual legitimacy that the church had previously provided him.

Conclusion

Mobility and immobility are not given states, but conditions, which are interpreted within an institutional, relational, and moral framework.

This explication means that social and geographic mobility and immobility can be understood as an articulation, which carries moral meaning. I have shown how rituals play an important role in bringing Ghanaian Pentecostals together and provide a sense of empowerment, albeit for different purposes. While Pentecostalism offers Ghanaians a rich ritual life that allows for new forms of stability and social continuity with the future, each ritual performance is also a conjunction of different prayer contexts that involves the Holy Spirit. As an ethical practice, spiritual prayer is not simply about embodied practices that cultivate an inner relationship with God. Neither is it always about correctly conveying what are considered by religious authorities to be sincere expressions of an inner transformation. Indeed, Pentecostal transformation as ethical practice exceeds both these models of change, as it looks at the different contexts through which prayer becomes meaningful and takes on an ethical force of its own. It also involves acts of balancing, on the part of the prophets, between an individual calling from God and the institutional boundaries for how the Holy Spirit and prayer ought to be expressed.

This chapter has also looked at how prophets in CoP help frame and facilitate international travel. However, as I have shown, transnational (im)mobility can be achieved and given meaning through many ways, and the same applies to the means through which Pentecostal prophets in Ghana come to demonstrate their own spiritual power and success. I have pointed out that the spiritual legitimacy and religious authority of the prophet to help believers achieve their goal of international travel extend beyond the mobility of the prophets themselves. Many prophets who help others with their ambitions of international travel do not leave Ghana. Instead, they participate in a sending discourse, submitting to the authority of the church institution and its leaders. In this way, they demonstrate obedience and patience, positive Christian virtues that are valued by church leaders and other members. I am not claiming that prophets never travel. Some leave the churches in which they developed spiritually and become more mobile within Ghana and overseas. Yet this activity also opens them up to (self-)scrutiny.

Looking at how mobility and immobility become framed within a moral and institutional framework illuminates the paradox between the transnational mobility people acquire through the services of prophets and the prophets' own relative (im)mobility. In developing my argument on the role of (im)mobility in transnational travel, I have taken a closer look at two Pentecostal prophets who have close associations with CoP in Ghana. While one prophet, Owusu Tabiri, travelled throughout Europe and America with CoP and later left the church to become a leader of his own international church, the other, Alfred, continued to submit to church authority and did not travel outside of Ghana. While Tabiri achieved a level of success and international mobility upon leaving CoP, his increased social and international mobility can be interpreted as "unsuccessful." He was ostracized by CoP and seen as lacking humility and discipline, was unable to overcome his differences with CoP leadership, and continued to hold a grudge against the church. Alfred's lack of international mobility, on the other hand, did not affect his popularity within the church or his reputation as someone who could help others become more internationally mobile. Instead, his spiritual authority was seen as embodying Christian virtues, such as patience and submission to God's Word.

It is important to understand how religious intermediaries become agents of change as well as subjects of power, where people's mobility or immobility become realities through the rituals of social institutions, their moral positioning, and the power of an external other called the Holy Spirit. Prophets and church members are constantly negotiating between individuality and dividuality, desires and obligation, rivalries and loyalties, individual charisma and institutional authority. In the next chapter, I take a closer look at two Ghanaian Pentecostal women and how their associations with prophets and traditional intermediaries allowed them to alternate between Christian individuality and dividuality. It is to the suffering of others and the multiple ways a Pentecostal individual identity is negotiated because of this suffering that I now turn.

Chapter Four

Individuality and Dividuality

Onnipa nnye abe na ne ho ahyia neho

A human being is not a palm tree, to be able to achieve self-sufficiency.
Akan proverb

It is from the notion of the "one" that the notion of the [Christian]
"person" was created ... indivisible and individual.   Marcel Mauss (1985)

I was browsing through the selection of Christian books in a well-known charismatic church bookshop in Accra when a man walked up to me. He introduced himself as a prophet of God and said that the Holy Spirit had spoken to him regarding my life. He was a confident man in his mid-thirties who seemed skilled at striking up conversations with strangers and never at a loss for things to say. After chatting with me for over half an hour, asking where I was from and what I was doing in Ghana, he told me that the Holy Spirit had given him personal information about my family's ancestral past. There was a curse on my father's side of the family, he said. This ancestral curse had tarnished my family name and had held back the men in my father's family from certain success for several generations. In this spiritual diagnosis, he presented me as someone who, while equally affected by this ancestral curse, would go on to break it. While I was not Christian, the Holy Spirit told him that I had secretly accepted Jesus into my heart and that I would become "a great man" and "the light of my family." God wanted me to know these things, he said, and that was why he had suddenly approached me. It is was his responsibility as a prophet of God to share this information with me, bringing an unknown ("forgotten") past into my present, with the hope that it would provide spiritual guidance to help me break with my ancestral past and change my life forever.

My encounter with the prophet destabilized me for a moment. My disequilibrium arose, in part, because he was not wrong in pointing out that my father's side of the family in Ghana was once relatively successful and had since lost their somewhat privileged status. However, his talk of ancestral curses was also part of a larger narrative of locating responsibility for the absence of a better life in spiritual agents that continue to haunt the present. It is not uncommon in Ghana or other parts of Africa for the dangers of ancestry and witchcraft spirits to continue to be keenly felt, and the Holy Spirit is important in limiting or alleviating these dangers. While this revelation about my family's past did not throw me into a state of Christian (dis)belief, it did provide me with an opportunity through which to better understand the importance of Pentecostal prophets in Ghana and their role in helping to trace and mediate unknown and forgotten relationships.

Even as Pentecostals are told that they are free from the sins and spirits of the past and from the negative effects of kinship relations – hence becoming "individual[s]-in-relation-to-God" (Dumont 1985) – they are continuously brought back to these same issues through the ongoing presence of the past in their lives. In such cases, Ghanaian Pentecostals are not only "remembering (their past) in order to forget" (Meyer 1998b, 332), but are also engaging with the possibility that they continue to be possessed by, or in relationships with, these spirits. Rather than a mere "belief in" particular agents – such as God, the Holy Spirit, ancestral spirits, vital substances, witches – relationships with spiritual entities continue to reflect a state of shared existence as well as provide "a set of methods for orienting one's own and other's sentiments and actions in relation to those agents that have an impact on people's well-being" (Klaits 2010, 25). Ghanaian Pentecostal prophets play an important role in bringing individuals and the dividualized nature of their relationships with others, human and non-human, into presence and in returning people to a sense of well-being. In the process of assessing relationships and resolving personal problems, Ghanaian Pentecostals have simultaneously to re-evaluate their identities as Pentecostal individuals, transformed, free from the traditional past, and as dividuals who are occasionally still connected to the spirits of their past.

In this chapter, I address the tensions involved in the ongoing composition of a Pentecostal Christian self through the contingencies involved in balancing individual aspirations for personal change against one's continuing moral obligations to others, a process of self-fashioning that can only be partially acknowledged in born-again language and ritual. Such processes of self-fashioning, in Michael Lambek's terms, concern "how much each of us is part of others and how much my self is determined by the self-making projects or the acts of others, as well as the acts I carry out for, in respect to, or inextricably interconnected with others" (2010a, 16). While fashioning themselves as Christians through technologies of the self, such as prayer, fasting, and Bible reading, Ghanaian Pentecostals must also take into account their relationships with multiple others. They have to appropriately balance what is entailed in breaking from the traditional past with what aspects of the past can be allowed to remain in the present. They have to evaluate their identities as Pentecostal individuals who are free from the traditional past and as dividuals who are still connected to the spirits of their past.

In what follows, I take the "individual" and "dividual" as co-constitutive. On the one hand, Pentecostals as individuals-in-Christ claim a rupture from the traditional past and acquire a personal relationship with God; on the other hand, they continue to participate in relationships that are defined by the openness of the self to other beings, signifying that this new beginning is experienced in the transitive mode. As such, I understand the process of maintaining "individuality" as an expression of distancing oneself from the control and moral expectations of certain significant others; and I view "dividuality" as the close proximity and the expected as well as the unexpected pull of others – human and non-human – in one's life, where persons are seen to be composed of relationships and substances. In doing so, I focus on two Pentecostal Christian women in Accra, Ghana's capital: Maoli and Mama. Both these women sought healing and spiritual help in times of personal suffering – one from a traditional priest in her hometown and the other from a CoP prophetess who ran a successful prayer camp and enjoyed a stable client base.

Maoli and Mama were both self-identified born-again Pentecostals who shared a common criterion for what it meant to be a Pentecostal: the idea that becoming born again meant leaving the African traditional past and the world of ancestors behind. Yet they differed in the way they aligned with their Pentecostal identities. Maoli was in her twenties and worshipped with more than one charismatic church; Mama was a woman in her sixties who had been a member of CoP before joining another charismatic church in Accra. They were both faced with personal illness and suffering caused by others. In the first example, Maoli was forced to seek the help of her ancestral divinities in order to end her physical suffering. It was only by achieving a balance between her personal desire for a healthy recovery and her duty to fulfil her ancestral obligations that she positively transformed the negative relationships that were causing her to suffer. Her example highlights another aspect of dividuality: her person was composed of different components or substances that could have a negative or positive effect on her. In the second example, I shift my attention to Mama, whose healing experience in a prayer camp resulted in her born-again conversion. Mama's ill health, caused by witchcraft, led her to seek the help of a prophetess from CoP. Unlike Maoli, she purposefully avoided the help of a traditional priest. Her case demonstrates how becoming a born-again Pentecostal is both a matter of individual choice and the influence of relationships. It is a relational effort that shows how relationships of trust, built over time, can result in interdependent actions between the self and others. By understanding Christian identity as a living tension between alternating states of individuality and dividuality, I am interested in the circumstances and contingencies that led Maoli and Mama to make different practical judgments regarding how to live their Christian lives.

The Case of Maoli: Sins of the Present and Ancestral Obligations

Maoli is Ewe. While the Ewe are an ethnolinguistic group who come from the Volta Region in southeastern Ghana, Maoli was born and brought up in Tema, where she smokes fish and sells them to markets in Accra. She is a born-again Christian who did not want to engage in any form of traditional worship. One day, however, she felt she was left with little choice. She had been seriously ill for a long time, and doctors could not find anything physically wrong with her. She was experiencing mood swings, and the money earned from her business suddenly declined sharply. A driver who transported her smoked fish from Tema to Accra noticed these drastic changes and suggested that they could be linked to a spiritual cause. She did not understand the problem because she considered herself a committed Christian who regularly attended church and prayed. She described her suffering as stemming from her naivety, trusting others, and falling into unhealthy relationships through which her health and business were attacked:

> You do not know anything when you are born and while growing up you do not know any better. You take everyone as your friend and you easily trust those whom you think are your friends. But you do not know what

they are thinking of what is in their hearts. The same people who walk
with you, eat with you, sleep with you, these same people who you learn
to trust and share your secrets with, these same people will try to destroy
you. But when you are young, you do not know any better until you have
experienced it for yourself. Spiritual sickness is worse than any kind of
physical suffering. It's even worse than having malaria.

While Maoli had never followed traditional rituals because Christianity taught that these things were of the devil, she told me experience
had taught her that certain spiritual problems require alternative spiritual solutions. She described spiritual suffering as more serious than
physical suffering: "Only you know what you are going through and
you feel like you are dying." Maoli had exhausted all other possibilities
open to her as a Pentecostal, including seeking the help of prophets.
Her biological father eventually asked her to return to the village to
seek the help of one of the traditionalists whom her family knew well.
Since her church had not been able to help her, she followed his advice
and returned to her father's hometown. It was there she realized that
her Nigerian boyfriend, who had recently gone to Benin, had performed some black magic or *juju* on her. The traditionalist wanted her
to conduct certain protection rituals. During the rituals, her ancestral
spirits spoke to her through a spirit medium. "Do you think that going
to church will help you? It will not solve anything," they told her. They
would continue to bother her until she fulfilled her ancestral obligations and duties. They wanted her to recognize where she came from:
she belonged to her father's house and thus to her father's ancestral
spirits. She should acknowledge them by buying some cloth to cover
them and some food to feed them. Eventually, Maoli did as the divinities asked. She apologized to them, three in total. She had not known
any better because she had grown up in Tema, and was therefore unfamiliar with her past and where she had come from. As a self-identified
born-again Christian, Maoli should have had no association with these
spirits. Instead, she decided to satisfy their demands and made a situated judgment based on her circumstances and the options available to
her at the time.

This pragmatism is a common feature in Ghanaian Pentecostalism.
In a similar example discussed by Elizabeth Graveling (2010, 45),
Kwaku, a Ghanaian Pentecostal who found himself in need of additional help in passing his exams, simultaneously aligned himself with
different powers that he was in relationship with: "God, spiritualist,

witchcraft (incited by the devil), and the family." Kwaku did not distinguish between them on a conceptual level, and his ability to tap into these seemingly contradictory discourses was made possible because he did not see them as mutually exclusive strategies. Similar to Kwaku, Maoli was not adopting a religious discourse or belief system; instead, she "[was] interacting with beings and processes" that she "[knew] to exist and to have effect" while attempting to live a good Christian life (ibid.). The need to protect oneself from present and future suffering provides a counter-narrative to Pentecostal distinctions between those who are saved and those who continue to sin.

Maoli's suffering forced her to recognize her kinship relations and her ancestral past before she could successfully live her Pentecostal identity. These ongoing connections with one's ancestral spirits are made possible through ideas of dividuality and partibility. Indeed, it is important to note that from birth, a child in Ghana is connected to both parents by more than a biological link. Blood (mogya) and spirit (sunsum) are important components of any symbolic relationship between family members in Ghana, and children receive elements from both their father's and their mother's sides, regardless of whether kinship relations are based on matrilineal or patrilineal lines. Thus blood and spirit are part of the very substance of Ghanaian ideas of personhood, according to which a human being is not necessarily separate and fully formed from birth.[1] Consequently, spiritual forces have an interest in the relationships that have been established through previous generations. The individual being essentially belongs to the spiritual world, and is here linked to the actions of others and the moral relationships that connect him or her to others – which is why deliverance prayers are important in disconnecting these relationships, even if temporarily. These ancestral spirits were an intrinsic part of Maoli's self, Christian or otherwise, and they demanded to be recognized.

Many Ghanaian Pentecostals continue to believe that while you may be born again and washed of all your sins, others, such as family members, business partners, or friends, still connect you to family spirits and witchcraft. The fear always exists that people in your hometown could mention your name, without your knowledge or presence, while pouring libations to the ancestors during a festival or communal event. Alternatively, unknown to you, your parents, or generations before them, could have sought the protection of a shrine before your birth, connecting you to the spirits of that shrine (see van Dijk 2001, 225). It is from such an experience of spiritual bondage that a Christian requires deliverance. While deliverance prayers are seen as spiritual weapons to take back what the devil may have stolen, to attack enemies, to spiritually cleanse places and persons, and to ward off evil spirits, when deliverance prayers fail or are seen to have little effect, other alternatives of spiritual power are sometimes sought in order to alleviate personal suffering.

Apart from prophets, traditional priests also have the power (*tumi*) to solve spiritual problems linked to witchcraft and ancestral spirits. While Ghanaian epistemology locates *tumi* everywhere, some people, places, and things can channel this ever-present power better than others (Hagan 2000). Whenever I asked Ghanaians about *tumi* in its local usage, they reminded me that I had to be more specific: whose power and authority was I referring to? More than a rational and individual pursuit of goals, power is a cultural resource that has to be understood through what it does (Breidenbach 1979; Arens and Karp 1989). Martin Lindhardt (2010), for example, has shown that traditional elders and born-again Christian youth in Tanzania share a cultural understanding of spiritual power, with regard to what it does, allowing them to respect each other even if they do not share the same religious identity. While Pentecostals describe the Holy Spirit as more powerful than traditional spirits, they are not immune from the effects of the latter. Rather than seeking a strictly Christian answer to problems of disease, finding a practical solution becomes more of a priority for those who are suffering. In another example, Alice Street (2010, 266), who looks at Christian belief among hospital patients in Papua New Guinea, writes about Clare, the sister of a patient, who was less interested in explaining her brother's sickness than in pursuing different ways of healing and positively transforming his body. In this case, Pentecostal Christian belief, as propositional ("believe in" statements), is less important than intervening in the situation and focusing on the possible ways of transforming such relationships (ibid., 268).

Maoli did not view her different options as contradictory, but simply as necessary. She continued to attend church regularly and considered herself a born-again Christian who prayed to Jesus Christ. She did not seem to have any problem with what she had done; for her, there ceased to be a right and wrong, just a need to recognize and acknowledge where she came from before she could walk in the present and carve out her own future as a born-again Christian. In mediating a simultaneous proximity with and distance from her ancestral spirits, her ethical judgment also speaks of the limits of born-again rupture. By satisfying her obligations to her father's hometown, she was free to worship God through Christianity again.

"Give to Caesar, what belongs to Caesar," Maoli told me in reference to her ritual reconnection with her ancestors, which had allowed her to freely pursue her Christian practices. By ritually acknowledging her "traditional" side, her "Christian" side was allowed to flourish. Cultural ideas of spiritual power and of the composite self continue to influence the ways in which Ghanaian Pentecostals like Maoli imagine their relationship with the Holy Spirit and with other non-Christian spirits. Maoli's case points to the practical decisions she made in reconnecting with her ancestral spirits. It involved a process of self-fashioning as well as of deciding when to follow her born-again commitments, when to depart from them, and how to evaluate between her competing commitments to the Holy Spirit and her ancestral spirits. Maoli was not making a strict distinction between God and the devil, but an ethical decision between living (happily) and suffering (miserably). In her case, a Pentecostal identity can also be viewed, analytically at least, as a way of ritually forgetting an ancestral past in order to remember the continuous presence of Pentecostal freedom. Her case also demonstrates how the jealousy of others can potentially pull a person back into unhealthy relationships that cause illness and the destruction of happiness through what my interlocutors described as witchcraft or the "dark side of the African." Rather than transcending the ambivalence of witchcraft power and uneasy family relationships, Pentecostalism in Ghana internally reproduces these discourses, as it simultaneously seeks to address the tensions of communal Christian relationships and the pursuit of one's individual ambitions.

Witchcraft and the "Dark Side of the African"

I was sitting in a café in Kumasi with a pastor whom I had met during a Holy Ghost Convention in Accra. Pastor Efa had travelled from Kumasi to Accra for the church event, and we had arranged to meet again when I was in Kumasi. Efa was also a prophet who helped people with problems of illness and ill fortune, which in many cases were linked to witchcraft. This ability to help others had recently paid off. A family member of a woman whom he had healed of paralysis promised to provide the necessary funding for his eldest son's plane ticket to the United Kingdom. He had identified this woman as a victim of witchcraft. When he met her, she was paralysed and had been suffering from all unknown illness. Efa eventually healed her by delivering her from the witchcraft causing her paralysis. The Holy Spirit revealed to him that the witch involved was a close relative of this woman. Like so many others in Ghana, Efa directly linked the cause of suffering to the witchcraft activities of family and friends who did not want to see the person succeed. The same people who are supposed to support and care for you are most likely the ones who also want to destroy you and cause you to suffer, not simply through neglect, but also by intentionally trying to do you harm. I asked him the question that was foremost on my mind: "Why is it that it is almost always someone close to you or a family member who tries to make you sick or fail in life?" His eyes became larger than before, as he stared at me with a knowing look, before replying:

> Jealousy. It is the dark side of the African. The ability to use black magic and other evil supernatural powers to bring their own people down … [T]hey do not like to see somebody else succeed or doing well in life so they create obstacles. This magic can be obtained from a priest or herbalist and then applied against the victim. Otherwise, the person causing the harm might be a witch, have an evil spirit enters her and takes over her life from a young age. That is where you draw the line, those who accept Jesus and those who do not.

Efa associated "jealousy" with the "dark side of the African," which is similar to a negative spirit, not wanting someone else to prosper. The witch was someone close to you who disregarded the limits of kinship and other moral relationships within society. In their relations with others, witches' personal envy and greed eat at them from the inside until they turn on those closest to them. Efa's answer was similar to a reply Adam Ashforth (2005) received from a Soweto healer or *inyanga*, Mr. Zondi, when he asked him why witchcraft was increasing in post-apartheid South Africa. Mr Zondi's reply is also telling of the social changes and the political and economic situation since post-apartheid independence in 1994.

> "Jealousy" he replied. "There's too much jealousy." But he was puzzled about the recent increase in jealousy. "The way things are now," he said, "when a person buys furniture, the other one gets jealous and wants to destroy him. You've got cows? They'll kill you. You can't buy a car. You can't even buy a pair of trousers. You can't do anything with your life. They

don't want any progress. This jealousy is too high, and it causes the witches to be more active." Mr. Zondi's view was that jealousy was running out
of control in recent years, since there has been freedom. (ibid., 128)

While witchcraft is sometimes described as an age-old phenomenon
found within family relations, others see the increase in witchcraft accusations as something that has emerged out of more recent social and
economic developments in postcolonial Africa. The literature has focused on witchcraft's embeddedness within increasing socio-economic
inequalities amidst promises of a prosperous future, especially with
regard to the tensions between communal obligations and the selfish
individualism associated with the new political economy (Geschiere
1997; Meyer 1995, 1998a; Weiss 1998; Auslander 1993; Ashforth 1998).
In Ghana, witchcraft is similarly associated with uncontrolled posses-
sive individualism and selfish behaviour, which are opposed to communal values and threaten the limits of what is socially and morally
appropriate. It is also used to address an inversion or a breaking down
of traditional structural roles and responsibilities, whereby young people and women increasingly have more power and authority in public
and economic life over men in society.

Witches are also, potentially, people who are close to you, either
through friendship circles or work networks. Through the intervention
of a witch, one's destiny could literally be "eaten" or "swallowed." One
could become bewitched through many means – food and sexual relations are among the most common ones – and these means are generally related to the experience of suffering and weakness, barrenness,
infertility, the immature death of someone, sickness, poverty, and the
unexpected loss of wealth. In Ghana, seeking the help of prophets is a
common way to protect and defend oneself from witchcraft. However,
traditional shrines also provide these same services to those in need.

Only when you leave the busy central urban districts of Ghana and
go into the smaller towns and villages do traditional religion and its
authority become a visible and dominant presence. One such trip took
me to a village called Noase, just a few kilometers from Wenchi, a town
in the Brong-Ahafo region. The village was famous in Ghana because it
was the home of *Kwaku Firi*, an Akan divinity who has come to dwell in
Noase for over three generations. I was there in 2003 to attend the annual Apoo Festival that celebrated the end of the crop harvest and ush-
ered in a new cycle of productive relationships and fertility. The power
of the shrine came from its past history of healing serious ailments,

Figure 4.1 The chief priest of Kwaku Firi during the Apoo festival. (Photo by the author.)

blessing women with children, and protecting people from evil. Its work was very similar to that of Pentecostal prayer camps in that divine healing and protection were offered to people who became members. People from all over Ghana and even other parts of West Africa made frequent trips to the shrine, becoming related to the divinity through a ritual sacrifice and consumption of food that made you a son or daughter of *Kwaku Firi*.

"But how does someone become related to a divinity?" I asked an Ewe friend who was initiated into the shrine and a "son of *Kwaku Firi*." He told me:

> There is a way to be a member, be under his protection, which is a ceremony or small ritual that they make. Some divinities they will give you something to eat. Others will cut you and put something in your blood, others give you a kola to eat. Here they do a small ritual and sacrifice a chicken and then immediately *Kwaku Firi* becomes everything for you.

Through consuming something or contact with blood, the person becomes a child of the divinity and is protected by the shrine. Although the shrine protects members of the immediate community in which it is situated, regardless of whether they come to pay their respects or believe in the shrine's powers, those who willingly choose to forge closer ties with the divinity receive a higher portion of power and protection. It therefore requires a choice from the individual, whereby he or she willingly decides to undergo a ritual aimed at making him or her into a son or daughter of the shrine. The power does not come from one's individual self, but from a stronger spirit divinity who enters into a relationship with the believer or who fills his or her person and acts through that person.

Many Pentecostals frequently spoke of their previous connections with traditional shrines, either in their childhood or before conversion. Mrs Amankwa (Mama), a friend of my paternal grandfather and a former member of CoP who lived in Accra, was one of them. Mama had started a Christian fellowship almost twenty years earlier that still met daily in the compound of her home for spiritual prayer and intercession. I had been to her home in Accra on numerous occasions, where we spent a lot of time chatting about her religious conversion and other experiences she had concerning her Pentecostal life. On one such occasion, we spoke about the progress of my research while sipping tea on her front porch. I told her about my visit to the *Kwaku Firi* shrine and my conversation with the chief priest of the shrine. She looked at me with bemused curiosity and promptly declared, "They are all witches." Then she asked me what I thought of the place.

I suggested to her that the shrines had their own moral conduct and principles, which appeared good. "It reminded me of the Pentecostal prayer camps," I said. The local divinity, like Jesus, was referred to as a Holy Spirit and a Son of God, and helped the people known as "sons and daughters" of the shrine with similar type problems of healing, deliverance, protection, and material success. The African priest, like the Pentecostal prophet, I suggested to her, served a similar role as the mediator between man and God. She shook her head disapprovingly at me and said, "You don't understand, Girish. These shrines are very smart these days. That is how the devil works. He knows the Bible and he has all sorts of methods to trick people. All shrines use witchcraft."

To Mama, the traditional shrines and the devil were one and the same. These shrines could not compete with Pentecostal power. She proceeded to narrate to me how her grandfather and her aunt had both been to this same shrine in the past. She started her verbal assault on the shrine by first questioning the strength of its power. Her aunt (her mother's sister) had gone there when Mama was young to seek power and protection. Upon the aunt's return to the village, the passenger car she was in met with an accident and went off the road. Mama's aunt was the only person to fall out of the car, she told me, while trying to make a point. On another incident, she and her aunt were returning from a neighbouring village and had to walk through the woods. When they came to a stream, they suddenly saw three bright lights travelling upstream against the flow of the water. She described these lights as witches travelling back from a mission. Her aunt screamed for *Kwaku Firi* in fear, asking for protection, but nothing happened. Mama told me that *Kwaku Firi* did not come to their rescue. Instead, several hunters who were in the forest heard their screams and came running to help. Needless to say, I did not mention to Mama that it seemed very possible to describe these same narratives as explanations for *Kwaku Firi* actually having come to their rescue: the hunters did help them, and although her aunt fell out of the car, she did not die.

What was important for Mama, however, was to show me how one could have relationships with these divinities, but that these relationships were all destructive and the work of the devil. From my conversations with Mama and many others, I realized that divinities or ancestors were thought to have a covenant with individuals, not necessarily of their own choice or doing, given that these relationships had been established since one's birth or even before. As much as these spirits could protect and help individuals at certain times, they always wanted something in return. They could physically take away your success, material wealth, and health. Mama also told me how her mother had gone to a village divinity to seek its protection and to ask for a smooth delivery before she was born. Since her birth, Mama has been associated with this village divinity, and the people of her village sometimes referred to her by the same name as the divinity. It was only years later that she was set free from this connection. After becoming born again, she was asked by a Pentecostal evangelist to make a list of all her past connections to shrines so that they could pray over them. Only then did she realize the long-lasting effects that the shrine had on her. Eventually, after much prayer, she was delivered from the divinity of the shrine.

This incident, like many others of the sort, proved the reality of her God and the power of Pentecostalism to her. "I now know the God I am serving, and He is not a small god," she declared to me. The local divinities and other spirits were represented by "stones," she said, but the power of the Christian God was beyond the representation of such material objects. Again, she offered a selective and partial reading of events by failing to recall the numerous times she had told me about the importance of the food items and gifts given to her by the prophetess of a CoP prayer camp, where she had received her healing, and by not mentioning the efficacy of this relationship and these objects as vehicles for miracles. I now turn to Mama's story of a woman whose individual choice to convert was closely tied to the dividual nature of her relationships to others.

Mama and the Edumfa Prayer Camp

Mama was originally from Kumasi, Ghana's Ashanti capital, where she met her husband, who comes from a royal lineage. After her marriage, she worked as a trader and made extra money buying cloth from Abidjan (Côte d'Ivoire) and selling it for a profit in Ghana. In her work on Kumasi market women, Gracia Clark (1994) has shown that for many West Africans, and for the Ashanti especially, financial independence is important for the personal dignity of an adult woman. Her ability to use her own income, without permission from others, is seen as "the basis for forging firm bonds of mutual aid" (ibid., 107). This insight gives some background to the importance of Mama's membership within a social group, her sense of financial independence, and her need to maintain good relationships with her business partners and neighbours. Such relationships carried significant moral weight as well as commercial advantages. However, these same group dynamics can also be harmful, especially when people become jealous of someone else's success. Mama's story is one of an ongoing effort to balance the pull of her relationships with Christian and non-Christian others and her own relationship to her Christian identity and ability to make decisions for herself.

In the early 1980s, after she had moved to Accra, Mama had a dream followed by a sickness that left her partially paralysed from the waist down. She was bedridden for six months and unable to carry on her business. She described the paralysis as a sudden occurrence following a visit to her husband's village near Kumasi, where she had prominently participated in a wedding:

> The night before, I had a dream about a certain woman in the village who I knew did not like me and was jealous of my success. In my dream, I saw

this woman standing error a big pot of boiling water, slowly stirring it. I asked the woman what she was doing but I got no reply I woke up in the middle of the night in a cold sweat and started praying. However, at that time, I was not a Pentecostal but a Presbyterian and did not know how to pray. When I woke up the next day I went to the post office to make a phone call to one of my children living overseas. Suddenly, in the post office, my legs gave way and I fell to the floor. When I regained consciousness, I was in hospital and paralysed from my waist down.

Mama's illness was interpreted as a spiritual intrusion into her life that was intended to control her future actions and impede her productive capacity to engage in business and trade. Her claims to financial independence were offset by the pull of moral obligations to others and the spiritual forces of others who wanted her dead. While seeking medical answers to her sudden illness, she began to ask other "why" questions regarding the timing of her illness and the dream she had the night before her paralysis occurred. Mama's business was very profitable; according to her, this led to jealousy from certain of her kinfolk in Kumasi and in her husband's village. During the wedding she had attended, one of the elder women in the village had become jealous of Mama and had criticized her publicly. She suspected that this woman was a witch and that she was the one who had appeared in her dream and made her ill.

It was a "spiritual attack," she told me. Her Christian identity and membership in the Presbyterian church could not help her fight the evil spirits sent by this old woman from her husband's village. As she told me her story, she emphasized her feeling of helplessness, her body's permeability to spiritual attack, and the lack of personal agency she experienced during this period of her life. She specifically linked her inability to pray effectively to her identity as a Presbyterian and to not yet having accepted Jesus into her life. She realized the risks and dangers of family relationships and negative spiritual forces on her health and well-being. After six months of being bedridden, Mama slowly began to walk short distances; eventually, she went to London to seek further medical treatment. She then spent an entire year in London trying to get an appointment for an operation, which was, however, postponed due to logistical problems. The doctors advised her to go back to Ghana for some sunshine and to return in a few months for her operation. On her way back, she stopped over in Abidjan, where she consulted a well-known traditionalist. The traditionalist told her that if she returned to Ghana, she would die from her illness before she could return to London, and then asked Mama for some money to carry out a ritual prayer for her recovery. Mama chose not to continue any further social transactions with this "fetish priestess" and returned to Ghana, still in bad health. Once in Ghana, she shared her story with a friend, who advised her to seek help at the Edumfa Prayer Camp, one of the most popular CoP prayer camps, where a powerful prophetess, Aunty Grace, would pray for her health. These different choices of healing reflect Mama's negotiation of various power relationships and identities as well as her ability to engage diverse social networks. Mama was less interested in explaining her illness than in finding a solution for it through the various networks available to her. However, as a Christian, Mama explained to me that she was not comfortable with "all" avenues and rejected the traditionalist's offer to conduct a ritual sacrifice for her.

Many important politicians, businesspeople, and foreigners, alongside the poor and uneducated, seek Aunty Grace's help and spiritual advice in interpreting dreams and seeking protection from witchcraft. Edumfa is known as a place where God hears people's prayers and where people's individual needs are met. The prayer camp itself is a place charged with stories of miracles and angelic visitations. Even before visiting the prayer camp, I had heard about it many times from several people in Accra, including church members, taxi drivers, and shop owners. The camp, people told me, is connected to heaven by a ladder whereby angels move up and down between heaven and earth. "Angelic doctors" come down to earth to heal the sick and suffering, and perform "surgery" on them while they sleep. People with all forms of sickness and all types of problems continue to journey there, staying for extended periods of time and praying for a solution to their troubles.

It was at Edumfa that Mama eventually received her healing, within an hour of her arrival. She made the three-hour drive from Accra to the prayer camp, arriving during the Thursday special prayer service called *Mpaebo Da* (Day of Prayer). She described the scene of her healing to me:

> When I arrived at the prayer camp, they were having their Thursday prayers at the church on top of the hill, so I drove up and joined them there. I could hardly walk, so I sat down on a folding chair just outside the church building. I was enjoying the songs of worship and music. The minute I got there, I heard a voice in my head telling me that I was healed.

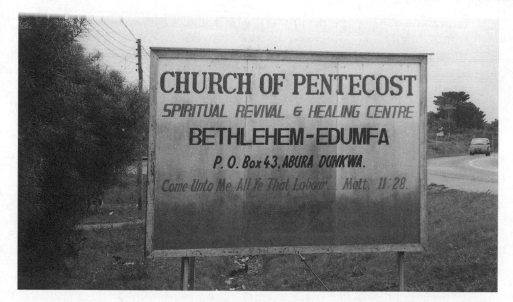

Figure 4.2 Edumfa Prayer Camp signboard. (Photo by the author.)

Then, suddenly, the voice told me to stand up and walk. I looked around but saw that nobody had spoken to me … [A]ll the people were concentrating on the worship. At first, I thought I was dreaming. But then I just stood up, walked into the church, and began worshipping with them. Now you must understand that I could barely stand on my own before that … It was through simply being there that I was healed.

This healing experience allowed Mama to experience the power of the Holy Spirit as an external force that came into her and took control over her situation. By listening to this inner voice in her head, she was healed. She later described the voice in her head as the Holy Spirit that filled her when praying. While this healing transformation proved to Mama that God is real, she made it clear to me that she did not immediately become born again upon being healed. After her healing experience, she continued to visit the prayer camp's Thursday prayer services in order to learn more about these new relationships. She stayed there for weeks, getting to know the prophetess better, listening to sermons, learning the songs, and listening to people tell stories of their own miraculous healings.

Figure 4.3 View of Edumfa Prayer Camp. (Photo by the author.)

Mama also made it known to me that she had various possibilities for action and that her decision to become born again was a personal choice. She stressed that this decision was not influenced by her healing experience or by the individual power of the prophetess, stating, "I could have chosen to stop attending the prayer camp after my healing and return to the Presbyterian church." It was only months after her healing experience that Mama eventually made the decision to renounce her affiliation with the Presbyterian church and to become born again and join CoP. While the object of her new commitment was Jesus, this commitment only manifests in social relationships (Englund 2004, 485). Since her decision to become Pentecostal resulted from the freedom to choose between different options, what followed was a period of self-examination over whether she could sustain her commitment in the face of other ongoing relationships.

Mama maintained her close ties with the prayer camp and Aunty Grace, visiting Edumfa as often as she could and financially contributing to the camp's development. She also became a source of spiritual protection for others in her own community. After successfully praying

Figure 4.4 Thursday prayer service at Edumfa Prayer Camp. (Photo by the author.)

for the full recovery of her neighbour's dying son, she converted her home in Accra into a prayer centre in order to help others deal with sickness and other spiritual problems, leading daily prayer sessions on her front porch. We spent many afternoons on that same front porch, discussing her conversion experience and subsequent affiliations with Pentecostal pastors, prophets, and churches. It was also there that I learned more about the limitations of Pentecostal power and how the actions of others can affect one's ability to spiritually protect oneself. Although her born-again identity helped Mama create new structures of relatedness, she continued to face limits to her new Pentecostal agency.

I visited Mama at home one weekday afternoon only to find her resting in bed. She was ill that day and could not get up. When I asked what was wrong, she said that it was difficult to explain and then proceeded to tell me that her spirit was weak. It was another spiritual problem, she told me. There were no outward signs of sickness, just her description of weakness and a feeling that all was not right. When I asked her to elaborate, she said she suspected that the early morning prayers she held in her house each day were causing annoyance to others, non-Christians, in her area. They had probably reacted to the presence of her prayer fellowship and the early morning prayers by sending their own evil spirits against her, causing her to fall sick. She pointed to the street and said:

> You know that Fadama is a Muslim area and there is a mosque nearby, as well as a Hindu church and a *malam* (Muslim spiritualist) who lives down the street from me … [T]he *malam* and I used to be friends. I even attended his daughter's wedding and brought gifts for them. But since I became born again and turned my house into a prayer ground, we do not communicate anymore … There are witches that live around this area and they do not like that we hold prayer sessions here every morning and sometimes all-night prayer meetings. It disturbs their peace and spoils their work.

Mama told me that she extracted herself from these relationships of mutual exchange in order to remain a committed Pentecostal. Although she prayed for the protection of others, Mama continued to be subject to witchcraft attacks that made her sick. She told me that she could not blame the Holy Spirit or God for the lack of protection surrounding her. Instead, she described this as her own fault – she had not protected herself sufficiently. She could not trust her prayer assistants to spend enough time cleansing the prayer ground of any ill will or witchcraft, or else their prayers were not powerful enough to protect her from spiritual attacks on her health. As she explained:

> These last few days, however, I haven't been attending the breaking and cleansing prayers that we usually have before the prayer meetings begin … [M]y prayer leaders have not been doing a good job and hardly spend a few minutes attending to these prayers … I suspect that that is why these spiritual attacks have made me sick.

Mama's example points to the importance of uncertainty and doubt, which serve to accompany and provide meaning to the subjective experience of Christian certainty. The limits or boundaries of Christian meaning are always put to the test, challenged, debated by Christians themselves, and at times fail to produce the intended result (Tomlinson and Engelke 2006). However, it is important to note that a preoccupation with Christian meaning only emerges in particular circumstances or when performances fail. In Mama's case, it was the shortcomings of her prayer assistants' words and actions, attributed to their "laziness" or "carelessness," which made their prayers less efficacious. Human weakness provided an entry point for uncertainty and for the worldly dangers of life to creep in. Within the next few days, Mama decided to make a trip to Edumfa Prayer Camp to pray and fast for her own recovery and to spend some time with Aunty Grace. Such a crisis served as a way to make Christianity meaningful again through more powerful forms of Pentecostal prayer. Her ongoing relationship with Aunty Grace indicates that the circumstances for her continued commitment to Jesus and her ability to help others were dependent on her relationships with both Christians and non-Christians, as demonstrated by her ability to take on the pain of another's suffering as well as by the permeability of her own body when others extended suffering onto her.

As I have shown, the personal freedom Mama experienced from her born-again transformation was based on her relationships with others that both tested and affirmed her Christian faith. Any account of Pentecostal identity as a process of self-fashioning must also recognize the different ways in which transformation is expressed as diverse alignments with the non-Christian past. While public acceptance regarding the definition of a Pentecostal identity is important to processes of self-formation, it does not always shape or determine how Pentecostals act in the world, nor does it conform to a single criterion for what identifies a committed Pentecostal subject. Mama's and Maoli's stories demonstrate that

Pentecostals are social actors, who make judgments about balancing their personal ambitions and communal obligations, and about how the individual and dividual nature of relationships ought to be expressed in a given cultural situation. If the boundaries of Christian meaning can be challenged, and if Christian performances can ritually fail to create the intended outcome, an attention to ethical practice allows for a closer examination of how Christian persons alternate between individuality and dividuality within these varied and shifting circumstances.

Alternating Personhood: The Individual and Dividual Christian

Thus far, I have shown how individual desires for positive change and the social pull of communal obligations were brought together differently in the lives of two Ghanaian Pentecostal women through a process of self-fashioning and judgment. These examples resemble Turnerian "social dramas," without the teleological assumptions associated with this term, and hence involve four phases: breach, crisis, reflexivity, and reintegration (Turner 1985). Maoli and Mama faced moments of personal dis-ease while they were searching for the best way out of their suffering and into the born-again life they were promised. In doing so, they had to weigh the various options available to them. By evaluating how to live as Pentecostals, they came to recognize the limits of their own Christian identity, its assumptions of freedom and rupture, and the difficulties in remaining consistent. While they both emerged temporarily victorious over their suffering and continued to see themselves as committed Pentecostals, they did not make the same choices on how to achieve the appropriate balance between their independence from and dependence on the world – between spirit and flesh.

Both Maoli and Mama claimed a born-again identity that entailed the acceptance of a specific history of salvation and a new moral relationship between man and God (see Engelke 2007; Cannell 2006a). How the Spirit of God and the body of man come together to create the presence of God in the world is the subject of much debate among Christians. It is precisely by participating in such debates over the correct convergence of spirit and flesh that Ghanaian Pentecostals become involved in the ongoing practice of defining their Christian self. The Pentecostal self is found in the movement or tension between the application of certain criteria regarding the spirit's embodiment and the recognition of its limits. This tension is closely associated with the fact that the promise of personal rupture and a new relationship with Jesus is complicated by the presence of other others, human and non-human, in the construction of the Christian self. For example, even after becoming Pentecostal, Mama's physical body continued to bear the brunt of spiritual attacks that made her own spirit and body weak. Her personal relationship with the Holy Spirit of God was at times insufficient to heal her body. She continued to seek the support of the prophetess, Aunty Grace, and to visit Edumfa Prayer Camp for more powerful forms of prayer. In her case, the question of appropriately mediating the presence of God was also about appropriate "relationality" (which persons could help her become whole again) and a question of "constancy" (whether she could consistently demonstrate her Pentecostal individuality effectively over time). In the case of Maoli, her body was both intrinsically linked to her ancestral spirits and open to the spiritual attacks of a jealous ex-boyfriend and business partners. She finally resorted to restoring forgotten family relationships and fulfilling her social obligations to her ancestral gods in order to recommit to her Pentecostal present. Her case also points to the "partibility" and composite nature of relationships in Ghana, where a person comprises elements of her parents and others in her life. These examples demonstrate that finding the appropriate or comfortable balance between dividuality and individuality, or between communal obligation and individual freedom, requires ongoing practical judgment and evaluation. Maoli and Mama demonstrated a pragmatic quality to their Pentecostal faith by looking for new ways out of their illnesses and by doing what they thought would be best in order to attain a renewed sense of well-being. Their examples also show how a Christian's life is fraught with spiritual intrusions, moral transgressions, and social dependencies that are unexpected and sometimes necessary to remaining a committed Pentecostal Christian individual.

If the "individual" is an important frame of value for Christian personhood, Pentecostals in Ghana cannot be understood through a Christian individualist framework alone. Joel Robbins (2004a) provides a good example of how Christian ideas of individual personhood and indigenous ideas of the self interact. In his work among the Urapmin of Papua New Guinea, Robbins describes the tensions and contradictions that these charismatics experience between individualism and relationalism (ibid., 290). The Urapmin are forced to make ethical decisions in finding the appropriate balance between the existing tensions of an individualism found in the Christian model of salvation and the Urapmin relationalist conception of social life. While the Christian individual is described as the sole unit of salvation, the Urapmin are troubled by a Christian individualism that does not also emphasize relationships of sharing and support between people. If charismatic Christianity places more emphasis on the individual as the moral unit and paramount value of divine judgment, a relationalist conception of social life makes it difficult for the Urapmin to completely embrace Christian individualism. Also writing on Melanesian Christianity, Mark Mosko (2010, 232) proposes another approach, suggesting that Christian individualism is inherently about the partibility of the total person, even if the "individual" occasionally becomes an important resource. He argues that while taking on a new identity seen as discontinuous from the past, Melanesians continue to understand their Christian identity through ideas of partibility, first. Christianity appeals to Melanesians because it possesses a dividual logic that is recognizable to Papuans. For Mosko, Christian conversion represents a change from one "dividualist" form of personhood to another (ibid.).

Ghanaian prophets present us with an understanding of Christian personhood that closely resembles Mosko's analysis. Theories about a plurality of invisible, disembodied spirits are uncontroversial for most Ghanaians (Appiah 1992, 135), and prophets are known for their special ability to channel the Holy Spirit as well as to help deliver people from the debilitating presence of demonic spirits in their bodies. After becoming born again, Pentecostals often continue to ask whether it is the Holy Spirit or other spirits that possess them, and whether their ancestral divinities continue to have a presence in their lives. This uncertainty happens because a Ghanaian person has multiple relationships and is usually made up of different substances and powers, some inherited and some acquired. For example, an Akan individual is seen to be composed of the *okra* (the soul, which comes directly from God), *sunsum* (spirit, which comes from the father), and *mogya* (blood, which comes from the mother) (see Opoku 1978; Wiredu 1980; Gyekye [1987] 1995; Atiemo 1995). Blood is linked to ideas of vitality, life, and sexuality, as well as to descent and the mother's ancestral line. Alternatively, "everything is or contains *sunsum*," where *sunsum* is inherently "an activating principle" (Gyekye [1987] 1995, 75), and one's divinities are transmitted through the father's *sunsum*. Ghanaian Pentecostals might claim an individual identity in Christ and experience a direct line with God through the Holy Spirit, but they are still wondering how much of themselves is still in the other, and connected to and affected by others and other spirits. This connection is partly why prophets remain very popular in Ghana. In his study of apostolic prophets in Botswana, Richard Werbner (2011) presents a model of alternating personhood that takes the cultural resonances of dividuality seriously. For Werbner's charismatic prophets, dividuality matters, especially during exorcisms and witch-finding sessions when their clients' selves are permeated by others' substances. Like Ghanaian prophets, these apostolic prophets take on the suffering of others, even as their personal sense of individuality and autonomy is strongly asserted. In their continuing orientation towards cultural idioms of personhood, these prophets are well situated to traverse the boundaries of dividuality and individuality.

Is conversion to Christianity in Ghana, then, merely a variation or continuity of a pre-Christian logic of relatedness? For Robbins (2007b), such a one-sided approach to understanding religious change as merely a replacement of old wine with new wine skins is tantamount to a problem of "continuity thinking" in anthropology, which does not acknowledge or take seriously Christian claims of discontinuity. After all, CoP leaders are deeply concerned if Pentecostals continue to positively engage with these spirits or, in some cases, claim to be possessed by them once born again.[2] Many church members I knew professed that they were no longer tied to the spirits of their past or only engaged with these spirits as demons who had to be cast out of people's lives and places.

This chapter does not define Christian personhood, but rather presents what my Ghanaian Pentecostal interlocutors claim it is, as they work either with or against competing and sometimes incommensurable visions of personhood and well-being. Perhaps the question is not so much "what" is a Christian person, but rather "how" and "when" is Christianity experienced as more or less in-dividualizing? Maoli's and Mama's stories reveal how both individualist and dividualist notions of relatedness work together to provide alternating frameworks of and for Christian personhood in Ghana. This idea of an alternating individuality and dividuality was shared by many church members, who believed that they were made anew-in-Christ as individuals but still connected to the spirts of their past. For them, deliverance continued to be a popular practice in weekday prayer services and in prayer camps. If their born-again status emphasized a new relational life, separated from their traditional family networks, a life that was also personally empowering, Maoli and Mama continued to struggle with a relational and dividual understanding of the traditional person, which reconnected them to their families and included the interpenetration of others in and on the self. While they claimed a new Christian individuality, they were not simply Christian individuals, no longer aligned in some way with the spirits of their past and with cultural ideas of dividuality and partibility. They both, in their own way, struggled with a traditional relationalism that they were supposed to have left behind, and were simultaneously involved in Christian relationships that emphasized the dividual nature of personhood.

While Ghanaian philosophers point out the importance of the communal and divisible nature of personhood, they remind us that the communal structure cannot foreclose moments of individual self-assertiveness, reflection, and evaluation (Gyekye 1992; Wiredu 1996). Similarly, some anthropologists argue that we should see all cultures as containing both individual and dividual modalities of personhood (LiPuma 1998).[3] However, individuality and dividuality also need to be understood through different levels of analysis and should be compared with cultural practice (Boddy 1998, 256; Coleman 2011a, 6). How, then, can we draw from cultural approaches to personhood without reproducing stereotypical ideas about Christianity as individualistic or reinforcing indigenous forms of cultural continuity of dividuality or partibility at the expense of a Christian identity? If Pentecostalism does mount an attack on what is regarded as the legacy from the past of dividuality, how can we understand a Christian personhood that takes into account different cultural models of dividuality without also endorsing dividuality as an artefact of continuity thinking?

Conclusion

This chapter has stressed the need to understand dividuality and individuality as interrelated concepts within a comparative anthropology of Christianity. The focus has not been on moments of moral instability or on a productive crisis of unsettling dominant discourses around personhood, but rather on the complexities Pentecostal Christians in Ghana face when making choices and decisions, given the range of possibilities available to them. I have suggested that alongside cultural assumptions about Ghanaian or Christian individuals and dividuals, we should allow the Pentecostal individual/dividual antinomy to emerge from the tensions between the multiple forms of personhood that surface at different moments and from the practical decisions people make about how to live their lives. No person is solely an indigenous or a Christian subject; nor can a person simply be characterized as either individualistic or dividualistic. Instead, it is important to look at how a Pentecostal identity can be experienced and achieved differently through a practical convergence of the individual and dividual within everyday life negotiations and contingencies.

Christians are not just host to the Spirit of God but also to other spirits, including ancestral spirits and the spirit of witchcraft. Ghanaian Pentecostals work towards achieving a comfortable balance between the influence of the Holy Spirit and other spirits in order to alleviate the suffering in their lives. These moments of evaluation, concerning how to live well and stay healthy, are accompanied by ambiguity and uncertainty regarding the appropriate action to take. I have focused on two Ghanaian Pentecostal women and their relationships with prophets and other religious intermediaries who helped them achieve personal goals. In discovering the reasons or powers behind their sickness or sense of well-being, they simultaneously drew on different ideas of the Christian self, in which the Holy Spirit and other spirits provided a charged space for reconstituting relations. Understanding the women's response to sickness and their decisions to seek spiritual consultation as ethical actions acknowledges the difficulties they faced in trying to remain consistent and to fulfil the criteria for rupture. Maoli and Mama were exercising judgment on how to solve the problems they faced as Pentecostals, sometimes in piecemeal ways, especially during times of crisis and indeterminacy. They were not merely involved in an individual relationship with God, but also with multiple others who needed to be accounted for, especially when evaluating how to negotiate with and draw from various Christian and non-Christian relationships that they were connected to. In this way, "when" is someone a Christian could, on occasion, become a more important question than "who" or "what" is a Christian. The different, competing, and sometimes contradictory roles that church leaders, prophets, and traditional religious intermediaries play in the lives of Ghanaian Pentecostals alert us to the importance of both the "individual" and the "dividual" as coexisting and alternating states of existence, and as a response to the implication of the presence of others in one's life.

The stories of Maoli and Mama are examples of the active balancing and negotiation between individuality and dividuality that deserve attention in any cultural setting (LiPuma 1998). But we also need to ask, what is "culturally specific" (Boddy 1998, 256) about them? To what extent do cultural notions of kinship feature into this balancing between dividuality and individuality? In the next chapter, I explore how genealogical reasoning becomes important in church members' experience of Pentecostal kinship, and how migration, both within Ghana and to London, affects their relationship with their family and with Jesus. I pay close attention to the different Christian relationships that help sustain a Pentecostal transformation in Accra and London, and look at how Ghanaian Pentecostals struggle to achieve a personal relationship with God, separate from the effects of destructive and undesirable relationships.

Chapter Five

Kinship and Migration

Wo Nyame a wosom no daa daa
Ono na obegye wo

Your God that you worship daily
He is the one who will save you.

Akan proverb

I met Rita during my visit to a CoP youth camp in Kumasi. She was a recent graduate of social sciences from the University of Ghana, Legon, where she had studied religion. This is how our conversation began:

R: Where are you from?
G: Well, I was born in India, grew up in Singapore, am studying in London, and have family in Ghana.
R: All that doesn't matter. You are from the place that you are born and that is your hometown. Since your family comes from India and you were born there, you are Indian.

She seemed very satisfied with herself for having explained my roots to me. It did not matter that I had only spent a few months in India after my birth, or that I had spent over twenty years of my life in Singapore, or that my family had been in Ghana for over three generations. I did not resist her continued attempts to place me.

R: So you should be a Hindu, right?
G: Not necessarily.

Whenever someone questioned me about where I was from or what my religious background was, I would start by saying that I considered myself to be "of this world" or "a part of humanity." However idealistic this might have seemed, I did not want my interlocutors to associate me with being from one place or having a religion. I would, however, be quickly, and sometimes rudely, brought back to the inherent differences between them and me. They would ask me questions: "Where were you born?" "What religion do you belong to?" or "Which god do you worship?" On some occasions, they would assume that I was a born-again Christian, a "white man" (*oburoni*) and a foreigner, who prayed with them and attended church religiously. This was not one of those occasions.

> R: So what are you doing in Ghana?
> G: I am here doing research on Pentecostalism.
> R: So are you a Christian?
> G: No, but I have read the Bible and attend church services while I'm here.
> R: So, then, do you believe in Jesus Christ as your personal Lord and Saviour?
> G: Not really

She stared at me with a confused, almost sympathetic, look.

> R: But how can you say that you're studying Pentecostalism, have read the Bible, attend church, and not have accepted Jesus Christ as your personal Lord and Saviour?

She asked me if I prayed in Jesus's name. Again, and to her dismay, I replied in the negative. Rita told me that, like my ancestors, her ancestors had practiced "animism," and had worshipped stones and other inanimate objects. But she no longer saw the use of such practices, given that the gods of her hometown were distant and had no significance in her life since she had become born again. Rita wanted me to familiarize myself with Jesus through daily prayer and reading the Bible. I would then come to have a "personal relationship with Jesus," which, for Pentecostals like Rita, changed the way in which social relations are subsequently conceptualized and practised. She hoped that Jesus would "touch my heart" in some way, cause a conversion experience, and lead me to leave my Hindu gods and not be bound by my Indian roots.

My conversation with Rita resonates with many other conversations I have had with church members in Ghana and London that emphasize very deliberate strategies of differentiation and discontinuity, as well as connection and continuity. My interlocutors considered themselves "like-kin" and often needed to identify me as either Christian or non-Christian. They wanted to establish my religious background and roots so they could help me create a new religion and past. In response, I always tried to move beyond the genealogical framework they referred to in their attempts to place me. In this example, Rita was having none of it. Rita's point to me was that unless I left my "Hindu gods" and "accepted Jesus," I would not be free of my ancestral past and its negative effects on my life and future. A new relationship with Jesus would establish a new logic of Christian kinship to replace the old. As I discovered over time, however, the personal freedoms promised on becoming born again were always located in, and in tension with, one's commitments and obligations to where one was from and other structures of relatedness, including the church and one's family.

The question I ask in this chapter is: "How do church members in Ghana and London negotiate the tensions of maintaining a personal relationship with Jesus while fulfilling their obligations and responsibilities to others, including the church and family members?" The chapter discusses the ways in which two CoP members dealt with these tensions by examining how their born-again identity was mediated by and negotiated with church "kin-like" relations, family expectations, and personal ambitions of migration. If born-again Christians in Ghana publicly demonstrate their identities as individuals-in-Christ, they also continue to experience kinship within the church. A productive tension between Christianity as "descent" (given) and Christianity as "relational" (made) sits at the heart of connections and conflicts within CoP. In order to better understand the different aspects of these connections and conflicts constructed by CoP members in Ghana and in London, I turn to the examples of Albert and Eben. A new relationship with Jesus allowed Albert to leave his hometown, go to live in Accra, and hold aspirations to migrate overseas, whereas Eben's migration to London was challenged by communal obligations in London and family pressure in Ghana. While their personal relationships with Jesus gave both these men a sense of security and a confidence in the future, the church also provided them with a surrogate family in times of distress and alienation. At the same time, both struggled with their own desires for personal transformation and their moral obligations towards their family and their church.

The importance of kinship thinking in Christianity lies in the way it allows converts to address the universal claims made about "origins." When people create kinship, kinship also invokes a cultural and genea-logical order in which relationships are valued, promises made, actions judged, and compromises reflected upon (Bamford and Leach 2009).[1] In this chapter, I show how aspects of constructivist and genealogical thinking permeate Pentecostal relationships in Ghana. According to Rita, I simply had to make a different choice. The choice to believe in Jesus and appropriate certain kinds of prayer actions would help create a new relationship, or friendship, with Jesus. Pentecostal conversion, however, also provides CoP members with a new Christian relatedness meant to replace traditional family relationships. Pentecostal transfor-mation allows for manipulability in making new connections and aptly demonstrates that kinship terms serve as "linking terms" to help con-struct the subject in and through its relationships to others (Faubion 2001, 3). Church members may see themselves as no longer confined to a traditional framework for relating to each other and as operating through a Christian morality that constantly calls into question tradi-tional family relationships. However, they rearticulate their Christian relatedness as a new form of kinship that resembles traditional family structures. As Albert's story shows, although he was born again and a member of CoP, he drew on a genealogical model of kinship to explain how witchcraft worked, why his father's family had abandoned him, and why relationships within CoP were important to him.

Albert Successful

I first met Albert at one of CoP's local assemblies in Dansoman, a devel-oping area on the outskirts of Accra where I lived. An elder of the church made him sit next to me during the predominantly Twi service to serve as my translator. He was intelligent and resourceful, and we became fast friends. I found him inhabited by dreams of travel and fu-ture success. He had travelled to Accra from his hometown, awaiting the fulfilment of several prophecies that spoke of travel. I was to dis-cover months later that his hometown had become too dangerous for him to remain there and that his relationships with his family were tenuous. It was the temporary breakdown of relationships with certain members of his immediate family and his subsequent friendships with Pentecostals, through which support and prophetic guidance came, that influenced the way he interpreted and described future aspirations

Figure 5.1: Albert praying. (Photo by the author.)

of and for change. His personal testimonies and stories helped weave tapestries of relationships that had brought him to where he was at the time and helped direct him to where he wanted to go. These testimonies were also performances, which helped him come to terms with the contradictory aims of being accepted into his father's family and living a life independent of his family's negative influence.

Albert was brought up in his father's hometown in the Brong-Ahafo region of Ghana. His mother returned to her village after his parents divorced when he was younger. Albert is Akan. Unlike Maoli (Chapter Four), who is Ewe and connected to her parents' gods and ancestors through a patrilineal descent system, Albert is connected to his through a matrilineal system. According to an ideology of genealogical kinship, he therefore inherits a relationship with his mother's blood (*mogya*), which encompasses relationships with the mother's blood clan (*abusua*), including ancestors, inheritance, and ownership rights over property.[2] Among the Akan, an individual is made up of the *okra* (the soul, which comes directly from God), *sunsum* (spirit, which comes from the father), and *mogya* (blood, which comes from the mother) (see Opoku 1978, 94–100; Atiemo 1995, 12). Thus *mogya* gives the child status and membership within one kinship group. The child also receives the father's spirit (*sunsum*), which binds him or her to the father's divinities. Responsibility for the educational upbringing of a child falls on the father. The *sunsum* and *mogya*, while attributed to the father and mother respectively, also have spiritual associations. Apart from linking the individual to the father's gods, the *sunsum* is associated with a variety of attributes, including dreams and psychic experiences, character, and intelligence (Atiemo 1995, 11–12). Only when a genealogical link with a kinship group is established can the individual claim an identity, including social status and inheritance. These ideas around shared substance and succession have implications for the ways in which Albert saw himself as a victim of witchcraft and family neglect, and for the reasons that led his stepmother to try to kill him. Albert believed that earlier predictions about his future and his blood ties to his mother's family threatened his life:

> When I was younger, my [step] father and stepmother, who were attending spiritual churches (*sunsum sore*) at the time, brought me to a pastor of their church to prophesy into my future. During the consultation, the prophet told them that I was going to be the light of the family and that a day would come when everyone in my family would come under me. He also explained to them that I was a child of God who should be brought up carefully and under good guidance. My father was initially happy on learning about my future, but my stepmother was worried that I now posed a threat to her children's future and decided to have me killed. My stepmother had shown me love until she learned of my destiny. She decided to consult with a man in the village who was spiritually powerful. If

you wanted someone dead, he could do it. You would not even have to leave his house and the person you wanted dead would have met that fate. He gave my stepmother some water to sprinkle over me. My twin sister and I were asleep at the time when my stepmother walked into our room and sprinkled what she later called "holy water" all over us. The next day I questioned my father about the reason for that night's strange visit. My stepmother explained that the man who gave it to her said that if I asked about the water, it meant that I must be a wizard and dangerous to the family.

According to Albert, this event was the first of a series of many attempts to have him killed. His stepmother later poisoned his food. She would make his favourite food, which later gave him severe stomach pain and cold sweats. After the first attempt at poisoning him failed, she went back to the man who had sold her the poison. He was surprised to learn that his poison had not worked and decided to check on Albert, using a mirror that could look into someone's life.[3] He saw a ring of fire surrounding Albert and asked the stepmother why she wanted to kill a child of God. Albert was no ordinary child, he told her. But she was determined to kill him, and so the witchdoctor gave her a stronger poison that she used in his soup. Only after eating the soup, and almost dying from it, did Albert and his father finally realize that his stepmother was trying to kill him.

Another strand of Albert's story included his genealogical relationship to his mother's hometown. While visiting his mother's house for a funeral, he received a vision. In this vision, he saw that, in 1824, his mother's family house had also been a mission house for a white Methodist missionary. The missionary prophesied that one day the house would break and the family name would fall into disrepute, because some of its members were witches. He also prophesied that a boy would be born and that this boy would raise the house and lift up the family. Maurice Bloch (1998, 115) makes the argument that individuals' autobiographical memory – what they experience during their lifetime – is not that different from their knowledge of a more distant historical past which they have not lived through. The difference between recalling and remembering stresses how people remember more than they have experienced. In this case, Albert remembered a family history before his own lifetime that had a direct impact upon his present. As Albert thought about his vision and wondered about who that boy was, he heard someone beside him say that the boy was Albert himself.

Albert told me that because of the missionary's prophecy, the witches and gods in the town were not at rest and were trying to kill him. In Ghana, it is not thought uncommon for malevolent spirits to interfere in a person's *nkrabea* (destiny). Neither is it uncommon for Ghanaian Pentecostals to see themselves as the light of the family, helping protect their non–born-again family members from harm.

A few years later, the mysterious death of Albert's twin sister, to whom both he and his father were close, left his father and him on bad terms. This event was significant, as it further emphasized Albert's marginalized position within his father's family – all the more since Albert himself might be accused of being a male witch. His father later blamed Albert and his mother's side of the family (*abusua*) for his sister's death.

When I was fifteen, my step-grandmother [mother's stepmother] came from my maternal village to take me, and my sister, there for the Christmas break. I did not go, but my sister reluctantly accompanied her and returned home bloated. She gained so much of weight that was not normal. She died two weeks later after a mysterious sickness. Her death was a shock to both my father and I. My father later consulted a traditional priest who was sure that my grandmother was a witch who had murdered my sister. After my sister's death, my father lost affection for me and soon neglected me completely. He blamed me, and my mother's side, for my sister's death. He loved my sister a lot and treated me differently after that. Later, I learned the truth – that this man is not my real father. My mother presented him as our father, and he married her and she bore him another boy, after her former husband divorced her painfully. He refused to pay my school fees after the death of my sister. He told me to return to my mother's place ... because of that I suffered a lot.

Albert and his mother's family were viewed as witches and as dangerous to his stepfather's family. Such narratives of witchcraft suspicions demonstrate a "darker side to kinship" that is not uncommon in Africa (Geschiere 1997). Among the Akan, witchcraft is, strictly speaking, hereditary only within the matrilineal blood clan (Debrunner 1959, 54). Hans Debrunner has written that witchcraft produces a stress on relationships and is usually followed by fears and quarrels, especially when someone in the family dies. The death is attributed to the witch, who is then usually abused (ibid., 83). Tom McCaskie (2000, 181), however, has described witchcraft among the Asante as a discourse of power and wealth in interfamilial and interhuman relationships, where witch-craft, like Christianity or education, aims at obtaining wealth and power at the expense of others. Witchcraft accusations in Albert's case resulted in the breakdown of long-term moral commitments between close kin and the withdrawal of protection and financial support. While Albert blamed his stepmother and grandmother, and believed them guilty of witchcraft, Albert himself was accused of witchcraft by both his step-mother and later his stepfather.

In Albert's case, witchcraft and earlier prophecies were used as a ra-tionale for explaining strained family relations and unfulfilled obliga-tions. Both sets of accusations against him allowed him to see himself as a victim of circumstances beyond his control. He saw his stepmoth-er's accusation that he was a wizard (male witch) as a way to cut him off from the family and any future inheritance. The undue stress of cer-tain individual relationships with members of his close kin group in his father's hometown left him in search of other relationships that could help him continue his education and succeed in life. After being thrown out of his father's house, Albert went to live in Tema with his maternal granduncle for a while, but was treated as a lowly servant and made to do all the household chores. It was around this time that Albert left the Presbyterian church and joined a Pentecostal church, where the pastor guided him and prophesied that Albert would be "a great man of God." Albert eventually went to live under the care of his maternal uncle in another village in the Brong-Ahafo region.

It was at his uncle's house that Albert became a member of CoP. His uncle, who was the presiding elder of a branch of CoP, taught him how to pray effectively, preach in public, and develop his spiritual gifts. Albert, in turn, assisted his uncle in healing and deliverance services, where the Holy Spirit was invoked to deal with people's problems. However, after a few months, Albert left the village and headed to-wards Accra. He was fleeing from the anger of the royal family of a nearby village, who were seeking revenge on him for speaking ill of their ancestral gods. His journey to Accra was punctuated by a visit to the Edumfa Prayer Camp, where Aunty Grace prophesied that Albert would leave Ghana – more specifically for Israel – in the near future. Through his association with these Pentecostal pastors and prophets and prophetesses, Albert came to regard CoP as his new spiritual home and acquired a confidence that allowed him to continue bravely in the midst of difficulties he believed were connected with witchcraft and traditional authority.

Albert's conversion and subsequent membership in CoP allowed him to escape tensions within his family and helped him address specific emotional and economic problems. He did not, however, completely sever his relationship with his kin. While Pentecostal practices in Africa allow younger converts like Albert to achieve a degree of individual autonomy in relation to their family and elders, in many cases these practices do so without challenging commonly shared ideas of moral personhood that are tied to the ways in which people relate to their families (Lindhardt 2010, 8). Members of Albert's family continued to be connected to him through the financial and emotive connections that long-term kinship obligations implied. Certain members of his family supported him on his journey from his hometown and when he arrived in Accra. In addition to his uncle offering Albert a home, a cousin from his stepfather's side of the family provided a place for him to stay, where he lived without paying rent for several months, until he was eventually asked to leave. Albert did not have a regular income when I met him, but depended on the financial support and hand-me-downs from church members. In turn, Albert did not completely neglect family obligations. He continued to send his mother whatever little money he could spare and occasionally spoke to his stepfather. He felt empowered and was no longer afraid of his stepmother, saying, "I now realize that she is a weaker vessel." He also wanted to return to his village eventually, as an important man of God, to help his family financially and to rid his lineage of witches.

In telling me about his past, Albert identified with certain characters of the Bible, especially with the stories of overcoming suffering, persecution, and betrayal by one's own family. He compared himself with Joseph in the Old Testament, who had been deceived by his jealous brothers and was forced to live in exile among foreigners. Like Joseph, Albert said that he would eventually go on to overcome all obstacles to fulfil God's destiny for him. What for Albert were previously incomprehensible experiences, both good and bad, became inserted into a Pentecostal narrative and "reintegrated into a system of meaning" (Stromberg 1993, 55). Narrative is an important instrument for the organization of present and future action that provides structural continuity with a traditional and Christian past (Peel 1995, 582). As I go on to show, becoming Pentecostal is more than just a strategy for inverting witchcraft accusations or ideologically addressing the promises and problems of modernity.[4] It is also about recreating kin-like relations and participating in rituals and roles that provide a new social life and a confidence in the near and distant future.

Pentecostal Kinship and Biblical Genealogy

Albert's example cannot be used to generalize about all members of CoP, since he did not become a member until later in his youth. He initially became born again through a prayer fellowship in his hometown, and later joined CoP while living with his uncle. Many other church members and leaders, however, consider themselves "born into the church" and participate in a reproduction of church history that goes back to before they were born. By this I mean that their parents or grandparents were members of CoP before them. They grew up seeing the church as an extension of their own family, attending Sunday school, and learning about Christianity under the guidance of certain elders and pastors, whom they commonly refer to fondly as their spiritual parents. Having said this, over time, almost all church members, including Albert, come to identify with CoP as an extension of their own family. They start to take on new roles and duties for the church, creating new Pentecostal kin alongside their already existing family networks.

For many Ghanaians, conversion to Pentecostalism is a second conversion, one that provides discontinuity from unproductive kinship relations, traditional religious beliefs, and a non-Christian past that are seen as holding them back from a good life and positive future. Remaining Pentecostal, however, requires recognizing and understanding the ideological commitments that bind church members together as a moral community through the blood of Jesus and the Spirit of God (see Englund 2004, 303–6). For example, after accepting Jesus Christ publicly, Ghanaian Pentecostals are symbolically washed in the blood of Jesus before praying to receive the Holy Spirit baptism. In this born-again transformation, Ghanaians are baptized in the Holy Spirit (*Sunsum Kronkron*). Other forms of ritual, such as sharing the Holy Communion (the consuming of the "body" and "blood"' of Christ) once a month and regularly engaging in prayer (including spiritual warfare/intercession), call into effect common notions of Akan identity and communality by means of blood (*mogya*) and spirit (*sunsum*). The church oversees important ritual ceremonies in a member's life, such as birth and naming ceremonies, water baptism, Holy Spirit baptism, marriage, and funerals.

CoP is also largely endogamous.[5] Marriage is encouraged between church members so that they remain in CoP and bring up their families within the community. Finding the "right" husband or wife was widely discussed among members, as it was felt that the wrong choice could "spoil" one's Christian life. One of the most important criteria was that he or she be a good Christian. I knew parents and pastors who encouraged the youth to marry other church members. Many of them interacted socially in church and through church activities and were willing to find a life partner within the church. In general, many parents and youth in CoP felt that they shared a similar upbringing and spiritual background. Some young people also found their prospective spouses in other Pentecostal churches, which was still acceptable in the opinion of most church leaders. However, some pastors feared losing their church members if they left CoP for their spouse's church. Pastors would strictly warn the young people in their congregations about the dangers of marrying non-Pentecostal Christians or, worse still, non-Christians. Many times, the elders and pastors would facilitate unions through recommendations and by acting as go-betweens in Ghana and even internationally.

One pastor proudly commented to me that the members of his congregation refer to him as *abusua panin*, which literally translates as "head of the family" in Twi. Among the Ashanti of southern Ghana, the lineage head (*abusua panin*), with the advice of the older men and women, watched over the welfare of the whole group while maintaining social and moral order (Fortes 1950).[6] The lineage head also had the power to settle private disputes between members of his group. It was common to call other members "brother" and "sister," while older or senior people in church were called "father" or "mother." Through new ways of becoming a family, Pentecostal transformation marks a discontinuity from being sinners and a continuity with a new line of descent and adoption into a new moral community.

Another way CoP members shared a new kin-like relation together was through identifying as "sinners" and as descendants of Adam. To many Ghanaian Pentecostals, the Bible confirmed their new genealogical origins and their identity as sinners. In this way, a Christian genealogical model gradually surfaced to replace the traditional one. Having inherited the sins of Adam and Eve, for which they were now forgiven upon accepting Jesus Christ as their personal Lord and Saviour, they were adopted into a new family. As a church leader put it:

> Because we are descendants of Adam, we partake of that same nature. All of us were sinners. Adoption starts with a choice and allowed us to transform from sinners, bringing us into our family … Before adoption can be done, some legal work must be taken care of. That is why Jesus had to die on the cross, to satisfy the legal criteria. Adoption is not free. There is some expense involved … an expensive price, the blood of Jesus Christ.

This language of adoption into the church community through the sacrifice and death of Jesus Christ interestingly draws on the legal discourse of bureaucratic institutional forms, invoking the symbolic potency of membership documents that CoP provides to its members. These documents help church members identify themselves to others outside their local church assembly, especially when they travel or migrate to other regions in Ghana and even overseas. Church members also claim an inheritance through the blood of Christ, using this blood in prayer as a weapon to take back whatever the devil may have stolen from them and to attack their enemies. As a church leader said in a service, "You and I are of the tribe of Judah. Our destiny is to walk in the abundance of God."

The words of another church elder during a prayer meeting nicely sum up the Ghanaian attitude towards the importance of inheritance and family obligations:

> Until you have identified your father, you have not discovered your inheritance. Only after you pin him down, only then is He under obligation to perform … He now has a responsibility towards you.

Becoming born again is therefore more than an abstract ideological relationship between Jesus Christ and believers. Church members are adopted into the church community, where they learn to identify with a new father, to "pin him down," and become part of a new kinship group that is henceforth seen as responsible for their this-worldly upkeep and the promise of a future inheritance in heaven.

In explaining to me what should happen to an individual after becoming born again, one apostle told me:

> Once you are saved, about forty things take place in people's lives … [M]ost importantly all your sins are forgiven. The power of Jesus Christ takes care of the individual totally once you are born again. They have become children of God, a part of His royal, heavenly family.

In helping me understand what was specifically Christian about sin, the same apostle continued to highlight the differences between Christianity and traditional African religion. He foregrounded the different interpretations of sin in Christianity and traditional religion, and deferred to a Christian's shared lineage with Adam and Eve as a way of comparing "Christian morality" with "traditional law." Salvation in the

Ghanaian (Akan) world view, he explained to me, was like the traditional law still found in many Ghanaian villages, and different from the biblical idea of salvation. According to him, the Akan world view limited the concept of salvation to "saving someone from trouble or harm's way" and "saving their life" (*nkwagye*). The Akan regarded the casting out of evil (*mmusu*), which is referred to as *mmusuyi*, as "reinforcing life." The absence of *mmusu* was an aspect of salvation (*nkwagye*). Salvation as *nkwagye* also meant "giving birth to a healthy baby and surviving, being healed, delivered from problems, and so on," he said. "The biblical concept of salvation is larger than in the African world view." It is "more inclusive."

In order to clarify his point, the church leader told me that as a child growing up in an Akan village, he found certain local practices strange and disconcerting. Ghanaians had their own traditional ideas around morality that were at odds with Christian morality. Sins in the Akan world view, for instance, were viewed as "antisocial acts," the punishment for which was either arbitrated through the community representative or the household elder, depending on the severity of the offence. While the social and moral order of the traditional system had its taboos and rules for governing (mis)conduct, the hierarchical order of these rules was misplaced. To him, this meant that the moral implications for certain immoral actions, such as adultery, were given less attention than what he considered less serious offences, such as having sex with your husband in the sacred forest or fetching water from the river while menstruating. Pentecostal Christianity in Ghana sought to address this imbalance of moral values through the genealogical idea of sin as inherited from Adam and Eve, which is subsequently washed away by Jesus. However, this transition and translation has never been easy, the apostle admitted. As Robbins (2004a, 219–21) similarly notes, for the Urapmin, giving up traditional taboos led to difficulties constructing themselves as moral subjects, allowing sin to become a new entry point into morality.

While Pentecostal transformation is achieved through a process of establishing discontinuity with a traditional morality and the unhealthy relationships thus constituted, it simultaneously provides a social continuity through a "spiritual kinship" and shared ways of becoming a new moral being (Englund 2004, 483; Shaw 2007, 76–7). Through the process of becoming a member of a new church community by personal choice, a genealogical bond between members of CoP is forged by means of obligation and the embodiment of a shared Christian identity and a new relationality. While being a Pentecostal in Ghana can effectively create a sense of embodied continuity with a church community and history, it also recreates continuity with the problematic aspects of kinship and with concerns over witchcraft. Church members in London formed another moral community through participating in church services and prayer performances. However, they also faced lasting concerns over the moral dimensions of church and familial obligations, as they interacted with a new work economy, ongoing duties to family members in Ghana, Christian obligations to evangelize, and the experience of a new freedom and personal relationship with Jesus.

Pentecostal Relationships in London

While London is seen as a land of socio-economic opportunity for my Ghanaian Pentecostal interlocutors from PIWC London, it is also a place of moral dissolution. The representation of Pentecostal transformation as a narrative of getting ahead in life is complicated by the problem of creating a life in London that is morally good and filled with loving relationships. On the way home from a church service one Sunday afternoon, an elder admitted to me that in London the prayer lives and evangelical zeal of church members took a back seat. According to him, the church's desire to build God's kingdom in London was juxtaposed with the members' need to work long hours and negotiate the financial constraints of living in London, while sending remittances back to Ghana. Many church members did not have enough time: for each other, for their families, or for their Christian lives. They were too busy, lived too far away from each other, and did not have the opportunities to build Christian relationships. Many newly arriving CoP members in London experienced a sharp drop in their social status. They had to take jobs that nobody else wanted, such as cleaners, security guards, supermarket cash clerks, drivers, mailmen, and nurses. As a male elder said, "When I came to this country, I was cleaning all over, but I told myself I would never clean women's toilets. I was adamant but eventually had to because I was desperate." Some church members experienced tensions between new forms of individuality that living abroad and the new work economy helped to forge and their communal obligations with the church in London and their relatives in Ghana. While the ideological connection between their economic migration to London and their Pentecostal transformation was articulated as a social fact in church services, their lives in London generated contradictions between their dual identities as Christian evangelists and economic migrants.[7]

The lack of time to pray together was a frequent topic of discussion, especially after the weekly Friday prayer meetings at PIWC London. These conversations articulated certain disappointments with the church in London and allowed personal opinions to be made explicit. It was at one of these prayer meetings in London that I first met Eben, a Ghanaian man in his early thirties. Eben always contributed passionately to discussions concerning the church in London. He spoke about how the church in London was too "rigid" or too "cold" because of the lack of time devoted to prayer. He compared this situation to prayer life in Ghana, which he associated with living close together and communal obligations. "If you didn't go to church in Ghana," he said, "someone would come over to your house and drag you along. There were more obligations to go to church. Your family and community applied pressure on you." The Ghanaian Pentecostals I knew in London would always idealize home (*efie*) as a place of kinship and spiritual life. Yet they also knew they could not return to Ghana without redistributing their earnings among family and friends. This reality created another rhetorical theme regarding Ghana as morally corrupted.

"Ghana is spoilt," Eben told me one day. He did not want to go to Ghana unless there was a special event that justified him spending his time and money on the journey there and back. He complained bitterly about how his extended family and friends in Accra had the misconception that he had lots of money just because he was living in London. What they did not understand was how expensive living and studying in London was. He held two part-time jobs while attending chartered accountancy classes. His family in Ghana would sometimes call him up in London to ask him to send money for a funeral in Ghana. "A funeral is like a big party to them," he said, "and they never even once asked me how I was doing. They simply wanted me to send money because I was now living in London." Such complaints are common among the majority of Ghanaians living, studying, and working in London. Some returning Ghanaians became patrons to their extended families and even villages, sending money regularly and helping to develop the places that they were from through the education and upkeep of their kin. Others found it very difficult, because they knew there would be no end to the demands made on them by their numerous relations in Ghana. Their eventual return had to be well timed and could only take place once they had accumulated enough money to purchase property, build a large house, start a business, and help take care of other members of their family.

While Ghana was portrayed as morally ambiguous and fostering relationships of extraction, it was also a place for remembering continuities with past Christian relationships, where people had more time for prayer and Christian relationships. Eben explained that London was a busy and bustling city with many more opportunities than Accra, but where communal prayer was less frequent and Christian relationships were weakened due to individuals' busy work schedules:

> The work schedule here is irregular and includes evenings and weekends. While in Ghana you can, not have a job and be supported, here you cannot not have a job and survive. Work takes priority here more than anything and many times we are too tired and worn out after work here to go to church … I wouldn't have believed it if someone told me this before I came here. You have to be here to know … [H]ere I don't expect help or that someone has to be responsible for me like in Ghana.

Eben was speaking about the precarious life that London presented. However, he also admitted to me that there was something to be gained from his experience of migration and living in London. In our conversations, Eben observed that for him, moving to London led to the establishment of a new independence from family relations and an even better personal relationship with God. He spoke to God personally, he said, and was able to say "no" to the many requests from his family. He refused his brother's demands to return home to help him with his church work, and postponed returning to Ghana several times in order to not be influenced by his family's expectations of him. Eben said he knew that the God who had spoken to him in Ghana and brought him to London had not yet told him to return. "If God tells me to pack my bags and go back to Ghana, I will go without hesitation," he said. But he felt it was not yet his time. He had a strong conviction that God had a specific plan for him and that he was eventually going to return to Ghana to share his experiences and knowledge about God. Eben was also convinced that Christianity in Ghana was becoming too materialistic and that Ghanaians had begun to take Christianity for granted. They had lost their initial direction and focus on the Holy Spirit, and too many people were walking into church on Sundays with demons inside them. Christianity was becoming a forced habit and haunted from the inside. He wanted to return to Ghana to re-educate Ghanaians about Christianity, to remind them of the initial spark that had brought them to Jesus, and to help purify the church of its un-Christian teachings.

He had grown more critical of his family in Ghana and the influence they tried to wield over him. Due to a stronger personal relationship with Jesus, which had developed since arriving in London, Eben said he had become more independent and relied more on God:

> They tell you what they think is best for you and want you to finish every-thing faster so that I will return to Ghana sooner. You know that my brother is a man of God, an experienced minister, and so he thinks that his words should be taken with authority. But I have my own relationship with God, and God has spoken to me for many years now and told me many secrets, many of which I do not share with my family ... I have to trust in the Lord and, more importantly, have patience. God works in His own time.

When his own family in Ghana became a distant voice on the other side of the phone and the Ghanaian church in London did not meet his expectations of a more cosmopolitan Pentecostal identity, Eben began interacting with Pentecostals from other ethnic and national back-grounds. As a migrant's social networks extend outwards through cre-ating affiliations and wider affinities with religiously defined groups, a migrant's loyalty to his or her place of departure begins to take a back-seat (Levitt 2003, 570). Eben demonstrated a wider affiliation to the Pen-tecostal community by starting a Bible study group with other students from his accounting course, and occasionally preached to Bulgarian Pentecostal immigrants in the hired hall of a motel in central London. Living in London put Eben in touch with a global community of Chris-tians from other nationalities.

On the surface, it would seem that Eben was practising a Pentecostal-ism free of unhealthy family relationships and the influence of the Gha-naian Pentecostal church, one in which his individual or inward relationship with God had become more pronounced. It would also seem that he had succeeded in transcending his ties to the intimacies of the world that he had come from. His family was no longer completely responsible for him, and neither was he bound to them. While there might be some truth to these observations, one cannot conclude that Pentecostal relationships in London result in a decreasing dependence or a complete discontinuity with the Ghanaian church and family rela-tionships in Ghana. Instead, the church and his family reasserted them-selves into his life when his new independence became problematic and the cause for some disappointment. In the next section, I demonstrate how Eben's Pentecostal transformation also addresses re-establishing relationships and maintaining continuities with CoP in London and with his family in Ghana. While many church members like Eben

emphasize their increasing independence and individuality, the moral
and authoritative strength of kinship and church relationships is never
completely absent, and is able to outlast, even tolerate, any short-term
lapse in commitment (see Bloch 1973, 84–5).

Continuities with Kinship in London

While Eben enjoyed more independence and freedom from the moral
obligations that living with family in Ghana entailed, he was still subject to their expectations and the authority of his older brother in Ghana.
His brother, who was the founder of a popular charismatic church in
Accra, wanted Eben to return to Ghana to help him run his church. He
threatened to stop sending Eben financial support if Eben persisted in
his attempts to stay in London. This situation led Eben to go against the
wishes of his family and stay in London longer, creating tensions between his brother and him. While in London, Eben also went against
his brother's choice of a marriage partner. Instead, he became involved
with and later engaged to a woman whom his brother had specifically
counselled against, eventually bringing her to London from Ghana.
This choice caused additional tensions within his family and with his
brother. They eventually went along with his decision when they saw
that there was no way to change his mind. However, an incident occurred after Gertrude, his fiancée, arrived in London, one that led him
to reframe his opinion of the importance of family and the role of the
Ghanaian church community in his life. Since the couple only had a
customary marriage and were not yet formally married by law and in
church, they could not legitimately live together. Gertrude went to live
with her cousin outside of London.

Eben complained that he did not get as many opportunities as he
would have liked to see Gertrude due to his busy work schedule and
the physical distance that separated them. Some months after Gertrude
came to live in the United Kingdom, Eben discovered that she was secretly seeing another Ghanaian man. He was heartbroken and angry
when he found out about her affair. He told me that Gertrude had taken
advantage of his foreign status in order to get a visa for London and to
seek further personal opportunities for herself. She had been deceitful,
and Eben blamed himself for not listening to his brother's advice and
for not taking his Christian relationships in CoP seriously. While he had
gained a certain independence from church and familial obligations,
the relationships connecting him with his family and the Ghanaian
church ultimately became more important in re-establishing emotional

and moral stability in his life. In other words, the nature of long-term moral commitments to family and to the Ghanaian church in London helped to mould the response to new short-term problems.

Eben and many other church members in PIWC London felt caught between their obligations to the Ghanaian Pentecostal community and family and a new work economy and other relationships defined by individualistic forms of production and consumption, which emphasized greater choice. This tension between values was reflected in Eben's experience of living in London and was symptomatic of his own changing relationship to a new work economy as well as to his recent subject position as an economic migrant who did not have easy access to the things and people he felt were important. It is precisely in such situations, when social and economic conditions shift and the new existential limits of relationships are experienced as tensions between engagement and alienation, that the discourse of witchcraft can (re) emerge (see Englund 2007b). If church members' expectations of intimate and social relationships were changing, so too was people's understanding of witchcraft.

While witchcraft is as real and remains as much a topic of conversation in London as in Ghana, it did not take the same public dimensions. The relative absence of prophets also meant that members were limited to weekly prayer meetings for resolving more personal problems. While in some other African churches in London, such as the Aladura church studied by Hermione Harris (2006), members could bring their personal problems to church and solicit assistance through visions, prophecy, and personal prayer, CoP did not allow such prophetic practices within its UK church. Problems of witchcraft and other related spiritual issues were addressed on occasion, but were usually confined to more personal conversations. According to many church members in London, people in Ghana had more time to think about witchcraft and about the possibility of others bewitching them because many Ghanaians were relatively poorer and did not have full-time jobs or busy work schedules. Christians in Ghana also expected miracles and wanted to find instant solutions to their problems, they said. They told me that in London there were fewer reasons to blame every failure on witchcraft and other demonic influences. They also admitted that there was less time for prayer and for a committed Christian life, and that patience, rather than miracles, was a virtue they had to learn to cultivate.

Eben, too, had become very critical of certain aspects of Pentecostalism found in Ghana, especially the important role prophets played in the lives of many ordinary Pentecostals. "Too much greed and materialism

Is caught up in Christianity in Ghana," he said to me. "Scripturalism is more important here [in London]. People have to be taught scripture and to accept Christ completely." While in London, he had come to see the prophets in a negative light. Faith in Ghana, he complained, had become overly concerned with instant miracles and belief in the power of the prophet, who were out to "eat people's money":

> Faith, faith is not about getting what you ask for now. That's the problem with Ghana. People there expect miracles, answers, and solutions to their problems. They go to the prophets who are out to eat people's money, prophets of Baal, and they give them money. They don't take time to read the Bible. If you spend time on knowing the Bible, you will not need all these prophets and ministers telling you what to do.

According to Eben, the prophets in Ghana represented selfish and financially extractive relationships not uncommon in descriptions of witchcraft. He explained that those who visited prophets lacked patience and knowledge of the Word of God. The Ghanaian church in London, Eben explained, should encourage people to understand the Bible first and then slowly cultivate a personal relationship with God, which is independent of Ghanaian culture and an overreliance on prophets. While these criticisms were not shared by all CoP members in London (indeed, many continued to visit prophets when they returned to Ghana), many church leaders shared Eben's belief that CoP members relied too heavily on prophets to solve problems, placing "their faith in men or in places" rather than in God (Onyinah 1995, 98–9).

The question of where a CoP believer put his or her faith reveals how a biblical genealogy of "origins" becomes an important consideration for Pentecostals. Whether to place one's faith in church leaders' interpretation of scripture, in the power of the prophets, or in the support and advice of church and family members were concerns and questions CoP members faced regularly. The development of Christian relations over time involved being simultaneously cautious about the origins of others with whom one associated; it also entailed deliberations and decisions made about whether these people were truly Christian or whether they were embroiled in selfish pursuits and unchristian-like behaviour.

PIWC London members speak about witchcraft when interpersonal relationships of trust are in question within the church. When I asked the resident missionary of CoP UK about witchcraft in PIWC London, he denied that witchcraft was a concern among members, and told me that it was only important in Ghana. His measured response came partly because witchcraft was seen as representing an aspect of African culture that CoP leaders wanted their international branches to disassociate from. According to the CoP missionary, talk of evil spirits and witchcraft was not culturally appropriate in London. Not only did it distract church members from the true source of salvation – Jesus – but more importantly, it was not a successful way to bring non-Africans into the church. In his sermon that day, and probably for my benefit, he said, "We are not interested in demons. We are interested in Jesus Christ. We give you the power of God, not prophetic messages for the individual." The character of the witch, however, was occasionally invoked in conversations and prayers in church. For example, at a child's baptism, the elder praying over the child said, "If any witches and wizards have met under a tree somewhere and made an evil covenant, in Jesus name, let that curse be removed and destroyed." On other occasions, I was told me that there was no certainty that the people who prayed alongside us were true Christians.

"The biggest witches and wizards are to be found within the church," an elderly church member said to me after a tea evangelism meeting. A group of older women were sitting around a table and sharing their testimonies of conversion. They told me that there was always a lack of trust and that some Pentecostal believers in church were witches disguised as Christians. Not long after, I attended the celebration for the birth of a church elder's baby. A rented bus picked us up from the church and took us to where the proud parents lived. Looking forward to witnessing the conviviality of such an event, I was curiously surprised when some women politely refused to eat any of the food that was served. The new mother looked uncomfortable but did not say anything and, instead, turned on some Ghanaian gospel music. People got up to dance, helping to break the awkward silence. Later, when I asked a church friend why these women had not eaten any of the food, she whispered back in a hushed manner that some church members suspected that our host, the baby's mother, might be a witch.

Sasha Newell (2007, 469) has argued that while Pentecostalism claims to be able to transcend the power of witchcraft, it recreates witchcraft discourse within the church, since the Pentecostal church is also a site for conspicuous consumption and the illicit accumulation of wealth by church members and pastors. Witchcraft represents not merely the unknown inner workings of an external force but also the suspicion and critique of corruption within the inner workings of an internal presence that church members were connected to. I found that the topic of witchcraft in the church was often accompanied by the question of whom to trust. In the introduction to his book *The Gift*, Marcel Mauss (1990) used a Scandinavian poem to make a general point: regardless of which society we come from, we engage in relationships of exchange with people we trust and with people we do not trust.[8] Ghanaian Pentecostals have a friend in Jesus, in whom they have trust and confidence. However, they also have to interact with people whose actions and words do not demonstrate the behaviour of a true or good Christian. This reality is the dilemma faced by many Ghanaian Pentecostals in London, who sometimes have little choice but to engage in relationships with non-Christians as well as with church members whose intentions they do not always trust. Issues of trust arise when people cannot predict what others will do and what will happen; when people do not have full information about others, their intent, and what is being offered, possibly allowing others to take advantage of vulnerabilities; and when their life is in under the control of others. Such occasions point to the limits of trust within the church and to the need to manage relationships in any given situation through deciding how to appropriately balance self-interested ambitions with disinterested behaviour.

I would sometimes find Eben watching church members in mid-prayer. Once, when I asked him what he was doing, he commented that he wondered whether they were truly praying in the spirit. According to Eben, some of these people who prayed alongside us could also be witches, who came to church for their own selfish reasons. The metaphor of witchcraft extended to others outside the church as well; witches were seen as people who benefitted from the marginal status of Ghanaian immigrants. After a Sunday church service, Eben commented on the supernatural ability of certain people to profit from new ideas and innovative business strategies. Eben's experience of London's new economy – its changing patterns of labour, market consumption, and economic and social inequalities – was characterized by unproductive social relationships and an immoral accumulation, which he attributed to London's "white witches":

> Practices of witchcraft and wizards in London are different compared to Ghana. Here, you don't see witches destroying and tormenting people, but you see that they are more into bringing out inventions, making ingenious things to make money from people. Almost every year, there are

new technology and inventions somewhere, upgrading products like computers and mobile phones. People are buying into it. That is the way the witches here channel the spiritual advantages they have.

This description of witchcraft in London evoked a different image of modernity, where witches were described as "white entrepreneurs" who had secret knowledge that they used to manipulate the economy and other capitalist relationships in order to profit from the gullibility of others. The consumer markets were presented as mysterious centres of wealth accumulation and exploitative circuits of economic exchange that London's white witches participated in to the exclusion of others. Economic migrants and British consumers in general were all victims of the new technologies and inventions that these witches brought to the market. Because of these witches, whose spiritual power extended beyond ordinary understanding, Eben and others like him were forced to spend their hard-earned money on such new inventions as mobile phones and the latest fashions.

Eben's description of witchcraft in London shares many similarities with general explanations of the mechanism behind a new moral economy of goods and services that Ghanaians share, according to which communitarian values and the individual accumulation of wealth are in conflict (Parish 2000, 2001).[9] In London, witchcraft continues to be reflective of changing relationships through which individuals come to understand the limits of their social and economic world. It also delineates the limits of Christian relationships in London, during the process of creating independent Pentecostal subjects who are still tied to social and cultural constraints that bind them to various genealogical inheritances.

Conclusion

In this chapter, I have focused on the personal changes a Pentecostal identity has made in the lives of two male individuals within the same church, and on the implications their born-again identity has for the ways in which they negotiate their migratory movement and the politics of their everyday lives. By presenting Pentecostal transformation in the light of the tensions between family relationships, a kin-like relationship with the church, and a personal relationship with Jesus, I have shown how Pentecostal transformation provides Ghanaians with an ethical practice that allows them to pragmatically address both changing interpersonal relationships and wider socio-economic changes stemming from migration. While migration provides evidence of success and discontinuity from a life of economic hardship, many church members acknowledge that Pentecostal faith cannot be reproduced in exactly the same way in London as it is in Ghana. This reality is reflective of church members' ongoing efforts at self-definition.

If conversion to Christianity is a tension between a new identity that is given and a set of relations that is made by the actions of people, then Pentecostal transformation can only be understood through the selective and situated ways in which a claim of personal freedom and individual choice is embodied and performed alongside genealogical relations and socio-economic constraints. For instance, a claim of discontinuity with a non-Christian past and traditional kinship structures is usually framed as a personal choice and as establishing a personal relationship with Jesus. This choice is usually accompanied by a comforting feeling of joining a new Pentecostal family who are like-kin, where one antecedent ("African ancestors") is replaced by another ("Adam and Eve"), and also stresses long-term moral obligations and the deference of moral authority to the elders and leaders of the church community. If church members who migrate to London gain more independence and distance from their families and the church community in Ghana, the moral criteria for how they should live good and happy lives is still, largely, determined by the families and church elders with whom they remain connected and who hold them accountable to these earlier promises and obligations.

Understanding Pentecostal transformation as an adoption into a new family that is not "really" family allows for a better look at the different ways in which the tension between individual aspirations and communal obligations varies across diverse personal, social, and economic contexts. The boundaries of what constitutes a good Pentecostal, of what is or is not virtuous action, shift and are being shaped by their contextual application according to who the speakers are, what the closeness or distance between them is, and where they are at the time, and by the changing nature of social relationships in which these boundaries are embedded. For example, if London is commonly described as a place of economic opportunities and for experiencing personal freedom, Ghana, in turn, is seen as economically backward and constrained by family obligations. However, the opposite is also true. When in London, Ghana is often described as allowing for closer family and Christian relationships, while London is filled with more anonymous exchanges that create a distance between believers and doubts as to whom to trust. I have also argued that while largely seen as a matter of individual choice, voluntary, and mainly positive, Pentecostal transformation is linked to other kinds of relationships that are determinate, communal, and sometimes negative. The ongoing problems of (mis-) trust within families and in the church in Accra and London demonstrate the limits of these same relationships and reveal the cracks in this social project. Talk of witchcraft in both Accra and London helps illustrate this point: if Pentecostal transformation in CoP is about kin-like relationships that resemble family ones, in that it allows church members to participate in a social project that morally binds them together in an exclusive way, it simultaneously projects an external world of danger and binary logics of difference through which the unexplainable and the extraordinary becomes explainable and ordinary.

Chapter Six

African Christians in London

> You know, if you have a friend
> In whom you have confidence
> And if you wish to get good results
> Your soul must blend in with his
> And you must exchange presents
> And frequently pay him visits.   Marcel Mauss (1990)

In Chapters Six and Seven, I shift focus from Ghana to the Ghanaian Pentecostal diaspora and CoP in London. The last few chapters revealed the multiple tensions and disconnections church members face within CoP and in the wake of alternative forms of Pentecostal practice and sociality. The next two chapters continue along a similar vein, showing how church members in London strive to attain religious continuity in their lives amidst experiences of social and cultural discontinuity and spiritual danger. Together they examine the disconnections within globalizing Pentecostal networks through the contradictions CoP members in London face, caught between their moral obligations as born-again Christians (to evangelize, for instance) and their own social-economic realities as Ghanaians and immigrants in London. As ethical actors and members of a virtue community, CoP members have to negotiate their call to evangelize to others with their new lives as UK residents. Such balancing acts ascertain the universal validity of a belief in a Christian God, which is also in tension with multiple and conflicting roles and identities.

This chapter addresses how CoP members in London define themselves as moral agents of change who participate in church and community politics through their Pentecostal Christian faith. I demonstrate that African Christians in London are not simply marginalized through their precarious positions as immigrant subjects. Ghanaian Pentecostals are also engaged in a "moral ambition" (Elisha 2011) to not only save themselves, but to save others and to protect the church community and its immediate environment. As I go on to show, many of my interlocutors shared concerns about the corrupting influence of British "culture," especially its effects on the church youth. Through focusing on the cultural diagnostics Ghanaian Pentecostal migrants made concerning the ethical challenges created by their lives in London, I look at how these Ghanaian Pentecostals strive to maintain a sense of continuity amidst so much uncertainty. Rather than generalize about African Christian "beliefs" or the "occult" in London, I argue that we need to examine how church members form a virtue community that serves as a religious counterpublic to media representations and academic generalizations.

A "counterpublic" is an ethical space for deliberation and action that is conceived in contrast to a secular and liberal model of politics (see Hirschkind 2006). The construction of a Pentecostal counterpublic in London involves an ongoing reflection on the ways in which church members perceive the possibility of transforming their own community, their social environment, and their circumstances for the better, based on the conditions for being a virtuous born-again Christian. Such a virtue ethics is concerned not only with liberal political value but also with ethical value, where one "moves beyond acts (making choices, following rules) to persons or character," shifting "the focus from having, to doing, to being" (Lambek 2008, 133–4). Ethical practice therefore becomes an important entry point for reflection and pragmatic judgment, for deciding when the "witch" and the "devil" become important characters in one's life and need to be acknowledged, and when "faith" becomes a prime form of social action and activism. Ethical practice is also based on what church members do to transform the limitations of the places and circumstances in which they find themselves and to balance what they can change with what they have little control over. Before describing the ways in which CoP members deal with the threat of uncertainty, I first turn to how the media represented African Christian churches in London.

Media Representations and Moral Evaluations

While I was conducting my research on PIWC London, African religious beliefs and Christianities were beginning to receive more media attention in the United Kingdom. Since 2001, there have been more publicized

Incidents involving African religious practice, witchcraft, and cases of child abuse and child sacrifice that have led to several deaths. These news reports tend to focus on the bizarre and the exotic, reinforcing Western stereotypes of Africa as the Dark Continent, where African Christian migrants are seen to belong to a distinct ontological ("occult") realm in need of further investigation and social control (Sanders 2003a; Caplan 2010).[1] The British media portrayed many of these churches as responding to (and taking advantage of) the cultural and social needs of marginalized African migrants in London. Many of these same African migrants, however, see themselves as agents who interpret the precarious nature of their new migrant lives through their Christian faith and who ask how they can work towards changing their new cultural environment as virtuous Christians. Their aspirations for a good life and their active attempts to change their surroundings and circumstances for the better usually sit uncomfortably with the simplistic and exoticizing ways in which the "African occult" is evoked in Western public representations (Ranger 2007; ter Haar and Ellis 2009; Meyer 2009).

One of the first cases to appear in the British media was that of a young African boy, later named "Adam," whose torso was found in the Thames in September 2001. The murder of Adam was later linked to voodoo rituals practiced in Benin, Yoruba ritual killings, and a West African trade in human body parts, and eventually involved pathologists and occult experts from South Africa (Ranger 2007). By 2005, a link between the exorcism of child witches, Congolese churches in London, and the abuse of children such as Adam had been made in the leak of a report to Scotland Yard. A new media spotlight shone on African Christian churches in London. The violent deaths of children, including Victoria Climbie in 2000 and Child B. in 2005 (as well as Kristy Bamu in 2010), led to investigative-style journalism and the production of a number of documentaries for the British Broadcasting Corporation's Channel 4 (BBC 4) that aimed at exposing African churches and witchcraft accusations against children. These documentaries, filmed for BBC 4's current affairs documentary series *Dispatches* in Nigeria's Niger Delta region ("Saving Africa's Witch Children" in 2008 and "Return to Africa's Witch Children" in 2009) and a Nigerian Pentecostal church in Tottenham, North London ("Britain's Witch Children" in 2010), have served to explicitly link hundreds of African Pentecostal churches in London to potential witchcraft accusations and child abuse.

These media representations of the occult in Africa point to the shared cultural belief in the spirit world and its unique ability to be the main explanatory cause for any misfortune that may negatively affect people's lives in the material world. As the documentary "Britain's Witch Children" (2010) asserted, "At its core is a widely held belief that nothing in life happens for natural reasons. And any misfortune you experience is down to the influence of evil spirits." This broad generalization of African religiosity depicts African Christian migrants as intensely religious and superstitious people whose journey to London leaves them morally disoriented and susceptible to trickery by opportunistic African pastors who earn money from their congregation's gullibility. According to the media, the pastors of these African migrant churches sometimes blame children for people's misfortunes, after which special prayers may be recommended. But even if some of these observations are true of a handful of African churches in London, as Terrence Ranger (2007, 276) points out, "[T]his is essentially the occult Africa of the BBC and of the British popular press."[2] Ranger also notes that although academic explanations for the "occult" have varied, ranging from millennial capitalism and the culture of neoliberal capitalism to a general crisis of modernity, grand theories problematically continue to be used to describe witchcraft in Africa. Ranger suggests that the "occult" needs to be studied in its own historical particularity and specific cultural context. I put forward that we also need to look beyond the "occult" and seek to understand how the religious practices in these African churches are critically assessed and weighed by church members themselves.

In their influential work on the "occult" in Africa, anthropologists Jean and John Comaroff (1999, 2000) have described Pentecostal Christianity as a response to global and economic events. They argue that those who are excluded from wealth and seek economic improvement and a better life come to attribute the hidden inequalities produced by the neoliberal market economy to the volitional powers of spirits and other unearthly creatures. This argument, however, has an inherent hierarchical division between those who see the inner workings of the economy as they are and those who are victims and merely responding to forces beyond their control. Others have argued that the adoption of Pentecostal Christianity cannot be explained as merely a response to social and structural shifts, and that materialistic interpretations of the "occult economy" should not be given precedence over religious motivation (Marshall 2009; Coleman 2011b).[3] What the "occult" does illustrate, in a graphic way, is the feeling of personal instability and uncertainty caused by forces considered to be outside the "social." In order to limit the effect these forces of instability could have on them and their loved ones, church members have had to name the forces, communicate with the chaos, and bring it under control. Rather than seeing these external forces as unknown forces, PIWC London members considered them to be extensions of an alternative form of sociality that they associated with life in London. In trying to re-establish a sense of control over their precarious lives, they would sometimes communicate with the "witch" or the "devil." Rather than assuming that seemingly irrational religious beliefs emerge from dire economic and social conditions, we need to understand the context of how, why, and when these religious worlds are created and put into practice.

We have to move beyond the "occult" framework popularized by the Comaroffs and consider the religious motives and actions of our interlocutors. We need to see them as political actors who are participating in the creation of their world and of the social and economic forces that characterize change. This frame involves carefully examining projects of self-fashioning that include the ethical lives of these same people, who are in the process of remaking themselves as members of a virtue community. It also means taking "faith" as action seriously. In describing the different ways in which PIWC London members engage with the witch, the devil, and faith, I provide examples of Pentecostals who experience a lack of trust and a lapse of social and moral control in their new environment. Through paying serious attention to ethics, we can begin to consider how an African Christian identity in London is negotiated in practice, and how prayer and evangelism serve to assess and balance the dangers and desires of multiple spiritual and geographical crossings and places of dwelling.

In the next part of this chapter, I discuss how the church youth have become a source of great concern for church members. The "problem" of the younger generation was one of the main topics of conversation. According to some Ghanaian parents, the leisure activities of their children and the lack of adult supervision in their lives have created opportunities for external and corrupt influences to take full effect. As newly arrived immigrants, many parents have little control over the new cultural and socio-economic environment. Disciplining young people, especially unmarried women, featured strongly as an issue among church members. This is partly why many Ghanaian parents either left their children in Ghana to be raised there by extended family members until they were older, or sent them back to Ghana to "learn respect."

Disciplining the Youth and Returning to Ghana

One of the first church services I attended in PIWC London in October 2002 brought into sharp focus the importance of church discipline and respectability. Some months before, a young unmarried woman named Alice was suspected of having an affair with a man. She was subsequently suspended from the church. It was only several months later, after having formally apologized and undergone pastoral counselling, that she was allowed to return. That Sunday morning she was publicly accepted back into the church congregation. The pastor told the girl's story to the church, emphasizing the importance of (self-)discipline in their Christian lives. He then announced that Alice was now engaged to the man whom she had been secretly seeing. To enthusiastic applause and loud cheers, Alice, her family, and the man in question were called onto the stage to celebrate their return. This incident left a mark on me. It revealed the generational and cultural tensions within the church regarding acceptable moral and sexual behaviour, and showed how certain activities by the church youth were under close scrutiny, or being described as immoral and in need of repair.

Too much free time was seen as a dangerous aspect of urban life in London for the church youth. Since many Ghanaian parents spent most of their weekdays working more than one job or taking part-time courses to upgrade their skills, they had less time for their children than they had had in Ghana. There were also fewer family members and friends to rely on for support. Ghanaian parents saw such unsupervised time as opportune for the corrupt influence of British culture to unfavourably affect their children. According to them, non-Christian friends and the cultural environment in London provided Ghanaian Pentecostal youth with the chance to pick up "bad habits" and to participate in illicit sexual activity. A church deacon with whom I held a conversation after a prayer service criticized unmarried girls and university students who came to London from Ghana specifically to earn money. According to him, these girls were sometimes involved in "prostitution." By this he meant that they would have many boyfriends and receive gifts and money in exchange for sexual favours. He complained that they accorded too much importance to acquiring wealth and therefore had a "false" sense of status. Another church member lamented that British people did not believe in marriage, which was causing problems with the youth. "The British law permits them to have sex at sixteen, and yet they wonder

Why there are so many under aged pregnancies, young mothers, and abortions? You should just stop the youth from having sex. Make it a law and enforce it," he said. He described the visible ill effects of "poor morals amongst British people" through their reluctance to marry but also by their willingness to have sex from a young age.

Many Ghanaian parents chose not to bring their children to London with them, even though they could afford to do so. Instead, they left their children under the care and close supervision of family members or friends in Ghana. In Ghana, the children would receive "a proper education," some church members told me. Another church member said that he kept his children in Ghana to be brought up "to have some sense." By this he meant that his children would be raised with Christian principles and would learn to have respect for their elders. Many parents were also reluctant to personally discipline their children in London. Children had a legal recourse to British child protection laws that prevented parents from using forms of punishment that would have been acceptable in Ghana. These parents experienced very concretely the thinning of social relations between themselves and their children. Ghanaian youth in London were in danger of becoming too independent and unmoored from the socially productive Christian relations and the necessary constraints of family and church.

The issue of deteriorating relationships of intimacy and care also arose in conversations concerning young people's susceptibility to demonic attacks. In one case, I came across a young girl, Jen, whose parents sent her back to Ghana because they could not effectively discipline her in London. She was labelled a "problem child," someone who would not listen to her parents or respect their authority. Jen told me that her parents were worried about certain habits she had picked up from her friends in London. She spent long hours out of the house, started smoking cigarettes, and sometimes stayed out late into the night "clubbing," she said. This behaviour was enough cause for her parents to worry. Jen, who was fifteen at the time, admitted to me that she felt neglected and was just trying to cope with her loneliness and to come up with new ways to get more of her parents' attention. They both worked several shifts during the week and had little time to watch over her movements. When she attempted to commit suicide by swallowing pain relief tablets, they became deeply concerned and contemplated the possibility that she could be a victim of witchcraft.

"You see, my older brother died several years before," she explained to me, and this unexpected loss had led her parents to fear that witchcraft was involved in his death. They assumed that Jen's behaviour and the attempt at taking her own life was another spiritual attack that could lead to her death. The possibility that witchcraft might be involved was a good enough reason to send Jen back to Ghana to live with relatives. While in Accra, she tried to escape from the family estate. She was eventually caught and sent to live in a small house with a Pentecostal pastor and his wife, who watched over her activities and restricted her movements. This close supervision did not stop her from trying to escape again on multiple occasions. Eventually the pastor's wife took her to the Edumfa Prayer Camp, where Mama (discussed in Chapter Three) had received her healing, and which was famous for its powerful prophetess, Aunty Grace, who could heal and deliver people from witchcraft.

At Edumfa, Aunty Grace sent Jen to a fasting shed located up a hill at a distance away from the prayer camp's daily activities, where she was chained and forced to fast and pray in order to purify herself. Jen described her companions in the fasting shed as either "mad" or "victims of witchcraft accusations." In an attempt to escape, the young girl feigned suicide. She tied a noose around her neck, and in the process ended up choking herself and fainted. When the guards were alerted to what had happened, Jen was released from her shackles and brought down to the main church building where the prophetess prayed for her. When the young girl eventually regained consciousness, the prophetess pronounced that she was freed from the effects of witchcraft. According to the prophetess, Jen was initially "dead in the spirit." The witches were going to "cut her up into many pieces and eat her for Christmas." The camp's prayers had broken the connection these witches had with the girl. She could return to living with others in the camp's main residence. Over the next few days, Jen was called up in church services and used as a living testimony to show others how "a girl from America" had been brought back to life and saved from the clutches of witchcraft by Aunty Grace.

Children of African descent in London, like Jen, who are seen as influenced by evil spirits, are deemed to be living outside the social confines of the church and the domestic authority of their parents and caretakers. This perceived deviance is interpreted as an opportunity for a witch or the devil to enter into and operate in the child's life. The church and the family provide regulatory forms of discipline in order to restore the youth to a state of purity by correcting their disobedience or by removing the spirits and demons from their lives and bodies.

Parental decisions to send children back to Ghana or to Pentecostal prophets suggest a sense of desperation and a lack of control, on the part of the parents, over the changes that accompany their new immigrant lives in London. Certain African churches knowingly take advantage of these fears and insecurities. If salvation represents a promise of return (a promised future or the return of Jesus), it also brings an experience of the limits of this promise for the immediate and near future. This dissonance and dialectic relationship between promise and pragmatics allows questions of trust and uncertainty to arise within the church and its community in London.

Christian conversion provided a promise of certainty that only Jesus could fulfil. In this way, uncertainty became a form of critique and a creative potential for change. It provided the impulse to act and to call upon the Holy Spirit to intervene in their personal affairs and the affairs of those around them. In dealing with the witch or the devil in their lives, church members put into practice certain actions and performances that helped recreate continuity with the security and safety that salvation promised. In the next section, I show how prayer and the involvement of the Holy Spirit also allowed for discontinuity and for the opening up of new possibilities.

Dealing with the Devil

While the witch was potentially "this" or "that" person, the devil was a more diffuse and global character, a more removed but equally intimate persona, involved in the personal affairs of all individuals. If the role of the devil in their lives was a common and acceptable premise, constantly spoken about and evoked in prayer services, church members did not always agree on when to make the connection between a problem they were facing and the role of the devil in that circumstance. The line between what required a "spiritual" solution and what required a "practical" one was something that church members discussed. I was privy to conversations on this topic during men's group meetings: when should a problem be interpreted as work of the devil that needed to be immediately dealt with spiritually, and when was it simply a "practical issue" that could wait? There was no need to pray over a practical issue or to cast out demons. However, the "devil is very subtle," someone said. The devil worked through the small things in life. "At what point do we draw the line and ask God to intervene?" he asked. For example, should a broken boiler, shower, or computer be considered the work of the devil? Should one pray over it or simply call a repairman? Prayer became an expression of faith but also a judgment call about whether to call the Holy Spirit or the plumber. The men's group leader responded by saying that everyone drew this line in a different place. Only "you" could know when your own resources were depleted, and only "you" could decide whether the Holy Spirit was needed.

Because Pentecostals believe they have the privileged capacity to serve as hosts to the Holy Spirit, they feel able to discern when to call upon the Holy Spirit to protect them and their immediate environment from the work of the devil. Ghanaian Pentecostals in London, therefore, do not see themselves merely as victims of circumstances beyond their control but as moral agents of change. By participating in spiritual prayer and acts of evangelism, PIWC members help protect and save other members of their community. Through their Christian faith, church members become socially invested and morally rooted to their city and country of residence.[4] They become actively involved in creating their own social and moral world, participating in the moral project of building, and defending, the church and their city of residence.

When I arrived at PIWC London in 2002 to conduct research, the resident missionary of CoP UK at the time explained the missionary aims of the church to me:

> We are working in the community here in Dagenham and Barking. But we want to broaden our tentacles to all of London. Since we are in this community, we have to help our own community, drug addicts, the homeless … We have a time of chatting with them, even a biblical chat to release some tension. It sets their minds right. We have organized tea evangelism, we have organized charity evangelism, where we collected used clothing and offered it to people in the area. Some are doing drugs because they don't see any love anywhere, but when they receive some love, their hearts open up to the Gospel. There is a generation that has no idea about the Jesus we are talking about. They are not interested about God. They are only interested in themselves.

The head missionary told me that the church was situated in a poor, working class neighbourhood for a reason. It was there to reach out to people and to open their hearts to the love of Jesus. Residents should benefit from the presence of the church in their midst. The passion to spread the love for Jesus seemed evident in both public and inspired speech. It was the Holy Spirit that brought the message of compassion and conversion to church members. For example, during one of the first church services I attended, a church member who was filled with the Holy Spirit shared God's message with the church community that re-iterated the church's mission in that neighbourhood:

> My anointing is with you. I am here to tell you that I have brought you to this vicinity for a purpose. I am here to tell you that you are not ordinary men and women. You are my children. You have been chosen, set aside with power and anointing to help the people around you, to bring these people to me.

Church members were instructed by God to bring the broken and poor people off the streets of Dagenham and into the church. God had confirmed that they were not just an ordinary Ghanaian community who meet in prayer, but were also there to positively transform the community around them and to bring new disciples into the church. Chris was a church elder who took these words seriously and stood out as someone who wanted to create change. Elder Chris often led the smaller but more focused weekly prayer meetings.

The members who met each Friday evening were known as the "engine room" behind the church and its weekly activities. They would meet to intercede for the church against any demonic influence. They usually began with opening prayers to spiritually cleanse the area and then prayed for a successful meeting and for the safe passage of others who had not yet arrived. This would be followed by songs of praise and worship, accompanied by clapping and the beat of musical instruments. The Word of God would come next, where a passage, mainly linked to spiritual warfare, would be selected and shared. Eventually the prayer leader would initiate the topics the group would pray about. In these spiritual prayers, "place" (whether in reference to other countries in the world, the city of London, or the neighbourhood the church was in) operated through the invocation and naturalization of specific kinds of entities and demonic beings that dwelt within it and which had to be defeated.

During a prayer meeting on the topic of "war," we were told that we were in a battle with the devil on earth. "There are so many witches people say," Elder Chris declared. "I answer, 'Witches?' Bring on the master. Witches are just constables. I am after the master, the devil." As another elder told the congregation, "The devil is working overtime to get you and me. The battle is raging within the household of God, within the church." Church members were tasked to protect the church from spiritual attack. In protecting the church as a community, they saw the devil as an influential figure, an enemy that had to be dealt with through prayer. The devil, after all, was the master of all witches. In that prayer meeting, a link between the food that was to be served at the church anniversary celebrations and the devil's involvement was made. Prayer group members shared personal messages from the Holy Spirit that the devil was trying to spiritually attack and poison the food that was to be prepared for the celebrations. We were promptly told to pray "in the Spirit" in order to bless the food, to "dip it in the blood of Jesus," and to block the plans of the devil. These prayers created an ethical field of interaction within, and an engagement with, the neighbourhood where the church was situated, through which the road that the church was on became a spiritual battleground.

"Let us pray and worship the Lord," Elder Chris said as he led the members of that Friday evening's prayer group. We were told to pray for the revival of the church, for the salvation of a church member's husband, as well as for the youth who wandered the streets of Dagenham. We prayed to cast the demons out of them and to help bring these "aimless and lost souls" to God. We were also told to move around freely, so as to allow the Holy Spirit to move among us. Some in the group walked up and down from one end of the room to the other, gesturing with their hands, eyes closed intermittently with a concentrated look on their faces. They were all praying in an angelic language, what Pentecostals call "speaking in tongues." An elderly woman went down on her knees in front of her chair praying aloud with her hands clasped together. The plethora of voices reached a deafening climax of sounds that rebounded off the walls of the room we were in. Eventually Chris clapped his hands sharply as an indication to bring the prayers to a close. He then explained to those present:

> These words uttered are not merely empty babble but are creative and powerful. We can use these words for our own benefit in casting out the evil spirits, in cleansing the church and the people. The battle is not a physical battle but a spiritual battle, where the war is on the spiritual plane and our words have the power to change our circumstances in the real world ... Instead Jesus has shown us that we can call forth miracles in his name. We only have to say "Come forth," and the spirit will return to the dead and the dead will be resurrected ... I do not know if any of you are aware of this, but this church, PIWC, is at spiritual war with evil spirits and demons in the form of a spiritual chicken that do not want the church to succeed.

Chris asked the group to pray for the church and to catch the spiritual chicken that was walking along the road in front of the church. He called upon us to spiritually "roast it and then eat it." Chris and others were concerned for the welfare of the church community and for the success of the anniversary celebrations. After the service, I spoke to Chris and asked him about the significance of the spiritual chicken. He smiled at me and said:

> There is a spiritual dimension in which God and the devil are at war. This spiritual dimension coexists with our physical one. Any defeats and battles have real effects in our physical reality. It is necessary that you are baptized in the Holy Spirit first before you can see the spiritual world and have an effect on it ... It was spiritually revealed to me that there were demons at war with the church and it manifested in the form of a huge chicken the size of a double-decker bus.

I was taken aback by the size of the spiritual chicken and asked him if he could see these spirits with his eyes. To this he responded:

> These things generally cannot be seen with the naked eye. Sometimes I can, and at other times it is revealed to me through dreams or visions when the Holy Spirit fills me from the inside.

The affective presence of the Holy Spirit inside them and in their lives was the reason Ghanaian Pentecostals gave for why they could step outside their precarious states of existence in London in order to participate in what they saw as "change" for the better. Pentecostals saw themselves as performing a specific biblical duty of interceding for others through spiritual prayer. When they went to war, engaging in spiritual warfare, they were expected to take on a different persona and to transfigure themselves into soldiers of God's army, allowing the Holy Spirit to take over in a communicative act that could only be achieved by those baptized in the Holy Spirit. Protecting the church, its members, and the people who lived around the church was a priority.

However, I was also privy to a conversation between two church elders after that prayer service. They were sceptical about Chris's vision and worried that talk of a "spiritual chicken" attacking the church might send the wrong message to other church members and to the anthropologist in their midst. The spiritual chicken Chris saw could be connected to several possibilities: the demonic character of the neighbourhood, the

evil intent to poison the food being prepared for the anniversary celebrations, or perhaps the association Chris unconsciously made with the
many fried chicken restaurants and take-away outlets along the road
the church was on. It was hard for the church elders to know which
explanation to accept, but Chris was a respected and dedicated church
member. His words had authority, even if others were sometimes
doubtful. In this prayer meeting, he was engaging in a politics of faith
that allowed him and others to do something and not simply believe.
By asking everyone at that prayer meeting to react to a provocation that
had already happened in the spiritual realm, to defend the church from
the attack that was taking place within as well as outside its front doors,
Chris was inviting them to act.

Acting on God's Boredom

Elder Chris often reiterated to me how his Christian life was not defined inside the church but outside of it, on the streets of London. He
lamented how PIWC pastors spent too much time organizing church
programs and not enough time spreading the word of God on the
streets. "We are spending far too much time in church when our calling
is outside," he said. He shared stories of how he had been able to help
others outside the church, such as the time he healed a deaf and dumb
boy in Hyde Park one Sunday morning. "This would not have happened if I was in church," he pointed out. He liked the idea that the
Holy Spirit could come into his life and disrupt him, taking him to
where he was needed most. He invited the "disruption and change" of
God rather than the security of religious institutions.

> God is not interested in us just meeting here every week, singing hymns
> and so on. God gets bored with this, especially when there are people out-
> side who are suicidal and in need of our help. God wants this church to go
> out and help these people. God wants the youth living around the church
> to disrupt the church.

Chris was one of a few church members who wanted to bring people
from outside the church to Jesus. According to him, a good Christian
does not simply attend church regularly and pray to God each week.
Faith was more than singing hymns and bathing in the comfort and
security of being with other Christians. He had what Omri Elisha (2011,
85) calls an "activist orientation": his Pentecostal Christian identity

consisted of a compassionate disposition to help (specific) others. PIWC London members like Chris discovered their Christian vocation by mobilizing others to join them in outreach. He received visions and messages from a communicative God who got "bored" by church routines, who wanted to "shake things up," and to change the community that the church was sitting in. "The young people who live around here are no longer wielding knives but guns now," he said. According to Chris, these youth lacked proper parental supervision, but most importantly they lacked Jesus Christ.

God's "boredom," and by extension the boredom Chris experienced in church, was a way of expressing a closing off of possibilities to act as Christian evangelists. An activist orientation becomes a form of religious activism when God as a social actor participates in unpredictable and impulsive ways to get his people to act. Writing about queer activism in India, Naisargi Dave (2012, 6) defines activism "as a kind of ethical practice, distinguished from moralism by its creatively oppositional relationship to the normalization of life and words." She goes on to say, "Activism as ethical practice is the creative, practical struggle against the drive to normalization ('normalization' in the sense of a narrowing of possibilities)." According to this definition, Ghanaian Pentecostals in London are also activists engaged in a shared sociality and ethical practice, struggling against the pressures of conformity, anonymity, and religious stagnation. The combined Christian imagining and the affective presence of the Holy Spirit (never fully manifest, not even in language) is why Pentecostals could step outside the church as an institutional structure in order to participate in what they saw as "change" for the better. My interlocutors had been charged with a divine mandate to preach the Bible to others and, while possessed by the Holy Spirit, to bring the spiritually dispossessed to salvation.

If God was bored, then church members needed to act "now." It was a creative struggle to act as Christians and to affect the world around them while living precarious lives. But their actions hardly produced the intended results. Their attempts to reach out to others in their neighbourhood proved terribly disappointing. According to Elisha (2011), who worked with Southern Evangelists in North America struggling to build charitable initiatives among local populations, social outreach is usually accompanied by a sense of frustration. During my time at PIWC London, although some church members like Chris shared a passion and ambition to evangelize to and help those less fortunate in their neighbourhood, many of these attempts were accompanied by failed performances that subsequently became devices for reconfirming a church member's own "faith."

On one occasion, a group of British youth walked into the church, disrupting a prayer session. They were invited to stay and join in the prayer. They did not stay, but Elder Chris invited them back for a youth club meeting, which was to take place the following Thursday evening. The following is an excerpt from my field notes for that day:

> I walked into the church building around six in the evening, half an hour late, having battled through London's rush hour commuter traffic. There were five local British youths (between ten and fourteen years old) from the Green Lane area sitting in a row in front of Elder Chris who was sitting there holding his guitar and a Bible. Ivy was sitting there with him, more a spectator and supporter than a participant. The boys watched my arrival with interest (probably because I did not look African), and we immediately introduced ourselves. Elder Chris introduced me as a member of the church. "Girish is one of us," he said, "a Christian." I did not try to correct him, as I was used to such methods, employed to raise a united front to hopeful converts. They all seemed genuinely interested in what Elder Chris had to say. They had walked in unannounced during the previous week's Friday prayer meeting, pushing against the front door, giggling in amusement as they watched us praying. They were invited in, but left soon after. Elder Chris had asked them to come again on Thursday evening for a youth club gathering. He was reading to them from Genesis and explaining how Adam and Eve committed the first sin by disobeying God and eating the apple from the tree of good and evil. That was a sin for which we, their ancestors, were paying for until Jesus Christ came down to earth and shed his blood to save us from our sins. He explained that all the boys had to do was to close their eyes and accept that they are sinners and say that they did not want to be sinners anymore. They then had to accept Jesus as their Lord and Saviour and that he died on the cross for their sins. He told them that if they believed in what they were saying, had faith in their prayer, then that would be enough. That would make you a Christian. And so when they grew old and died and when they left their physical bodies, their spiritual bodies would take flight and be received in heaven.

While the youth from Dagenham estates said the born-again prayer of salvation with Chris, they did so in a comical fashion, teasing and laughing at each other. For Chris, this was not good enough. It was a failed performance. They lacked the commitment to their new identity and did not have the most important ingredient, faith. Chris made it clear to us that "faith" was not the same as "belief," and that experience or speech alone was not enough for someone to have "faith." Belief, according to him, was simply a reference to thoughts and words that lacked conviction. Faith, on the other hand, meant acting on these words and thoughts with commitment and without the prior evidence of experience.

The Dagenham youth remained unconvinced by their conversion experience. They returned to PIWC London once more, but were not seen after that. This missed opportunity for a sincere conversion, however, led to a series of discussions at future youth club meetings concerning the nature of "faith" and what it "does." Chris wanted to teach the Ghanaian youth at these meetings that having and acting on faith was not the same thing as believing in God. At one of these meetings, Chris told us:

> There is a difference between belief and faith. When I believe, it is a state of mind. When I have faith, I act on what I believe. Faith acts, belief does not necessarily act. It is that act of confessing that is called faith. You have to act on what you believe. If you believe it, then you have to say it. In the book of Psalms, it says, "Let the redeemed of the Lord say so." Turn to Mark, chapter 11, verse 22 ... [someone reads]. "And Jesus answering said unto them, 'Have faith in God.'" Faith is something that you do, you have it ... "[W]ho so shall say unto this mountain be thou removed ... and shall not doubt in his heart but believe those things which he say shall come to pass. He shall do whatsoever he says" [claps his hands]. That is the difference! If you have doubt, you won't say it. That is the problem. God has faith. When we are walking in faith, we are thinking and acting like God. He has no doubt whatsoever.

According to Chris, faith was not simply "knowledge about God," which came from the Bible. It was biblical knowledge applied without question and without doubt. If we had faith, he said, we would become "like God." By this he meant that the Word of God had to be studied and embodied through practices of listening and reading, but more importantly it had to be acted upon through speaking and acting like God. God was likened to a social actor who could intervene in our lives and with whom we could communicate. He was a character whom we could emulate through our actions. Only then would experience of God follow. Chris's activism, his attempts to bring others from the neighbourhood and around London into the church, required having faith. If belief was merely a product of the mind, faith was a commitment to action that served to disrupt the stability and institutional security that the Ghanaian church in London provided its mainly migrant community.

Conclusion

An ethical analysis allows me to move beyond the reductive and exoticizing ways in which the "African occult" is evoked in Western public representations (Ranger 2007; ter Haar and Ellis 2009; Meyer 2009). For the British media, "African Christian" becomes an important symbol for all that is different and strange about recent African immigrants who continue to believe in witchcraft and spirits. The construction of such a distinct realm allows "African Christianity" to become abstracted from social and historical processes and to be turned into a category that can be judged by others (as "good" or "bad"). These immigrants are seen as bringing the beliefs and practices of their exotic localities with them to London. They exemplify the "African" who has yet to fully integrate and assimilate into British culture. For my interlocutors, London is a place of opportunity but also a place where the "witch" or the "devil" can act upon people and those they care about. It thus becomes a place that is in need of saving and protecting.

As members of a virtue community, my Ghanaian Pentecostal interlocutors spent a lot of their time in prayer, protecting themselves and the church from spiritual attacks. In spiritual prayer, they transformed the forces of uncertainty into forms of communicable spiritual entities. For example, the negative effects of British culture and the demonic potential of the city to corrupt their youth were important factors for determining how London and Ghana were perceived. When problems of ill-discipline or lack of respect emerged, Ghanaian Pentecostal parents saw them as potential dangers and entry points for immorality and sometimes witchcraft. The changing nature of relationships and cultural practices in the United Kingdom were seen by some to be a moral poison that could potentially infect their children, and their fantasies of a better life in London were projected alongside feelings of alienation, apprehension, and fear. While a shared rhetoric of "getting ahead" is an implicit part of the upward class aspirations of a migrant trajectory, migration also overlaps with another spatial-temporality that links the present to a series of potential threats to one's "morality, sociality, and tradition" (Dick 2010, 275). Rather than generalize about "African Christians" or the "occult" in London, ethical practice places more attention on the religious practices and practical judgments of church members regarding how to live a good life and deal with incommensurable values, especially when faced with limits and constraints that are interpreted as undesirable.

What remained constant was the Holy Spirit, described as a presence that could act in unexpected ways to help these immigrants counter their sense of estrangement from Ghana and the alienation they experienced in London. God's boredom was an important aspect of the affective force of faith that is centred on total openness to the presence of the Holy Spirit, especially in the end times where one has to hasten to fulfil God's plan. For some church members, boredom became a sign and an invitation that required the believer to look beyond the church and "belief" as paradigms of explanation. God's boredom calls upon the Holy Spirit, which provides an orientation for action that extends beyond the individual and the church. Rather than a politics of radical structural change, however, Pentecostal prayer and evangelism are a response to three forms of uncertainty: (1) a theological question of uncertainty that emerges from a Christian narrative of the Fall (of Adam and Eve) and the assumed distance between humans and God; (2) an economic uncertainty and a sense of precarity where dreams are born out of inaccessible opportunities; and (3) an accountability to act on behalf of the divine in the time of the "now," before the end of time. Pentecostalism becomes an activism that quickly folds back onto itself and therefore closes off new possibilities as soon as it creates them. The spiritual battles my Ghanaian Pentecostal interlocutors engaged in took on a different scale when church members transformed into citizens of heaven and members of a global Christian diaspora.

Chapter Seven

Citizens of Heaven

May you be cursed! From now on you will always be servants
who cut wood and carry water for the house of my God.   Joshua 9:23

But we are citizens of heaven, where the Lord Jesus Christ
lives. And we are eagerly waiting for him to return as
our Saviour.   Philippians 3:20

Imagine a Sunday morning in London. Most people are still fast asleep.
But if you were to venture out and take London's infamous public
transport, also known as the London Underground, you would see
many well-dressed Africans holding Bibles in their hands, making their
way to church. During the week, they are part of London's invisible
workforce – economic migrants who have travelled to England in
search of better lives. Now consider a gathering of Ghanaian migrants
in east London at a place called Dagenham. Once a white working class
neighbourhood, it is now interspersed with immigrant communities
from South Asia and Africa. A Ghanaian Pentecostal church sits in the
midst of this changing community. Hundreds of well-dressed Ghanaians, men and women in suits and patterned shirts, some women wear-
ing bright traditional cloth and headdress, merge onto this landscape,
changing it even if just for a day. These Ghanaian Pentecostals from
PIWC London consist of first generation economic migrants and their
children, many of who have grown up in London.

PIWC London is a religious home to many Ghanaian migrants and
their families. Situated in a former cinema and bingo hall, this two-storey building has served as the headquarters of CoP UK and its

International Assembly since 2002. On weekends and at weekday prayer services, the church becomes a place of meaningful performance and moral conviviality for its mainly Ghanaian congregation, who gather here in their numbers from different parts of London to demonstrate their faith in the Judeo-Christian God through songs, dance, sermons, and prayer. "There is power in the name of Jesus. Like a sword in our hands, we declare in the name of Jesus, we shall stand, we shall stand ... Life's enemies will be crushed beneath our feet, for there is no other name that is higher than Jesus," sings the choir, accompanied by a live band, as church members sing along, clap their hands, and dance to the music. Their musical performance is recorded by the church media production company, "Still Moving Pictures," and then uploaded onto YouTube, where one can also find videos from other branches of the church around the world, including branches in various states of the United States and in European countries such as France and Denmark. Flags from these diverse countries are lined up against a red curtain, where the pulpit also stands, pointing to the international success and presence of the church around the world and, as such, making the church into a microcosm of the world.

The church in London is a locus where a global Christian citizenship is embodied and performed, and where new missionary relationships with specific communities and nations are situated.[1] Through spirit-filled prayer and worship every week, Ghanaian Pentecostals project an outward consciousness of global reach and an imagined Christian community that extends beyond the boundaries of the self and individual nation-states (Coleman 2004, 2010b; Maxwell 2006). Pentecostalism possesses what Thomas Csordas (2007) calls a transposable message of salvation and portable practices that include prayer, speaking in tongues, and prophecy – homogenizing forms that travel across space and time through processes of missionization, migration, mobility, and mediatization. It is a global religious force that successfully adapts itself to the range of cultures in which it is introduced (Robbins 2004b, 119). According to Simon Coleman (2010a, 800), Pentecostalism in its global form constitutes what he calls "part cultures," holistic cultural forms that are also in tension with the local milieus they are transmitted through.[2] In this chapter, I seek to revisit how we may understand the "global" in the globalization of Pentecostalism through the self-identity church members share as "citizens of heaven," whose prayers extend beyond the church community and towards the United Kingdom and other Christian nations, and through the simultaneous tensions and limits that arise from church members' interaction and engagement with "culture."[3]

PIWC London is a site where the "near future" (as migrants in London) and the "distant future" (as Christians in heaven) (Guyer 2007) are embodied and simultaneously negotiated. The near future for my interlocutors in London concerns an "attachment to a world in which they have no controlling share," where, as migrants, they exist in a state of what Lauren Berlant calls "cruel optimism," part of a projection of a sustaining but unworkable fantasy in an age of late liberalism (Berlant 2011, 177; see also Povinelli 2011). Here the question ceases to be whether citizenship is a guarantee of social reciprocity and becomes how other kinds of identities possibly operate to temporarily alleviate this sense of pervasive uncertainty. It is in the church in London that my CoP interlocutors gather weekly in order to transform from immigrants and Ghanaian citizens living on the edge or margins of diverse cultures and a new work economy into "citizens of heaven" and saviours of their host country. It is during church services that their sense of precarity and uncertainty become productive of alternative forms of citizenship. As Christian citizens, they are members of a religious diaspora that spans the globe but who have yet to return to their true home in heaven. The Pentecostal imperative to look "beyond" the nation-state, the world, and towards an "elsewhere" when imagining home plays an important role in subjectively framing the ways in which Ghanaian migrants think about the present and see themselves as Christian citizens of heaven.

Christian Citizenship

If the nation-state is a significant player that mediates people's political and socio-economic lives, Christianity plays an increasingly important role in the migration of people from the global south, where it has come to replace the state in providing national and supranational forms of identity (Jenkins 2007, 13).[4] A Pentecostal identity allows the Ghanaian traveller, the economic migrant, and the international student to tap into transnational church networks, linking them to a larger Pentecostal community of believers that extends beyond the confines of Ghana. For example, when speaking about travel to Europe, some CoP members see themselves as "citizens of heaven," exploring Ghana's links with the places from where earlier Christian missionaries first came. Others describe themselves as African missionaries who are bringing the line of Christianity back to these European centres in order to bring the spiritually dispossessed back to salvation.

While much writing on citizenship has been tied to the legal-political aspects of the nation-state, largely ignoring the processes of subject-making and contradictory experiences involved in claims to citizenship (Ong 1996), more recent work on the relationship between citizenship and Christian subjecthood have provided an insightful lens through which to look at the ways in which Christians govern themselves and take responsibility, by participating in styles of self-regulation, as citizens of a nation-state and on a transnational level (Marshall 2009; O'Neill 2009, 2010; Fumanti 2010). If African Christian migrant claims to equality and national citizenship in the United Kingdom are often complicated by questions of illegality or by racial and cultural stereotypes, many such claims also continue to be rooted in the country through moral ideas and values about virtuous citizenship (Fumanti and Werbner 2010; Fumanti 2010). For example, Mattia Fumanti describes Ghanaian Methodists in London as diasporic citizens whose membership in the Methodist church provides a sense of "virtuous citizenship" that "is achieved by being law abiding, hardworking, and actively involved in … fellowships through acts of caring, charity, nurture, and human fellowship" (2010, 16).

Many of my Ghanaian Pentecostal interlocutors similarly participated in church fellowships and in embodied practices of prayer, fasting, and Bible reading that allowed them to develop themselves spiritually and to better govern themselves as "citizens of heaven." During a Sunday sermon in Ghana, a church elder said, "We are guaranteed miracles and extraordinary things because we are citizens of heaven and an extraordinary people." At other times, their claims to being citizens of heaven superseded their citizenship to any nation-state. As another church member in London, said to me after a Friday prayer service:

> I walk majestically because I know where I belong. I am royalty of heaven. This is only a rented body, a temple of God. If you look at me inside, I am beautiful, big and strong. We are not citizens of the United Kingdom. We are aliens here on earth. We are actually angelic beings in exile from the Kingdom of God.

In his ethnography *City of God*, Kevin Lewis O'Neill (2010) describes how Pentecostal doctrines and practices are central to informing and subjectively framing the ways in which everyday citizenship is practiced in post-war Guatemala. O'Neill shows how the neo-Pentecostal church-es in Guatemala City, using practices such as prayer, fasting, and exami-nations of conscience, provide an embodied morality through which church members perform their Christian citizenship. These processes of subjectivation demonstrate the important microphysical links between born-again Christian practice and a "politics of spirituality" (Marshall 2009). Apart from being good Christian citizens, and thereby virtuous citizens, Ghanaian Pentecostals in London also see themselves simulta-neously as accountable to others in the world.

As citizens of heaven, CoP members shared a confidence and ethical compulsion to pray for and preach the gospel to others. The call to evangelize is intertwined with the paradoxical notions of an uncondi-tional "compassion" that emerges from the sacrificial love of Jesus and from a conditional "accountability" that involves reciprocal obligations towards the divine (Elisha 2011, 155).[5] Like a Maussian "total" social act, the gift of salvation is at once this-worldly and other-worldly, si-multaneously interested and disinterested. Jesus's act of giving his own life (like the act of God, the father, to give his only son's life) enables the subsequent reciprocal obligation of his followers to return this ultimate gift by sharing the Word of God with others. As I go on to show, the individual's duty to reciprocate the gift of salvation is presented through divine prophecies of church expansion and as a "love" to which church members are accountable. The moral reasoning through which religious subjects navigate between an interested and disinter-ested evangelism is another aspect of ethical practice.

PIWC: Accountability and the Authority to Evangelize

PIWC is an amalgamation of what started as English assemblies set up in the mid-1980s. As Birgit Meyer (2010, 119) suggests, while the earlier mis-sion churches advocated for local appropriations of Christianity, the more recent Pentecostal and charismatic churches strive to create global con-nections, using English as the main language.[6] The purpose of these inter-national worship centres was partly to retain younger members of the church who preferred to worship in English, as well as to provide a place of worship for English-speaking foreigners and expatriates. As men-tioned in Chapter One, many church members of a later generation were not content with what they called the traditional aspects of CoP. Within PIWC services, the generally hard-and-fast church rules associated with traditional aspects of CoP, including head-covering, conservative dress for women, and congregation of the sexes, were no longer strictly adhered to. PIWC services focused on Bible study and shorter church services, as opposed to the lengthy sermons and prayer services usually associated with the local assemblies. There was also a renewed emphasis on Bible literalism. While it would be wrong to assume that the PIWC model has been the only evangelical tool for reaching out to a non-Ghanaian community, it has been the most suitable for including second-generation Ghanaian migrants living abroad as well as non-Ghanaians in general.

The concept of an international worship centre had now spread to other cities in Ghana and to overseas countries, where they largely attracted the university-educated and English-speaking generation of CoP. The aim of PIWC, as an apostle put it, was "to attract the postmodern generation." Speaking about why PIWC was important for addressing generational and cultural differences, Apostle Onyinah said:

Because they had been used to English and … the world is now the status of a global village. Now see that the youth have adopted all kinds of cultures … Yes, Western culture … sometimes even from the East, oriental culture, and so we cannot say that this is Ghanaian culture … when they go to the traditional church they find it difficult.

With the world becoming "a global village" and with new expectations of change due to the increased influence of multiple cultures on Ghanaians, the PIWCs were formed. The PIWC was linked to a changing culture in Ghana since the 1980s that had emerged from travel and exchange between Ghana and the rest of the world. The modernity of the new church elite was based on a more cosmopolitan lifestyle, new forms of consumption, and an easier access to education, all of which previous generations lacked. The PIWC was also home to church members who saw their missionary role as central to their travels and migration.

In most cases, church members who went overseas for business or long-term employment started prayer fellowships with other church members. Once there were enough people, they made a request to church headquarters in Accra to officially start a branch of the church there. The church's authority to spread the Gospel came not only from biblical authority to spread the Good News but also from earlier prophecies that this church would expand throughout the world. In a CoP book of songs (CoP 2000), we find an addendum entitled "God's First Covenant and Promises with The Church of Pentecost (Revealed)." It begins with the following statement: "The spiritual growth of The Church of Pentecost and its spread throughout the world is a fulfilment of God's Covenant made with the founders of the Church at its beginning (from 1931)" (ibid., 147). The first three of eight promises of the covenant, entitled "God's Part," are as follows:

1. That He God would raise a nation out of Africa that would be a spearhead and light to the world, heralding the 2nd Coming of Christ Jesus our Lord;

2. That the Gold Coast has been chosen to fulfil this eternal will and purpose of God;

3. He God would accomplish this through a White Missionary from Europe who would come to lead the group in the future, and the group … would become a great International Pentecostal Church, which would send out missionaries from the Gold Coast to all parts of Africa and the world as a whole. (ibid.)

These and other prophecies have become part of the church's collective identity. Church leaders occasionally refer to these prophecies when validating the church's worldwide spread and speaking about evangelism in other countries. Pentecostals, as Christian citizens, are divided subjects who move between the city of God and the cities of this world. For example, due to their special status as Christian citizens, church members are told to pray and intercede for the different countries within which the church has a missionary base. While deterritorializing in its attempts to evangelize outside of Ghana, the church is also reterritorializing in its attempts to specify how each country's evangelism efforts should be targeted and what role Ghanaian Pentecostals should play in the global spread of the Gospel.

While in Ghana for the annual church conference in 2003, an apostle of the church gave a sermon that coincided with the tenth anniversary of PIWC Accra. Apostle Addison was the head of missions for the church in Australia at the time. In his sermon he said:

We have to make a kingdom for ourselves outward. We are not here just for that first group we formed. We have to be led by our first love, Jesus. PIWC is going all over the world [reads from Matthew 5:5–20]: "Those who are chosen to preach and lead should expect to be persecuted but you will find a place in the kingdom."

Apostle Addison spoke on the theme "Thy Real Love." He was ordaining new deacons and elders into the church assembly that day. These church members had "character," he said, demonstrated by "a love for God and their fellow men." They were also "not lazy, baptized in the Holy Spirit, and participated in church all-night prayers." He then reminded members to nurture their love for Jesus in the same way that they would court their first and only love. Marriage, he said, did not only speak of a serious commitment but also represented accountability towards that first love:

> Accountability to our calling is even more serious today. [For] anyone who is called to serve … sacrificial love must take place. As soon as a man sees himself as different and knows his calling, he will do extraordinary things … [F]or example, within nine days in Nigeria I was able to plant five churches from Abidjan to Ibadan. When things seemed difficult, I took the authority vested in me as said by God [reads 1 Timothy, chapter 3]. 1973 was the first time I travelled abroad to represent the church witness movement in a Billy Graham revival in London. It was then that I got my first suit made. After the concert, Billy Graham asked all of us to go out and preach in the streets of London. It was in preaching that I remembered my first love. I said to an old man, "Papa, let me pray one second for you, and Jesus will come into your heart straight away." Five passers-by stopped and listened, and accepted Jesus as their personal Lord and Saviour that very day.

By becoming accountable to their first love – Jesus – church members would answer the divine call to evangelize and act with a sense of moral passion. Making Christians accountable to that "sacrificial love" was a way to create the expectations and conditions for this unconditional compassion to work in the real world (Elisha 2011, 161). Their love for Jesus not only spoke of an inner relationship with God but also included an accountability to prepare others for God's heavenly kingdom. Apostle Addison then suggested that while others in the West may be more technologically advanced, PIWC members have something even more important to share. They have spiritual power and a divine authority to spread the Gospel. According to the Apostle, all they have to do is claim it:

> A delegated authority is given onto us through believing and accepting Jesus is our saviour. That power is transferred from his authority into us.

We are given the rights, the assets, the power, the handing over of equipment to do business for the Lord – see Romans 13:1. Through him we become a chosen people, a royal priesthood, and a special generation. I stand on this authority. This authority, which is handed to us from above, must be used and taken by us. Many may have run ahead of us, but our authority is special. Let me tell you, they may have the machine but we have the power. They may also have the goods, but we have the power. By this heavenly authority, He will use His church to cover the world.

Apostle Addison used the inclusive "we," bringing his listeners into a shared social world as God's "chosen people," while calling for the church to continue to move forward and outward. He described the words that underlined authority for him, such as "power," "charged," "covenant," "force," and "influence." The Apostle also reflected on the earlier logo of the church, which consisted of a map of Africa with a dove flying down inwards and towards the African continent. While this logo represented the movement of the Holy Spirit into Ghana, and into Africa as a whole, it no longer seemed fitting for a church that was expanding out of Africa. He felt that the logo was too inward looking and did not represent the direction the church was headed to "make disciples of all nations" (Matthew 28:19). According to the Apostle, CoP was not just moving forward and outward into the world, but was also bringing people upward towards heaven:

It was not what God's covenant with the church was about. The covenant with the church was a covenant to move into the world and take the world, so authority must be taken immediately. I told the Chairman at the time that I see that our vision is not only for Africa. We do not belong to this logo anymore. The new logo should tell all those who are abroad – "We are coming" – and that authority went along with that. We can't go out into the world with a Gold Coast mentality. Everywhere a PIWC businessman goes, he will make breakthroughs there and plant a church there. What God has given us has elevated us to a higher pedestal.

Ghana was no longer the Gold Coast, and CoP was no longer just an African church. From the 1980s, CoP began a reverse mission to the West, with many of its members migrating to Europe and America as economic migrants and students.[7] Many Ghanaians at that time left Ghana in search of jobs, with a substantial number of professionals, such as teachers, lawyers, and public administrators, leaving the country for a better life elsewhere.[8] The new logo depicted the Holy Spirit, represented by a white dove, descending onto a world map With the expansion of the church to spread the Gospel to countries outside Africa, the icon of the map changed accordingly. "PIWC has been given power and authority to affect the whole world internationally, to shake the whole world," Apostle Addison proclaimed.

If CoP had been ordained by God to become an international church, my interlocutors in London were also dealing with questions regarding the repercussions of such church expansion and their own roles as missionaries. Many church members in PIWC London wrestled with questions of how to balance their personal expectations of missionary work with the new cultural environment in which they found themselves. It was certainly a topic of many church sermons.

Understanding Cultural Change

> Together we protested, we asserted the equality of all men in the world …
> And then the occasion arose when I had to meet the white man's eyes. An unfamiliar weight burdened me. The real world challenged my claims.
>
> Frantz Fanon (1952)

The theme of a Sunday church service in PIWC London was "Change." Elder James stood behind the pulpit. He reminded church members of the importance of a Pentecostal identity, which had helped them in their migration to London and was responsible for their present achievements. He spoke about his own poor, rural past in Ghana, and compared it to his present level of comfort and increased social status in London. While he had come from a mud hut in Africa, he said, he now owned several houses in Accra, a mansion in his village, and a home in London. Like others in CoP, God had called him and transformed him.

Elder James spoke about the positive changes that had taken place since his born-again transformation in Ghana and his move to London. He told us that on his birthday a few days earlier, he dug up a photograph of himself taken in 1996, when he had first arrived in London. He described himself as a country bumpkin, dressed in gloves and warm clothing, and spoke about how London had seemed so strange to him. So much had since changed. What he had economically achieved with his migration to London was not enough, however. Other Christian obligations persisted. He told church members that they were in London to build God's mighty church and to spread the Gospel. They were not just economic migrants from Ghana – God had chosen them for a higher purpose.

> We are not just Ghanaians here to work and earn money and then go back to Ghana. I was from a small village in the Central Region in Ghana. I had no money, but God made it possible for me to come here. The fact that you are poor, that you are feeble, not handsome or beautiful, that is why God called you ... He said, "I have chosen the weaker things in the world to shame the mighty, rich, and powerful."

Elder James's sermon supported the commonly held image of African Christians in Europe as unnoticed poor migrants, but it also proposed another powerful self-image as missionaries, foregrounding the positive role of Pentecostal churches among the diaspora in London.[9] He then spoke about a sign he had seen in Ilford, London, close to where the church was situated. It read, "If there is a God, why hasn't he shown himself?" In reply to this, Elder James told his audience that God was indeed present, that "the Lord has revealed himself so many times ... [H]e has revealed himself in me." A genuine transformation should result in a complete change in form, personality, and character, he said. Such an idea of transformation also meant that God had turned church members into members of his household.

> God has made me a citizen of Israel. Before, I was a gentile, a foreigner, and a non-citizen of Israel. I am looking forward to heaven. I know I am a child of God and that I am going to heaven. How many people can say that? To become a part of the household of God! If the Queen asked me to be her son and join her household, I will be jumping up and down in happiness. I won't have to put toothpaste on my toothbrush anymore. What more, joining the household of God?[10]

Such references to themselves as members of a "household of God" provide Ghanaians in London with a Christian-centrist or a Pentecostal-centrist cosmological map (Robbins 2010b, 63). The map allows Ghanaian Pentecostals in London to align themselves with an imagined global community of God's chosen people. As citizens of heaven, they can temporarily escape the confines of other kinds of bounded identities such as African and immigrant. To become a member of God's household was the dream James shared with other Pentecostals around the world.

Elder James's sermon pointed to their identity as diasporic Christian citizens whose true home is in heaven.

While PIWC London included a minority of members from the Caribbean or other African countries and encouraged people of all nationalities and ethnicities to participate in church services, the sizeable majority of people in this church were Ghanaian and mainly Twi speakers. According to church members, their new cultural environment had changed the way they related to each other. It had changed the "mindset," "attitudes," and "culture" of Ghanaian Pentecostals in London. Increased mobility and overseas migration also brought negative aspects of "culture." Culture in Pentecostal discourse has a double explanatory purpose. While culture can serve as a vehicle for helping people experience Christian salvation and for evangelism, it can also create a situation whereby it becomes a corrupting influence. Overseas migration and the ways in which Ghanaian Pentecostals critically engage with issues of British and Ghanaian culture foreground this point like no other.

Many traced the problem of culture to their first contact with what one church member described as the "white traditional churches" in London. Ghanaian Pentecostal migrants from CoP who arrived in London in the early 1980s worshipped together with white Pentecostals in a British Pentecostal church that had missionary links with Ghana. This arrangement did not last long, as differences between the Ghanaian and the British Pentecostals disrupted the ideological assumption that all Pentecostals were equal and part of one Christian family. While my interlocutors placed less attention on their ethnicized citizenship, cultural differences between Ghanaian members of CoP and white members of the Elim Pentecostal Church, UK, were highlighted as reasons that led to the breakup of this arrangement. One church elder said to me:

> Most of the traditional churches were not receptive … you know the white churches. The way we relate to ministers and members back home, that kind of closeness we were not getting it here. People came to church like visitors and they would go, even the local Pentecostal churches in London … Our main aim was to provide a born-again Christian forum for all these people to come together and worship in the Ghanaian language, and for matters of welfare … that there will be leadership who are closer to them.[11]

The imagining of a more expansive Christian identity that would unite them with others in the United Kingdom remained largely unrealized. What seemed missing in London was a sense of "closeness" or intimacy, which included the knowledge of a Ghanaian language, an understanding of shared economic and social welfare issues, leaders who could serve their personal interests, and, finally, the need for Pentecostal prayer that addressed their specific concerns. When these differences became issues of concern for church members, CoP members started organizing themselves to better represent the needs of Ghanaian Pentecostal migrants in London. This task made it necessary for them to form their own church congregation, separated from, yet still in alliance with, Elim Pentecostal Church, UK. As a church leader explained to me:

> Some of their cultural needs were not being addressed, and the people there could not understand some of their issues. Because our people there have special interest in funerals, in naming of children, education, and our way of supporting one another. So in that presence we started that association in 1987 April which we call Pentecost Association in United Kingdom and Eire, or PAUKE.

It was not until 1989 that an international branch of CoP was established in London, and 2002 before the church acquired its own building. Culture and hierarchical cultural evaluations between white and African congregations became an important way of creating distinctions between themselves and others in the United Kingdom.

Culture is not simply an articulation of group boundaries that are accompanied by shared attributes and their assumed naturalization. Culture also serves as a counter-discourse to Pentecostalism, providing material for explaining everything that falls outside the boundaries of a shared transcendental discourse. According to Kirk Dombrowski (2001, 123), who worked with newly converted members of an all-native church in southeast Alaska, "Pentecostal church practice allows people to not only stand outside of and against any particular culture, but against culture more generally."[12] The problem of culture for Pentecostals is also a problem of locating continuity in their new environment. It is a direct reflection of how Pentecostals view their relationship to the local, from a pre-commitment to a transcendental position of Christian "faith." In other words, Pentecostalism provides believers with a "transcendental vantage point" through which to view, be sceptical of, and criticize their relationship with the local while allowing them to continue being a part of global culture (Robbins 2010b, 69). I now turn to one such moment of critical distancing during my field research in London.

The Limits of Evangelism in London

As I proceeded to make my regular walk to church from Goodmayes train station in Dagenham, I decided to pay more attention to the sights and activities going on around me in this suburban district of east London. I had grown accustomed to this walk over the last few months of attending church services and prayer meetings with PIWC London. The church's present site was formerly a cinema hall that also housed a bingo entertainment centre. Pentecostal churches were fond of converting former secular places of "sin" into sacred spaces for worship. This area was like most other suburban areas outside London's inner city area. I passed two other local English churches on my way to CoP. I had never actually seen more than a few people outside these churches, even on Sundays, and there was hardly any activity around their premises – a stark comparison to PIWC that was filled with worshippers on Sundays. This time, however, a priest and two young boys were putting up a sign, which read "Jesus – The Prince of Peace."

The sign immediately brought to my mind references to the then impending war with Iraq that was on everyone's lips. The three archbishops of England's mainline churches had only the day before met with their Prime Minister, Tony Blair, to oppose the possibility of war with Iraq. They felt that it was their duty and responsibility as national church leaders to make a show of defiance, representing certain tenets of Christianity and presenting it as a religion of peace. This doctrine of Jesus Christ – Peace – was becoming more important at a time like this, especially when war loomed around the corner. Just the previous week, there had been peace demonstrations and marches in London, and before that in Australia and America. This global response was not surprising, but I started wondering what my Ghanaian Pentecostal friends thought about the possible war with Iraq. My train of thought was interrupted by the number of fried chicken restaurants and take-away outlets along the road the church was on.

I soon spotted Deacon Sammy and four other young church members walking along the street, across from the PIWC building. They had been distributing evangelical pamphlets and Bible tracts. Like Elisha's (2011) evangelists who prioritize social engagement as an important aspect of their own religious conversion, PIWC London members like Sammy discover their Christian vocation by mobilizing others to join them in outreach. Sammy was holding a loudspeaker in one hand. He had used it to get the message of salvation across to slightly bemused and annoyed passers-by. The group was returning to church to pray over their day's work. They asked me to join them, and we found ourselves a quiet corner in the church building. We prayed over the "success" of the day's evangelism, and Sammy gave a summary of the afternoon's events. He spoke about the way people in the area responded to them. One woman had yelled and threatened to call the police. Others were rude and paid no attention to them. "This is nothing!" he said to us. "I have experienced worse reactions. But we have done God's work, and now we have to leave the rest in His hands."

Sammy told the youth that he enjoyed street evangelism and explained why it was important. Sammy, like other church members who had arrived in London, complained that the Ghanaian Pentecostal church in London was "cold" compared to the church in Ghana. Ghanaian Pentecostals in London were so busy taking care of their own community and their economic and cultural needs that they were no longer "on fire" to preach the Word of God to others. Sammy explained how, upon arriving in London from Ghana, he had quickly become disappointed by CoP's cultural continuities with a Ghanaian culture and the lack of evangelical work outside the church community. He was upset by the use of Twi, an Akan language widely spoken in southern Ghana, in church services. While the church strove to maintain continuities with certain aspects of Ghanaian "culture" that had served earlier church members in London well, aspects of these same continuities caused problems for others like Sammy who were more interested in preaching the Gospel. According to Sammy, this attempt to hold on to Ghanaian culture prevented church members from spreading their universal message to British people and challenged certain assumptions of their religious transformation.

While some church members remained nostalgic for Ghana's "Christian" identity and the Christian relationships that had pervaded their lives there, others like Sammy lamented that the Ghanaian church in London continued to be too "Ghanaian," becoming an obstacle in their attempts to belong to a wider, non-Ghanaian, Pentecostal community and to evangelize to British society:

> When I first came to this country four years ago, I was very excited. I thought I was coming to the heart of the fire – England. I had great expectations upon arriving. But when I got here, I called up the local Church of Pentecost and asked them when the next service was. I got my reply in Twi. I was shocked and disappointed. "Why was Twi being used in

London?" I asked myself. When I attended the Twi service, I prayed to God that I could help bring the church forward and move beyond Twi. How else are we going to evangelize to others? God loves us all. The colour of our skin is not important to God, and I felt that others had to be brought to God. The church has to become more accessible.

Many later migrants who were concerned with evangelism considered the Ghanaian language and the culture of CoP as antithetical to a global Christian identity. According to Sammy, if "God loves us all," his Pentecostal identity should have allowed him to transcend both racial and cultural associations with Ghana. However, this was not the case, and, according to him, it made evangelism even more difficult.

While there were fewer opportunities for prayer and evangelism in London, Sammy pointed out that the residents of the area in which the church was situated and, more generally, people in the United Kingdom were fortunate to have the church and its members in their midst. The prayers of Ghanaian Pentecostals were powerful, he told us. Ghanaian Pentecostals were good people who prayed to God, and their intercessory prayers helped keep the United Kingdom safe from God's wrath. "But why would God be angry with the people of the UK in the first place?" someone asked.

Sammy worked as a nurse in south London and said that he had experienced first-hand the social problems associated with British culture. He complained that his work brought him into contact with many young people who were on drugs or were suffering from HIV/AIDS, as well as with many young girls who had experienced teenage pregnancies. In these cases, the negative aspects of British culture were associated with lifestyle choices that were considered un-Christian and morally dangerous. As I mentioned in the previous chapter, the possible moral corruption of the Ghanaian Pentecostal youth in London was a subject of concern for church members.

According to Sammy, some aspects of British culture, especially those related to freedom of sexual behaviour, posed an impending threat to church members' special status as Pentecostals. He often cited the freedom to have sexual partners before marriage or to adopt a non-heteronormative sexual orientation as important examples for all the things that were wrong in the United Kingdom; these views were not dissimilar from the opinions of church leaders in Ghana, as described in Chapter One, or from the opinions expressed by other church members in the previous chapter. Sammy said:

Such acts of gayism, homosexuality, and gender adjustments are common here in the UK. In the Bible, God hated these acts and even came down himself to see if they were true. Things are much worse now as men can chop off their manhood, implant breasts, and act, walk, and talk like women. Wouldn't God be more furious by these acts? But why hasn't he done something about this sooner?

In this case, rather than God's "boredom," it was God's "anger" that compelled Sammy to act. Sammy distanced himself from the aspects of British culture that he thought were immoral. He told us that he did not go out on "dates" and declined invitations to go to pubs and clubs with his British colleagues. However, Sammy's distrust concerning the continuity of Ghanaian culture and the immoral behaviour in the United Kingdom was accompanied by his faith that Ghanaian Pentecostals were God's chosen people, who were in London to fulfil a larger mission of protecting the country where they now lived from harm. To explain what he meant, Sammy cited the story of Sodom and Gomorrah from the Old Testament:

> In the Bible, God allowed the land of Sodom and Gomorrah to survive because he had said that if he could find at least ten righteous men in the land, he would not destroy it … In the same way, our presence in London and our prayers for them as Christians have helped saved England from God's wrath. Again, why doesn't he just ask us to go back to Ghana? It is our presence here that protects England.

Ghanaian Pentecostals were in London for a purpose beyond economic opportunity and social mobility. Their special status as citizens of heaven allowed them to intervene in Britain's destiny. As another church member remarked, "There was a time in Britain when the country was filled with the fire and zeal of God's missionaries. Britain is now referred to as the world's second most ungodly nation." "At the end of the day," Sammy told me, "the prayers of Ghanaian Pentecostals" were providing a moral buffer for the sins of the British people as well as protecting their own Ghanaian youth from immorality.

Ghanaian Pentecostals like Sammy believed they had been chosen by God to evangelize, pray for, and protect their host nation. The outreach activities of church members were instructive moments for observing when Pentecostal faith met with its own limitations and in understanding how such limits were rationalized retrospectively.

In their transnational movement to London, Ghanaian Pentecostals such as Sammy use the criteria for their self-transformation to turn the tables on the conditional aspects of their citizenship and on their status as economic migrants. Through their participation in technologies of self-transformation and through performances such as prayer and evangelism, they help their hosts by fighting against evil and by protecting their host country from further harm. In the next section, I look at how prayer acts in a transnational way to protect the United Kingdom and other Christian nations in their war against the devil.

The War in Iraq: "We Are All a Part of It …
It Is a Part of Our Destiny"

It was 2003, during the American invasion of Iraq. Fifteen members of a prayer force from PIWC London were participating in the course of the war through spiritual prayer. They prayed for the successful victory of the "Christian nations" (America and Britain) over their "Muslim" (Iraqi) enemy. The members of the prayer group compared themselves to the Jewish people of the Old Testament, fighting a war against the enemies of God's chosen people. They believed that they were living in the end times and that this war was a necessary part of their global destiny. They were acting within religious terms, while participating in the political circumstances of their time as members of a Christian nation. Elder Kofi led the prayer in this way:

Exodus 17:8 reads "The Lord is my banner." The first war that the people of Israel faced after crossing the Red Sea was the war with the people of Amaleh … A war was planned to set the people of Israel off course and to confuse them. But God is in control. Currently there is a war looming in Iraq. Maybe there is good reason for it, maybe not. God must have known about the coming of war against the Amaleh. But He wanted to cause confusion and take away Moses, their shepherd. There is a carrier leaving from Portsmouth going to the Gulf. The government, politicians are sending people to war. Like a modern day prime minister or president, Moses sent Joshua to war. It was our war, a war for the people of Israel, God's own war … The reason they succeeded was that a hand was raised to the throne of God [referring to the staff of Moses]. These days, people are full of criticism for others but you don't realize that "we are all a part of it." People don't come to realize that it is a part of our destiny … We all have that staff of power. We have power in us. Let us raise our hands to the throne and something will happen.

Kofi's prayers were indicative of a millennial utopianism in which Christians and Christian nations have been chosen by God to lead the war between good and evil. Elder Emmanuelle took over from Kofi and reiterated a similar point:

> While the American and British troops are being sent to war and its leaders have to make decisions, we can send our own message from here. We can use our own weapons, prayer.

Church members were doing more than simply taking on the burden of another group's national history and destiny. Through invoking the Holy Spirit to fill them, they became fighting soldiers in God's army. Instead of merely "immigrants" or "Ghanaians" in the United Kingdom, they were also citizens of heaven, aligned with Britain (as a Christian country) in their war against evil. Such spiritual warfare is central to born-again "political theology," which plays out through strategies of domination that also propagate forms of exclusion and revenge (Marshall 2009, 204). Spiritual prayer also translates into a feeling of responsibility to act on behalf of the nation. In witnessing the events of war and in collectively praying over it as God's chosen people, Ghanaian Pentecostals in London were embodying the moral weight of a Christian historical conscience. They were also increasing their investment in a nation that did not necessarily meet their moral expectations or return their love (Ahmed 2004, 131).

Such prayer performances illustrate the importance of Walter Benjamin's ideas of linear "homogenous, empty" time, which penetrates church members' lives as citizens of nation-states, and of "messianic" time, which allows them to recall a heroic Judeo-Christian past into the present (Benjamin 1968).[13] Pentecostal prayer performances, like messianic time, do more than simply remind Ghanaians of their new relationship to a new Christian past. They also commit participants to establishing relations of likeness between themselves and biblical characters, including the Jewish people of the Old Testament. It is through such prayer that ritual and myth become integrated as two sides of one action (Mauss 2008, 22–3). By identifying themselves as exiled beings from the kingdom of God and by participating in spiritual prayer, these

Ghanaian immigrants created a shared destiny with specific Christian others and with the countries from where Pentecostalism in Ghana first arrived – namely Britain and America.

Aligned with these countries as born-again Christians, Ghanaian Pentecostals see non-Christians and non-Christian countries as the true strangers or as enemies to be treated with hostility – reproducing the assumption that there are always conditions, boundaries, and barriers to any invitation of hospitality (Derrida 2000). This protection of and love for a group of Christian nations was a love for likeness and not for difference. In this "fantasy of love as return," the non-Christian other became the "obstacle" that allowed these Ghanaian Christians to "sustain a fantasy that without them [the non-Christians], the good life would be attainable, or their love would be returned with rewards and value" (Ahmed 2004, 131). This form of "love" and global alliance (as uncompromising self-sufficiency and mastery) is contradictory to the very condition of plurality. But if the non-Christian other is a symbol for all that is different, it is also a symbol of hope, a symbol for what can potentially be made into the same through conversion. According to my Ghanaian Pentecostal interlocutors, the Judeo-Christian God is the master of the heavenly kingdom and thus the master of Britain and America. Ghanaian Pentecostals, as legal guests, create another door to British society through tracing their own born-again Christian identity. As true believers, they now come to hold the key to the door of the house because they remain faithful to God's Word and because the house is no longer in Ghana or the United Kingdom, but in the kingdom of God.

Conclusion

Pentecostalism can be described as both global in its reach and local in its application, thriving off the tensions between its own values and the values of its host societies and cultures. This chapter has provided a practical specification to global Pentecostalism, highlighting the different inclusions and exclusions involved in negotiating Pentecostal migrant identities. I have restricted my analysis of Christian citizenship to the ethical practice of my Ghanaian Pentecostal interlocutors in London and focused on how they provide the criteria for and the limits of a shared virtue community within a larger British society. I have also shown how the tensions that arise from the simultaneity of different roles, as both citizens of heaven and residents of national and cultural domains, become productive arenas for establishing and destabilizing the global reach of Pentecostal networks. While CoP members in London see themselves as citizens of heaven, the reality on the ground is that as newcomers to the United Kingdom, many Ghanaian Pentecostals experience new forms of exclusion and discrimination in a society where their Christian identity no longer holds the same importance as it did in Ghana. Their situation in London reflects the limits of a transcendental authority in this world. A critique of culture is a moral commentary on the limits of this transcendental force, providing self-mechanisms of order and regulation.

It is important to understand how a concept like culture is a powerful way of marking absences. Ghanaian Pentecostals in London rationalize the difficulty of their dual role as economic migrants and Pentecostal missionaries by addressing what is absent in London. First, the absence of a sense of closeness and an understanding of Ghanaian culture initially led CoP members in London to separate from their white Pentecostal brethren and form their own church. Second, Ghanaian Pentecostals in London who believe they are bringing the fire of Pentecost back to Europe quickly become disappointed by the persistence of Ghanaian culture in CoP UK. The absence of a Pentecostal identity that transcends the social classifiers of race and language becomes frustrating for those with a missionizing goal. Third, Ghanaian and British cultures provide opportunities to speak about the absence of a Pentecostal morality and world view. It is then up to the Ghanaian Pentecostal church in London to help fill the gap between Christianity and culture.

Once in London and among a community of other Ghanaian Pentecostals, church members continue to live within and between multiple spatial-temporalities, between their status as economic migrants and as diasporic members of a heavenly kingdom. If "transnationalism"[14] acknowledges that people who aspire to move across and through geopolitical borders are still caught within and are embodied by the limits of hospitality, "diaspora" is a useful term with which to understand how transnational Christians imagine their home in the world and simultaneously in heaven.[15] One of the defining features of diaspora is the dialectic relation between integrity and discontinuity (Barber 2011, 54–61). If Christian integrity unfolds as a reproduction of one's self through technologies of the self and through an account of one's self (as "royalty of heaven"), then discontinuity emerges through the effort to establish an accountability to others through the interparticularities of everyday life in a new place of residence. At the same time, the nostalgic longing to return home or this "homing" desire is not necessarily the same as wanting to return to a physical place (Brah 1996, 180). Instead, diaspora evokes an idea of rupture and sacred time, which foregrounds ritual performances and embodied practices that allow people to connect with and to create home, wherever they may be. As members of God's household, church members have the ability to defend themselves and transform their environment and community through spiritual prayer.

The church in London is demonstrative of a Christian citizenship that is both distant and intimate, both global in its reach and firmly situated within specific discourses of culture and nation. By outwardly expanding CoP through overseas migration, Ghanaian Pentecostals are fulfilling their personal ambitions to lead a more successful and prosperous life abroad, moving forward into the future. They are simultaneously carrying out their responsibility as born-again Christians to bring the Gospel back to the lands in which it is now in decline. They do so through performances that collapse the world of the Bible into the world of economic migrants in London. While real happiness, health, economic success, and relationships are to be found in an "elsewhere," Ghanaian Pentecostals are also ethical actors engaged in acts of spatio-temporal balancing between Ghana and London, as well as between the near future and the future that is yet to come.

The Future Will Fight Against You

The Sankofa is a mythical bird in Akan culture that is depicted flying forwards into the future, with its head turned backwards towards the past and a golden egg in its mouth. The egg is symbolic of a treasure or wisdom that can be found in the communal past of one's ancestors or shared lineage. In a conversation with a Ghanaian academic who works on traditional religion, I suggested that the Sankofa could also represent an inward journey taken by an individual to find some personal treasure or hidden truth. He strongly opposed my interpretation. There is only one way Ghanaians traditionally look at the past, he told me. They see the past as a moral community looking backward, not as individuals looking inward. The wisdom of a people lies in a shared communal past; the individual has no moral standing separate from the community with which he or she identifies. It is only once you acknowledge where you are from that you have the strength and wisdom to move forward.

The symbol of the Sankofa has much to offer to my conclusion on Pentecostal transformation and ethical practice in CoP. Although the leaders of CoP might not agree with the Sankofa as a symbol of Pentecostalism in Ghana, given its association with an African traditional past, they would certainly recognize that church members, while encouraged to look inward, are also constantly looking back to a non-Christian and Christian past and to church history as a part of their personal journeys. Pentecostal transformation is productively understood as a reflective process that involves dual movements of looking back reflectively and moving forward in time through an ethical practice that is located in the conjunction or movement between explicit commitments to shared Pentecostal values and implicit local practices and changing circumstances.

Figure 8.1 The Sankofa. (Photo by the author.)

My time in Accra, Kumasi, and London alerted me to the diverse values and experiences that shaped CoP – among its church leaders, prophets, and ordinary members. I realized that these various groups and individual actors held different views about what Pentecostal transformation is and what kind of change conversion signals. Understanding Pentecostal transformation as ethical practice illuminates the ways that the rhetoric of rupture selectively emerges through a moral framework in which Pentecostals are mediating and evaluating everyday situations, different cultural and socio-economic environments, their ambitions of travel, and their relationships with multiple others. Pentecostalism in Ghana is not a religion of complete rupture, since rupture is only possible in relation to the past(s) it invokes and to the explicit criteria and implicit circumstances in which it becomes made possible.

Like the Sankofa, CoP and its members make a double movement, proceeding forward into the future while simultaneously looking back onto not one but multiple pasts that coexist, converge, and sometimes collide. If conversion is accomplished in a single event of transformation, this event only exists at the time of its unfolding. Everything that follows is an ongoing reflection and citation of this singular transformation. This new beginning is understood as meaningful in itself by virtue of a philosophical labour that reconsiders the circumstances through which the event happened and after which creatively imagines new ways to move on with life. If in dealing with present and past problems CoP provides its members with self-disciplinary practices to maintain continuity with a virtuous self and a Christian future, church members also encounter moments of indeterminacy that may destabilize and question the boundaries of what is acceptable or what is real.

A Pentecostal life is not merely the product of the weight of the past(s) on the present, but is also the result of how the future comes to bear upon the present. Church members make decisions about their near and distant future by either reinforcing church values or finding creative means through which new norms may eventually develop. The near future introduces inconsistencies, uncertainties, and dilemmas to the present and to the distant future simultaneously. Such an element of unpredictability or surprise is characteristic of an ethical life, serving as an invitation to act or respond to a set of decisions that have to be made. Dedicating attention to ethics within the lives of Christian believers therefore involves taking into account that (1) religious life is never fully consistent with any specific theological or philosophical logic; (2) religious life does not provide a complete answer to the complexities of life and its non-human elements; and (3) people ask questions pertaining to the application of specific values, rules, and content.

For many in CoP, ethical relations are not necessarily limited to achieving Christian certainty nor to alleviating Christian uncertainty where uncertainty and certainty are dialectically related, where they are described as phases of liminality that present opportunities for Christian subjects to struggle with and to work on themselves, with the goal of experiencing certainty (again) or rediscovering faith in God and his future promises. Instead, many in CoP are making ethical decisions between living happily and suffering miserably, or even living miserably and suffering happily. Neither is ethics solely defined by the orbit of the human self as enclosed or bounded. Rather, it engages with the opening of the self to multiple conversations (with oneself and with others) and to the presence of multiple spiritual others, including the divine, spirits, and the Holy Spirit, as social actors who enter into ethical relations with the self. At the same time, ethics addresses difficult questions and complex situations involving the demands of these multiple others, towards which the self becomes responsible. Ethical practice therefore involves the continuous work of adopting, redefining, and contesting norms and values in response to these same relations.

If Pentecostalism in Ghana includes an alternative sociality that emphasizes personal choice over genealogy and individuality over dividuality, it also reintroduces a myriad of other ways to provide its members with kin-like relations through ideas of partibility and dividuality, through providing spiritual protection, prophetic direction, and healing, as well as through a sense of continuity with a new family of Christian relations. As it builds foundations for itself in the here and now, the church allows members to look back to a Christian past by drawing from a collective ethos in the present. This construction of social memory and genealogical continuity with a biblical identity allows the church and its members to authoritatively claim to move on from a non-Christian past and to confidently confront an un-Christian present, while partially reproducing both these "non-" and "un-" Christian ideas within themselves. For instance, the prophets within CoP and the charismatic churches in Ghana are seen to be powerful mediators for the power of the Holy Spirit and for the fulfilment of the promises of Jesus. Yet they are also commonly viewed as acting to reproduce aspects of a traditional religious past or advocating a self-maximizing neoliberal agenda. CoP leaders and members spend much time and philosophical labour scrutinizing their own practices in order to differentiate the acceptable from the unacceptable and the genuine from the fake.

This book has brought together the anthropology of Christianity and the ethical dimensions of a Christian life in order to shine light on the multiple issues and ambiguities that a Christian identity holds for Ghanaian Pentecostals and to allow for a better understanding of how they evaluate the limits of a shared Christian identity. In doing so, it complements approaches that aim at understanding how these same actors are concerned with attaining coherence in their lives. Agreeing on the rules and boundaries of Christian practice does not provide a sufficient answer to other questions concerning the inconsistencies of practice or personal misfortune and suffering. A focus on Pentecostal transformation as ethical practice allows for the weighing of multiple considerations in the face of the multiplicity and the heterodoxies of religious experience and practice.

If Pentecostal transformation is implicated in the ways value is assigned to certain practices and material forms, distinguishing between what counts as Christian and on what grounds – a dialogic process that involves mutual relationships of institutional hierarchy and interdependence – is also concerned with the problem of continuity in regard to what ought to be done in particular encounters, situations, and circumstances. Many of the ethical concerns church members face manifest as questions relating to the problem of continuity: "Why is this happening to me (us), why here, and why now?" "When" are we more or less Christian? and "What comes next?" Alongside locating the church as a social institution and key site, where techniques of domination come into close contact with techniques of the self, my analysis of the ethical practices within CoP provides an understanding of how church leaders and members subjectively deal with the tension between the application of specific criteria for achieving transformation and the dilemmas involved in the recognition of their limits. Taking seriously the ethical dilemmas involved in assigning value does matter, because they complicate the notion of a shared Pentecostal identity.

Moving into the future is always a reflective process. As much as the distant future is determined by God's promises regarding salvation and entry into heaven, the near future, in retrospect, is always changing. Ghanaian Pentecostals have to wrestle with their own personal destiny and the present expectations of a future-in-this world. They have to act now, in the time before the end of the world, for themselves and for others. The near future, and the role of the Holy Spirit in this future, is an unknown presence that interrupts a Christian life and sometimes surprises church members in unexpected ways. It can be a creative force that guides the believer and provides him or her with unexpected opportunities. It can also be a barrier to mobility and an oppositional force that prevents the believer from achieving his or her desires and dreams. Many of my reasons for using ethics as an analytical framework were confirmed several years later, when I returned to Ghana and caught up with many of my Pentecostal interlocutors.

In 2012, Albert and I met up again and spoke about a number of issues bothering him. He was clearly frustrated. His Pentecostal Christian identity was not sufficient to help him succeed or change his life completely. His life was filled with personal betrayals and financial worries. A few years earlier, in 2007, he had managed to acquire a passport and almost succeeded in travelling to Malaysia, getting as far as Botswana's Gaborone airport before the middleman arranging his travels absconded with his money. Although he had completed his secondary school education, he continued to live off the charity of others, as the little paid work he received was insufficient. His Pentecostal identity and the relationships it consisted of continued to be central to his ability to survive in economically hard times and influenced the decisions he made about his future and his response to the ongoing challenges in his life. But this identity and these relationships also proved frustrating. Ghana had changed, as had Christian relationships.

Albert lamented what he saw as worsening social and economic changes in Ghana and the increasing lack of support church members provided:

> Everybody is complaining in Ghana. Nobody calls you to find out whether you are sick or whether you have travelled. Ghana today is not like the Ghana I used to know. Today is different. People used to sacrifice themselves to help you, but not anymore.

His employer at the time continually sought to take advantage of him. Albert was working for a retired civil servant he called Daddy. The father of a CoP member, Daddy was the West Africa representative of a British company that sold computer accessories and printed exams for the West African Examinations Council in Ghana. Through this new job, Albert had now travelled to Abuja, Nigeria, and helped broker deals with representatives from other West African countries. However, he was also expected to clean Daddy's house, wash his car, and run his errands. He was fairly certain that Daddy was pocketing a share of his monthly income that came from the British-based company. "He realizes that I have nowhere to go. He is taking advantage of me," Albert complained to me at the time. Daddy was not the only one who Albert felt had cheated him out of a future. Prophet Alfred, on whom Albert had depended for spiritual protection and sometimes emotional and financial support, was also no longer a benevolent character in Albert's life. Prophet Alfred had reneged on his promise to compensate Albert for his help in the prayer centre's activities and had misguided Albert on several occasions so as to prevent him from leaving his service.

Albert's destiny was intrinsically linked to his relationship with his employer, who did not pay him his promised salary, to other church members who were less helpful, to the church prophet whom he assisted in prayer but whom he felt was more interested in controlling him than helping him, to his mother whom he continued to support financially every now and then, and to others who provided him with advice about his future education and business plans. Yet his relationships with them had changed. His plans for the future had also changed. He no longer dreamed of leaving Ghana, but wanted to become a Christian motivational speaker and start a Christian chat show on television. He had started his own non-governmental organization (NGO) and was giving motivational lectures to youth groups on a church circuit. However, when I asked him for clarification about his destiny to travel overseas, he paused for a moment and replied:

> Travelling is not everything. You need to find a place to stay when you get there. People from overseas are complaining that they are not getting jobs. What you do today, you will reap the outcome tomorrow. If you have the opportunity to travel, and you get the visa to travel, and you overstay, find ways and means to stay illegally, the future will fight against you. Now I have discovered that this is not my ultimate purpose in life. I can make my life here and build myself here.

Albert had come to realize that he would have to do the right thing in order to bring his present circumstances in alignment with his new future. What might have seemed good for him once may not be good for him now. I asked him, "But what about your vision and the prophecies from others?" This is what he said to me:

> When you are young, you see things differently. I am beginning to understand certain things, now that I have grown older. I am just beginning to get certain things. There is an Akan proverb that goes like this: "When a child sees a crab's eye, he thinks it is a stick." If you tell someone else that

your vision in life is to travel, others will think you are a fool! Even if I had
that vision, did others achieve something from this? You need to criticize
the vision and challenge yourself. Travel is not unachievable, but it is not
a good vision. It is a selfish vision to just consume, consume, consume. We
need to have bigger visions that will also help others. None of the successful people I know had an easy start.

For Albert, a university education was a more important ambition
than migration, one that could, according to him, fashion him into a
certain kind of Pentecostal subject who could then go on to change his
community. Yet, due to his financial circumstances, this ambition was
still out of his reach. In 2013, Albert made a move that startled me. He
left CoP. The church, according to him, had become too focused on filling the financial coffers of the church leadership and had lost its traditional bearings. He cited several personal reasons for his resignation.
However, one stood out. In 2012, CoP made a daring initiative: it decided to no longer require women in all its churches, not just in the PI-
WCs, to wear the headscarf during prayer services. It was not biblical,
the church leaders argued. They provided a formal statement to church
members, gave interviews to the media, and even published a book in
order to justify what became a controversial decision. CoP was changing with the times and with the changing generation. What seemed an
insignificant change to me had a significant impact on many of its
members. Some committed church members felt that this decision be-
trayed a sense of history and biblical tradition that distinguished CoP
from the rest of the Pentecostal and charismatic churches. CoP was one
of the oldest Pentecostal churches in Ghana, and to many, the rule for-
bidding women to leave their hair uncovered in church was not only
biblical but also one of the few remaining cultural symbols that separated CoP from the rest. "There is almost nothing distinguishing CoP
from the charismatics now," said Albert with a heavy sigh of despair.

An understanding of Pentecostal transformation as ethical practice
does not aim to define Christianity as merely characterized by the application of specific rules or values. Instead, it is a recognition of the
problem of continuity that constantly faces Christians when discerning
what to do and how to act in changing and sometimes radically new
situations and circumstances. The actions of Christians are not without
cultural criteria for how change and continuity should be conceptualized or for the forms in which they ought to be mediated. However,
even as rupture is important for born-again conversion and the

cultivation of an inner self central for its maintenance, these criteria can only be understood within social circumstances that interrupt and alongside the creative and unexpected ways that Christianity becomes an object that is known.

In retrospect, Albert was able to look back at his own past and decide on how to conceive of his future and remake himself, given his personal circumstances, changing ambitions, and his born-again identity in Ghana. Older and wiser than when I met him in 2003, Albert told me that he was able to leave certain idealistic expectations of travel behind and focus on making a life for himself in Ghana. He was more knowledgeable about the world and about how to make his Pentecostal identity benefit others. If Pentecostal transformation brings with it uncertainty, certainty is only achieved at a point in time that is captured by the anthropologist. Reflection is ongoing and requires the ability to continually reassess one's life and changing life situations, and to make judgments – sometimes between incommensurable values – about how to best move forward. Otherwise, as Albert said, the future will fight against you.

Notes

Introduction

1 The anthropology of Christianity has focused on what Christians them-selves say and do, and has provided a theoretical commitment to the comparative and cross-cultural study of Christianity (Robbins 2003a; Cannell 2006a; Bialecki, Haynes, and Robbins 2008). One critique is its focus on Protestant and Pentecostal formations and neglect of Christian Orthodox churches (Hann 2007) and Catholicism (Napolitano and Norget 2009). More specifically, scholars have particularly focused on the re-pressed presence of Christianity within anthropology (Cannell 2006a), on Christian belief (Catholicism) as a method in the work of anthropologists such as V. Turner and E.E. Evans-Pritchard (Engelke 2002), and on the characterization of Christians as "repugnant cultural others," due to their simultaneous proximity to and distance from the seemingly secular world of anthropologists (Harding 2000).

2 Ghanaian Pentecostals use certain words and phrases when describing Christian rupture: they present it as a salvation that is "complete," an "accomplished" or "finished" work of God, a "dramatic transformation," a "total change," and a "total break" or a "cutting off" from the past.

3 According to the 2000 Ghana population census, 69 per cent of all Ghana-ians considered themselves Christian.

4 Some of the first Pentecostal missionaries in West Africa were a group of African Americans connected with the Azusa Street Revival in Los Angeles who went to Liberia in 1907 (Anderson 2004, 115). David Maxwell (2006) notes that the American Assemblies of God, a church in Springfield, Missouri, had been "operating in sub-Saharan Africa since the 1910s" (ibid., 386). It was in the early 1930s that Pentecostal church missionaries

from the American Assemblies of God entered Ghana, followed by
missionaries from the Apostolic Church, UK, in 1937. The latter grew out
of the Welsh Revival of 1904, and also appeared in Nigeria around the
same time as in Ghana (Peel 1968, 105). The three major Pentecostal
denominations in present-day Ghana that emerged out of the earlier
missionary efforts of the Apostolic Church, UK, are The Church of
Pentecost, the Apostolic Church of Ghana, and the Christ Apostolic
Church.

5 In reply to a district commissioner of the Gold Coast, who asked him why
   he was not building schools or digging wells, McKeown supposedly
   replied, "What the Africans need is not education: they need rivers of
   living water flowing out of their hearts and lives" (Leonard 1989, 76).

6 An exception to this rule is Rev Dr Mensa Otabil and his International
   Central Gospel Church (Gifford 2004). Unlike leaders from many other
   charismatic churches in Ghana, Otabil promotes a "rationalist critique of
   the spiritualizing tendencies in much contemporary African Pentecostalism" (de Witte 2012, 152).

7 Webb Keane (2007) and Matthew Engelke (2007) point out that (1) studies
   in linguistics, semiotics, and pragmatics have shown that signs are
   intrinsically material phenomena and that one cannot properly understand
   them without taking into account their materiality; and (2) this conclusion
   leads to a shift in the metaphysical assumptions of semiotics itself. Indeed,
   semiotics was for a long time dominated by a Saussurean paradigm that
   tended to disqualify the material aspects of sign systems as secondary to
   what was seen as the more fundamental and essential abstract rules and
   mental concepts governing sign systems. The paradigm has more recently
   shifted to one that acknowledges the crucial, determinant importance of
   the materiality of sign systems.

8 In the 1990s, more attention was dedicated to the contexts and conditions
   of missionary encounters with Africans. Through a historical analysis of
   the religious ideologies and practices of white missionaries in South
   Africa, scholars John and Jean Comaroff underlined the former's efforts to
   colonize the consciousness of the latter through the symbolic and hege-
   monic appropriation of (Tswana) signs and practice (Comaroff and
   Comaroff 1991, 1997). These latter works were deeply influential in that
   they provided a historical voice to missionary archives and nuanced
   cultural encounters. Yet they have also been criticized for ignoring the
   intricacies of how a Christian narrative could be appropriated by local
   parties differently over time (see Peel 1995, 2003; Maxwell 1999; Marshall
   2009).

9 The idea of rupture as a radical break from the past is problematized by scholars of Christianity in Africa, who underline the importance of understanding the historical continuities between earlier Christian movements and the more recent Pentecostal-charismatic churches (Maxwell 1999; Peel 2003).

10 Early studies by Wendy James and Douglas H. Johnson (1988) suggested that anthropologists should consider what makes Christianity vernacular in African society. A vernacular Christianity involves an understanding of the syncretistic process of incorporating indigenous cultural elements into Christianity, as well as the concomitant African appropriation of Christian elements. If Christianity is always syncretistic in its historical formation, anthropologists were advised to remain sensitive to the structural attempts of believers to construct "authenticity" via interconnected processes of anti-syncretism (Shaw and Stewart 1994).

11 Drawing on Badiou's ideas around the "event" and the "divided subject," Robbins (2010a, 647) suggests that, just as Paul's relation to the Jewish law and his Jewish past is not a simple one, the transformed Pentecostal subject may "have to struggle against the particularities defined by the situations in which it lives and against its own investment in them."

12 The work of anthropologists associated with the Manchester School has helped evaluate social change as process and advocated for a situational analysis approach that studies events over a longer, extended time dimension and not merely as a single case (Mitchell 1956; Turner 1957, 1968; Van Velsen 1967; Kapferer 2005, 2010).

13 While Michael Lambek (2000) and Saba Mahmood (2005) both seek to better understand religious subjectivity by drawing on an Aristotelian virtue ethics, they do so in different ways, raising important differences between a Foucauldian virtue ethics and a first-person virtue ethics (Mattingly 2012).

14 Foucault's idea of ethics as reflection refers to the work one performs as a process of becoming (*ascesis*). It is this understanding of philosophical labour that I ultimately draw from (see Dave 2012, 7).

15 In writing about "ethics," I consider "morality" and "ethics" as part of the same ethical practice my interlocutors are involved in. For Jarrett Zigon (2011), while morality is the embodied knowledge that subtly influences our actions in life, the ethical is concerned with reflective moments that cause us to stop and take stock of things. Zigon's use of ethics, what he calls a "moral breakdown," is felt when the implicit moral assumptions associated with institutional and public discourse over what is a good or right action are questioned and become cause for concern and conscious

reflection. By bringing both morality and ethics into dialogue with one another, a study of the "ethical practices" of Ghanaian Pentecostals in CoP focuses the ethnographic attention on the values that are shared within the church, as well as on the moments of reflection and dilemmas in the lives of individual church leaders and members.

16 The "why" question runs deep in the Africanist literature on witchcraft and the occult. As Edward E. Evans-Pritchard (1937) pointed out, just because the Azande believed in witchcraft did not mean that they did not understand how the world actually worked. Rather, witchcraft helped them to address the inconsistencies between "what" actually happened (the causal reasons for the event) and "why" it happened to a particular person at a specific time and place (the variable conditions of an event). These extra-causal factors continue to be important in understanding the presence of witchcraft and magic in post-independence Africa. My use of the "why" question acknowledges that theories about a plurality of invisible, disembodied spirits are uncontroversial for most Ghanaians and should not be viewed merely as a response to global and economic events or to the hidden inequalities produced by the neoliberal market economy.

17 The postcolonial period in Africa has been characterized by widespread political and economic crises and the continuing prevalence of "witch-craft" and "occult practices" that raised doubts concerning the Western character of modernity (Comaroff and Comaroff 1999, 2000; Geschiere 1997). This characterization underscored the problems associated with the singular or linear assumptions of historical time associated with modernity.

18 Margaret Peil (1995) estimates that ten to twenty per cent of the Ghanaian population lived abroad in the 1980s and 1990s. Two million people left Ghana between 1974 and 1981, of which the majority were from southern Ghana (van Hear 1998, 74; Koser 2003). Emigrating was seen as a way to survive the political and economic turmoil of the 1970s, a situation that was later exacerbated by the structural adjustment programs of the 1980s. This was a migration mainly of single individuals – mostly men, but also women – rather than of households (van Hear 1998, 76). At present, the largest Ghanaian communities are to be found in European cities such as London, Hamburg, and Amsterdam.

Chapter One

1 Taken from *Ai Weiwei: According to What?* Exhibition, Art Gallery of Ontario, 17 August to 27 October 2013.

2 A focus on historical continuity within African Christianity is in line with attempts to make historical connections between the earlier transnational Pentecostal movements and the more recent charismatic churches (Maxwell 2006).

3 At the beginning of the twentieth century, after an experience of "speaking in tongues," a small group meeting at a Bible school in Topeka, Kansas, grew more interested in the miracles of Pentecost as described in the Bible (Acts 2:1–4). This chapter in the Bible describes how the disciples of Jesus were filled with the Holy Spirit and bestowed with power from above – the spiritual gifts of speaking and interpreting unknown languages, prophecy, and healing. These gifts of the spirit allowed Pentecostal believers to compare themselves to the founders of the early Christian church. Led by Methodist healer Charles Fox Parnham, the group initiated a search for a more expansive spiritual experience. William J. Seymour, who then took this message on, started preaching about the power of Pentecost and sparked another religious revival in 1906, which later became famously known as the Azusa Street Revival.

4 These churches have been variously described as "independent African Pentecostal churches" (Hollenweger 1972, 151), "prophet-healing church-es" (Turner 1979, 97), and "Spirit-type churches" (Daneel 1974, 285).

5 Many prophets and anti-witchcraft shrines such as the Tigare cult com-peted for members and provided similar spiritual services, including producing pregnancy in barren women, prosperity, protection against witchcraft and poison, protection against thieves, detection of adultery, and curing sickness.

6 In Ghana, these independent churches appear in the literature as "Spiritual churches." They belong to the same category type as Nigeria's Aladura ("praying churches") and South Africa's Zionist churches.

7 Maxwell (2006) illustrates how an international Pentecostal community from Europe and America was already participating in transnational and institutional networks of the print media and of people as early as the beginning of the twentieth century.

8 The Apostolic Church, UK, grew out of the Welsh Revival of 1904 and also appeared in Nigeria around the same time as in the Gold Coast (Peel 1968, 105).

9 The story goes that a member of the Faith Tabernacle church from a small town in eastern Ghana called Asamankese had gone to the bush to pray for the recovery of his sick baby (*kokoase mpaebo* or praying under cocoa trees). During these prayers, he experienced the baptism of the Holy Spirit. The news of this outpouring of the Spirit quickly spread to the church

leader, Peter Anim. Within a short time, a revival that lasted almost two weeks had been launched in Asamankese. These revival movements provided a rupture from the previous Christian relationships Anim and his followers had with the mainline churches and Clarke's American-based group. They also provided continuities with a Pentecostal emphasis on the emotionally charged experience of the baptism of the Holy Spirit and on the search for divine power.

10 With the exception of the Wesleyan Methodists, whose main aim was to "implant Christianity and civilization," all the other early missionary churches employed the "school as the nucleus of the Church" approach to evangelism. For a more detailed examination of the missionary activities and organizational contradictions of the Basel Mission, see Jon Miller's (2003) book *Missionary Zeal and Institutional Control: Organizational Contradictions in the Basel Mission on the Gold Coast, 1828–1917*. Scholars such as T.O. Beidelman (1982) and J.F.A. Ajayi (1965) have described how Africans elsewhere used the early missions for their own social and economic advantage.

11 Divine healing was a common feature of the radical wing of the holiness movement in the late nineteenth century, a movement that historians see as the precursor of early Pentecostalism (Baer 2001, 735–6). Some of the earlier proponents of divine healing "insisted that Christ secured full bodily healing through his atoning sacrifice on the cross and that embracing this form of healing entailed rejecting doctors and medicine" (ibid., 736). A similar controversy with the apostolic missionaries in Nigeria broke out around the same time, between 1939 and 1940. George Perfect, the superintendent of the Apostolic Church, admitted to taking daily doses of quinine for protection against malaria. This led to a break-away by D.O. Odubanjo, the leading African apostle of the Apostolic Church, Lagos Area (see Larbi 2001, 11; Peel 1968, 112).

12 In his famous essay "The Social Psychology of the World Religions," Max Weber (1958, 287) writes that as much as ultimate values and their corresponding subject positions are "*religiously* determined," they also come to be affirmed in their "*ethical* rationalization."

13 Discussions concerning Pentecostal agency arise from within two main factions of the CoP: the church intellectuals and leaders, who focus on doctrine and theology; and ordinary members and prophets, who seek empowerment from the Holy Spirit. These moral debates within the church are based on organizational and sociological lines, closely resembling the distinctions Peel (1968, 287–8) has made between the two branches of the Nigerian Aladura churches: the Christ Apostolic Church

(CAC) and Cherubim and Seraphim (C&S). Peel describes how, while both CAC and C&S were interested in the benefits of spiritual power, they emphasized different ways in which to obtain it. Similarly, while some within CoP emphasize a more doctrinal form of faith, others are after a spiritual power that is found in the prayers of the prophet. As chairman of CoP, McKeown encountered a series of dilemmas regarding the appropriate forms that Pentecostal practice should take in church. His main adversaries were the prophets of the church.

14 The "Latter Rain Movement" began in a remote part of Saskatchewan, Canada, in 1948. Their teachings and practices of praying in tongues, prophecy, holy laughter, healings, and all-night prayer meetings spread to the United States and other parts of the world. Practices that the Apostolic Church, UK, and other mainline Pentecostal denominations at the time disapproved of and later rejected included the imparting of specific gifts of the spirit by the "laying on of hands" and the personalized prophecies made to individuals in order to transform their lives (Synan 1997, 212–13).

15 An additional feature that emerged out of the SU, from 1973 on, was the Prayer Warriors Ministry (PWM), which started out in the guise of prayer retreats organized by the town fellowships. An example of a book published by the SU was *Delivered from the Powers of Darkness* by Nigerian preacher Emmanuel Eni (1987). A video, which was later published as a book and attracted a lot of attention, was the testimony of Victoria Eto, a Nigerian who studied in Ghana: *How I Served Satan until Jesus Christ Delivered Me: A True Account of My Twenty-One Years Experience as an Agent of Darkness and of My Deliverance by the Power Arm of God in Jesus Christ* (Eto, 1981).

16 During this time, there was a backlog of "A-level" students who were waiting to enter university as a result of the new National Service scheme. Many students had to wait between one to two years before being admitted to university; it was also difficult to get jobs. This situation may have freed up time for these young people to spend with the charismatic ministries.

17 As Meyer (2004a, 453) writes, the charismatic churches of the 1990s "are characterized by a distinct form, in terms of scale, organization, theology, and religious practice, and this distinct form warrants investigators seeing them as a new phenomenon."

18 This response by mainline churches, coined the "Pentecostalisation of Christianity" in Ghana, has become a topic of scholarly interest (Omenyo 2002, 2005).

19 Some of the related questions Divine Kumah (2000, 1) asks are "Why is Ghana so blessed in human and natural resources, yet our people so

poor?," "Why do we produce such great brains yet have to depend on foreigners to make major decisions that affect us, especially in the areas of finance and economics?," and "Why have we become beggars?"

20 While modernity has been described as "multiple" and as an extremely vague and slippery concept (Cooper 2005), its underlying moral premises continue to have purchase.

21 In a national survey by the Ghana Evangelism Committee (1993), conducted between 1985 and 1989, CoP had the highest "average church attendance" ratings among all the churches in Ghana (ibid., 16). Also, when it came to "church planting statistics," CoP again ranked the highest, having established 1,594 new churches in the ten-year period before the survey, followed by the Presbyterian and Methodist churches, which established 499 and 460 new churches, respectively, within that same period (ibid., 24).

Chapter Two

1 Apostle Koduah pointed to the 1980s as a time when more Ghanaians became involved in traditional religion. This, he explained, was due to the changing political scene following Flight Lieutenant Jerry Rawlings's rise to power. President Rawlings, for the next ten years, consciously set out to promote African traditional religion, with the aim of teaching Ghanaians about their traditional religious past. This and other governmental interventions attempted to curtail the rising Christian activity in the country.

2 Onyinah's message is that, once born again, the believer cannot be possessed by demons and the curse of the family chain is broken (Onyinah 1994, 52; 1995, 38). In making a distinction between "Christianity" and "culture," Onyinah (1995) also distinguishes between the work of the Holy Spirit in Christianity and the work of other spiritual powers that include the use of "divination, sorcery, spiritism, or fetishism" (ibid., 87). For Onyinah, spiritual power outside the Holy Spirit and "culture" creates "extremes" in Pentecostal Christianity, and too much emphasis on prophets, miracles, healing, and deliverance creates "weak Christians" (ibid., 87–100).

3 The traditional concept of sin as *mmusu* in Ghanaian (Akan) epistemology is about the ongoing relationships Ghanaians have with their ancestral past, and different from ordinary evil or what is seen as bad (*bone*). While every *mmusu* (evil) is *bone* (bad), not everything that is *bone* (bad) is *mmusu* (evil). Sin understood as *mmusu* relates to the Akan idea that human beings are fundamentally linked with various other components that make up the universe, including other individuals, the ancestors, the divinities

of natural elements, other spirit-beings, and the Supreme Being (cf. Atiemo 1995). *Mmusu*, therefore, is more than simply bad actions and its results, as it has a spiritual component known to have the ability to remove any protective powers that the person already possesses and expose him or her to forces of evil (Atiemo 1995: 23).

4 In his work amongst the Urapmin of Papua New Guinea, Robbins (2004a, 218) similarly describes how Christian and "traditional" moralities point to different ways of constructing the person, with Christianity focusing on the "inside"' as a place of moral evaluation.

5 Keane's work aims to bring together the ways in which the material and symbolic were previously seen as separate in social theory. Through his idea of "semiotic ideologies," he reflects on "what signs are and how they function in the world" (Keane 2003, 419). Keane (2007) has shown how the Protestant quest for certainty unfolds through moments of uncertainty and debates that aim at distinguishing where human freedom can or cannot be located. For example, according to Sumbanese Protestant converts, sincerity in speech and prayer is a condition identified with a state of interiority and involves concrete practices such as affirming one's faith in public church ceremonies and praying with one's eyes closed.

6 The negative objectification of matter is what Matthew Engelke calls "thingification," which is "a move toward a particular understanding of that relationship in which the object in question becomes recognized as problematic," and is also "a process through which the object in question is divested of immateriality" (2007, 27). While the Friday Apostolics of Zimbabwe do not use the Bible, it is acceptable and common stance to be possessed by the Holy Spirit, use pebbles, blessed water, and blessed honey in prayer and healing.

7 While I consider a phenomenological approach to morality and ethics important (Zigon 2009), I also find that it complements a more structuralist intervention, which takes values as a central organizing principle (Robbins 2009b).

Chapter Three

1 In these sermons, all three components of Austin's ([1962] 1975) speech acts – (1) locutionary acts, (2) illocutionary acts, and (3) perlocutionary acts – are apparent. Locutionary acts consist of sermons as descriptions or reports that can be verified as true or false, for example, the poor state of the Ghanaian economy or the shared hardships that economic migrants in London face. Illocutionary acts bring the listener into a new state of affairs,

for example through a renunciation of their will or the renewing of their commitment and acceptance of Jesus again. Perlocutionary acts persuade listeners to take on new orientations in their lives or to become committed to act in new ways.

2 While some members of the church have been formally called to the full-time office of "prophet" and given a stipend, appointments to such evangelistic and prophetic offices were discouraged between 1962 and 1975 by CoP leaders (Onyinah 2002, 211). The strict position of the church with relation to prophets was relaxed somewhat when Prophet M.K. Yeboah became chairman of CoP in 1988. The term "prophet" has become widely used within the local assemblies to refer to ordinary members of the church (sometimes elders or deacons) who believe that they have been called into a prophetic ministry. There was a resurgence of the position of prophet within the church as the prayer camp phenomenon proliferated in the 1980s and 1990s. While CoP had thirty-eight recognized prayer camps in 1990, by the end of 1999, there were fifty-six.

3 Prayer centres operate for several hours at a time on certain days of the week. People normally return home the same day after these prayer sessions. Prayer camps, on the other hand, are locations that provide accommodation, allowing for a longer duration of prayer. Many people attending these prayer camps stay for weeks, sometimes months, praying for the solution to their problems while "waiting on God."

4 In 2003–2004, while I was doing fieldwork in Ghana, Ghana Airways, the state-owned airline, was in severe financial difficulties and faced strong public pressure to close down. The directors decided to fly in a famous London-based Ghanaian Pentecostal evangelist to conduct special deliverance prayers with the airline staff. These prayers were publicized in the media, and the company's financial difficulties became publicly linked with spiritual causes and the possible effects of witchcraft. On a national level, this set the stage for a transformation and the new start hoped for by the management of Ghana Airways. While Ghana Airways continued to suffer from financial difficulties, the prayer performance that involved both the direct participation of the airline staff and the general interest of the public provided the enactment of transformation.

Chapter Four

1 Earlier colonial scholars, such as R.S. Rattray (1927) and H.W. Debrunner (1959), had slightly differing explanations and acknowledged the ambiguous nature of some of the terms used.

2　For instance, deliverance was a problematic practice for some CoP leaders, who believed that the Christian self, once born again and baptized in the Holy Spirit, cannot be possessed by demons and that the curse of the family chain is broken (see also Onyinah 1994, 1995).

3　In studying ideas of social interaction and relatedness within different cultural settings, anthropologists have taken indigenous ideas of person-hood seriously in rethinking the pervasive assumptions of Western individualism in the study of others (Marriot 1976; Strathern 1988). They have helped us to realize that a Euro-American world view, which includes ideas of dualism between mind–body, individual–society, and subject–object, still persists in thinking about the relationships and transactions between people. In response, they have suggested that we temporarily suspend such Western-inflected dichotomies and allow our analysis to arise from within the cultural milieus of our interlocutors, from the ideas they have of themselves and their social lives. Rather than conceptualizing people as simply autonomous and self-sufficient "individuals," anthropologists have argued that persons in Africa, Melanesia, and India are also "dividuals" or divisible, taking other cultural ideas of personhood and volitional action seriously. Similarly, ideas around the convergence and the boundaries of spirit and flesh invoked in conversations among Pentecostals in Ghana, therefore, cannot be understood through an atomic Christian individualist framework alone.

Chapter Five

1　More recent literature has helped shift the focus of kinship towards the processes of negotiation in the widespread use and application of idioms of relatedness (Carsten 2000). For example, Janet Carsten's (ibid.) use of the concept of "relatedness" rather than "kinship" moves away from a genealogical model to conceiving kinship as constructed in practice. As illuminating as a social constructionist perspective can be, it also has the potential to exaggerate the broadness of kinship relations and their manipulability, as well as to underemphasize the continuity of genealogical thinking and the practice of compartmentalization (Bamford and Leach 2009).

2　While the Akan are known to have a matrilineal kinship system, other ethnic groups such as the Guan, the Krobo, and the Ewe, for example, display a patrilineal descent system. In matrilineal Akan societies, a child belongs to its matrilineage, and property is transferred from a mother's brother to a sister's son (*wofaase*).

3 This magic mirror is commonly known to come from the north of Ghana and other states in West Africa and is used by diviners to look into someone's life.

4 The Pentecostal churches in Africa are more popular among the relatively powerless, including young educated people and middle-aged women, who are attempting to move up the economic ladder through business or trade (Meyer 1998a; Maxwell 1998).

5 The Church of Pentecost resembles a patrilineal descent group, where God the Father, God the Son, and God the Holy Spirit all take on male forms and characteristics. Also men hold all the important offices such as elder, presiding elder, pastor, and apostle (see Introduction).

6 He was its chief representative in its political and legal relations with other lineages and with the community (Fortes 1950, 256).

7 This experience is shared by many African migrants in Europe (McGregor 2007; Nieswand 2005; Akyeampong 2000). It is linked to what B. Nieswand has called the "paradox of migration," whereby Ghanaian migrants are "living in two systems with contradictory attributions of prestige at the same time, which is deeply rooted in the process of migration itself" (2005, 255).

8 Trust, as a concept, has been largely ignored in the literature on Pentecostalism (for an exception, see Englund 2007a).

9 According to Jane Parish (2000, 2001), a defining feature of witchcraft practices in Ghana today is the conflict between two moral economies: global market commodification and local reproductive relations. The moral economies of traditional witchcraft, however, cannot always directly explain the mysteries of a new capitalist economy that amasses material wealth from distant places in exactly the same way (Sanders 2003b); neither does it suffice to limit witchcraft to group dynamics or "imagined kin-groups" (Englund 2007b, 297).

Chapter Six

1 Historically, "Africa" has had a special place in the moral imagination of travel writers, colonial administrators, missionaries, and anthropologists – as a dark continent in need of saving and further investigation. A more contemporary autochthonous African identity has been described as closely associated with "narratives of victimhood and with an interpretation of history as sorcery – that Africans have been accidentalized and mutilated by historical processes over which they have had little or no control" (Quayson 2002, 585; Mbembe 2002).

2 I do not want to ignore the influential role of African Pentecostal pastors among the diaspora community in London. Nor do I want to deny that accusations of witchcraft can realistically lead to child abuse and even death. Instead, I want to shift the mode of analysis to a mode that is less orientalizing, moving from one, based on examples, that summarizes the experiences of many to one that examines the diversity and complexity of the few in their struggle to build relationships of trust and redefine London for themselves.

3 As Sally F. Moore (1999, 306) wrote in her response to the Comaroffs' lecture on occult economies, "[t]he idea that the contemporary configuration of these phenomena is attributable to present forms of capitalism is to turn contemporaneity into cause, general context into particular explanation." Ruth Marshall's (2009) work on Nigerian Pentecostalism is also a useful critique of a secular, Western frame of analysis that does not take religion seriously as a political force. She criticizes the tendency of certain works in anthropology (including works by the Comaroffs) to reduce value to its objectified material and functional dimensions or collapse the value of acts into the value of productive labour (see also Coleman 2011b).

4 This does not mean that there was no difference between living in London and living in Ghana. Many of my interlocutors differentiated life in London from life in Ghana and simply "living" from "living well."

Chapter Seven

1 Arjun Appadurai's work on globalization has opened up a space for theorizing about the shifting interconnections between "local" and "global" and for indexing the work of the *imagination as a social practice* (1996, 31). Appadurai reminds us that the world today is rhizomic, largely characterized by displaced and deterritorialized populations and by the disjunctive role that mass media plays in these movements across borders. Electronic mass mediation and transnational mobilizations are doing something different through the formation of various new publics that operate at different scales. There is, however, an unresolved tension in Appadurai's work between universal claims of disjuncture and the particular contexts in and by which they take place. With regards to globalization, what is important to understand is how people make themselves both local and global in specific ways (Moore 2004, 81; Heyman and Campbell 2009, 135). The "global" and "local" therefore shifts according to the interpretive coinage it provides for different authorities in specific locales (Cunningham 1999).

2 The Christian idea of an expanding macrocosm provides a universalist way of participating in, and engaging with, the world; at the same time it is still tied to a bounded microcosm of identity (Horton 1960).

3 Harri Englund (2002a, 2002b) has described how inclusion and exclusion are also facets of transnational Pentecostal networks in urban Malawi. Not only do these networks empower and provide opportunities; they also create new hierarchies. Rijk van Dijk (1997, 2002a, 2002b), in looking at Pentecostal networks that stretch over Europe and Africa, concludes that these networks cannot be understood as pursuing a single trajectory. He subscribes to an "anthropology of transnationalism" that focuses more on opportunities than constraints, celebrating transnationalism as liberating and as freeing the person from constraints and relations to others (van Dijk 2001, 218).

4 These religious forms of post-national membership are usually associated with the move towards cosmopolitan citizenship and the notion of citizenship based on personhood (Delanty 2009, 127–31).

5 Marcel Mauss (1990) famously taught us that within gift economies, objects are seen to partake of something of the personality of the giver. While Mauss shows us that there is no such thing as a free or pure gift, Jonathan Parry (1986) suggests that Christianity's universalistic conception of disinterested giving, and its devaluation of the material world by a transcendental other, provides the ethical reasoning for the universalized idea of the "pure gift."

6 Church leaders realized that these English assemblies were "in content and even outlook functioning just as any other local assembly of the Church of Pentecost, the only difference being the use of English as the lingua franca" (Apostle Opoku Onyinah quoted in Larbi 2001, 202). In 1993, these English assemblies merged into one assembly in Accra, the Accra International Worship Centre.

7 Margaret Peil (1995) argues that migration became a common household strategy in Ghana and estimates that around 10 to 20 per cent of Ghanaian nationals were living abroad in the 1980s and early 1990s. Migration to other countries in West Africa, especially Nigeria, became a survival strategy for individuals and families, helping them cope with difficult economic conditions. However, it is estimated that of the two million people deported from Nigeria in 1983, between 900,000 and 1.2 million were Ghanaians. Since the 1990s, large numbers of Ghanaians have moved to major cities such as London, Amsterdam, Hamburg, and New York.

8 In the Ghanaian context, gender is a strong determinant of migration; men have a higher propensity to migrate, and women tend to migrate in order to join their husbands.

9 These churches are viewed as bringing an effective compensatory religious status to black minority groups, providing them with a moral code and a community environment to support them in alien surroundings (see ter Haar 1998; Mercer, Page, and Evans 2008, 59–60; Hunt and Lightly 2001, 105–6; Kalilombe 1997, 317).

10 This link between Israel as the chosen nation and Christian citizenship is not uncommon (O'Neill 2010, 7).

11 Marcus Banks (1996, 100) notes that an important issue that was ignored in the 1970s in the United Kingdom, and that remains unresolved today, is the importance of the role skin colour plays in relations among minority groups and between minority groups and the host "white" population. A demand for churches that were more likely to express the interests and sentiments of the West African community in London increased when early immigrants were not treated very warmly by native congregations of the already established denominations. The more reserved forms of "British" worship also contributed to this demand (Roswith Gerloff, *A Plea for British Black Theologies* [Frankfurt: Peter Lang, 1992], 11–12, quoted in Hunt and Lightly 2001, 106).

12 Dombrowski goes on to say that "this anti-Cultural stance is clear in two aspects of Pentecostal practice – in speaking in tongues and other 'gifts of faith,' and in absolute insistence on a transcendent notion of divinity" (2001, 123).

13 In writing about the importance of "messianic time" for our understanding of how ethno-linguistic "nations"' are formed within nation-states, Patrick Eisenlohr (2006, 242) points out that the emphasis here is not on a linear idea of progress but on the continuing presence of heroic and virtuous ancestors.

14 According to Peggy Levitt (2003), scholars of transnational migration have until recently ignored how religion influences the processes of transnational migration. For example, the ties between migrant communities and the home country have been studied with a focus on economic issues, remittances, political organization, and identity formation related to ethnicity (Smith and Guarnizo, 1998). Much of the work on transnationalism has highlighted the ways in which migrants relate to their home countries through their political identities and their cultural forms of practice, as well as through their participation in labour markets (Basch, Schiller, and Blanc 1994; Schiller and Fouron 2001). There have been an increasing number of works that acknowledge the religious motives and identities of transnational actors and their attempts to resolve the paradox of migration (Corten and Marshall-Fratani 2001; Clarke 2004; Maxwell

2006; Geordas 2007; Hüwelmeier and Krause 2010). The religious lives of African migrants in Europe and America have been a focus of few studies (Kalilombe 1997; van Dijk 1997, 2004; ter Haar 1998; Adogame and Weissköppel 2005; H. Harris 2006; Pandolfo 2007; Olupona and Gemigani 2007).

15 The word "diaspora" evokes a form of dispersion from a central location or place of origin that results in scattering over various locations (often times more than two countries). "Diaspora" is a category no longer confined to the description of the forced dispersal of certain ethnic groups such as the Jews, Armenians, and Greeks from their "homeland," but has come to also include others migrants who consciously self-identify or have become identified by academics as "diasporas" (Clifford 1994). Where an anthropology of "the transnational" might be inadequate in analysing the relationship between people and places (Wilding 2007, 343), "diaspora" becomes useful for understanding the work of the imagination and social memory and for underlying notions of "home" and "nation" as connected and also beyond these movements across space (Ramji 2006; Horst 2007).

Bibliography

Adogame, A., and C. Weissköppel, eds. 2005. *Religion in the Context of African Migration*. Bayreuth African Studies Series 75. Bayreuth, DE: Breitinger.

Adubufuor, S.B. 1994. "Evangelical Para-Church Movements in Ghanaian Christianity: c1950 to 1990's." PhD diss., University of Edinburgh.

Ahmed, S. 2004. *The Cultural Politics of Emotion*. New York: Routledge.

Ajayi, J.F.A. 1965. *Christian Missions in Nigeria, 1841–1891: The Making of a New Elite*. London: Longmans.

Akyeampong, E.K. 2000. "Africans in the Diaspora: The Diaspora and Africa." *African Affairs* 99 (395): 183–215. http://dx.doi.org/10.1093/afraf/99.395.183.

Anderson, A. 2004. *An Introduction to Pentecostalism: Global Charismatic Christianity*. Cambridge: Cambridge University Press.

Appadurai, A. 1996. *Modernity at Large: Cultural Dimensions of Globalization*. Minneapolis: University of Minnesota Press.

Appiah, K.A. 1992. *In My Father's House: Africa in the Philosophy of Culture*. Oxford: Oxford University Press.

Arens, W., and I. Karp. 1989. "Introduction." In *Creativity of Power*, edited by W. Arens and I. Karp, xi–xxix. Washington, DC: Smithsonian Institute Press.

Aryeetey, E., J. Harrigan, and M. Nissanke. 2000. *Economic Reforms in Ghana: The Miracle and the Mirage*. Oxford: James Currey.

Asad, T. 2003. *Formations of the Secular: Christianity, Islam, Modernity*. Stanford, CA: Stanford University Press.

Asamoah-Gyadu, J.K. 2005a. *African Charismatics: Current Developments within Independent Indigenous Pentecostalism in Ghana*. Studies of Religion in Africa 27. Leiden: Brill.

– 2005b. "'Christ Is the Answer': What Is the Question? A Ghana Airways Prayer Vigil and Its Implications for Religion, Evil and Public Space." *Journal of Religion in Africa. Religion en Afrique* 35 (1): 93–117. http://dx.doi.org/10.1163/1570066052995834.

Ashforth, A. 1998. "Witchcraft, Violence and Democracy in the New South Africa." *Cahiers d'Études africaines* 38 (150): 505–32. http://dx.doi.org/10.3406/cea.1998.1812.

– 2005. *Witchcraft, Violence and Democracy in South Africa*. Chicago: University of Chicago Press.

Assimeng, J.M. 1995. *Salvation, Social Crisis and the Human Condition*. Inaugural Lecture delivered at the University of Ghana on 27 July 1989. Accra: Ghana University Press.

Atiemo, A.O. 1995. "Mmusuyi and Deliverance: A Study of Conflict and Consensus in the Encounter between African Traditional Religion and Christianity." MA thesis, University of Ghana.

Auslander, M. 1993. "'Open the Wombs!' The Symbolic Politics of Modern Ngoni Witchfinding." In *Modernity and Its Malcontents: Ritual and Power in Postcolonial Africa*, edited by J.L. Comaroff and J. Comaroff, 167–92. Chicago: University of Chicago Press.

Austin, J.L. (1962) 1975. *How to Do Things with Words*. 2nd ed. Cambridge, MA: Harvard University Press. http://dx.doi.org/10.1093/acprof:oso/9780198245537.001.0001.

Badiou, A. 2001. *Ethics: An Essay on the Understanding of Evil*. Translated by Peter Hallward. London: Verso.

– 2006. *Being and Event*. Translated by Oliver Feltham. New York: Continuum.

Baer, J.R. 2001. "Redeemed Bodies: The Functions of Divine Healing in Incipient Pentecostalism." *Church History* 70 (04): 735–71. http://dx.doi.org/10.2307/3654547.

Baëta, C.G. 1962. *Prophetism in Ghana: A Study of Some "Spiritual" Churches*. London: S.C.M. Press.

Bamford, S., and J. Leach. 2009. "Introduction: Pedigrees of Knowledge." In *Kinship and Beyond: The Genealogical Model Reconsidered*, edited by S. Bamford and J. Leach, 1–23. New York: Bergahn Books.

Banks, M. 1996. *Ethnicity: Anthropological Constructions*. London: Routledge. http://dx.doi.org/10.4324/9780203417935.

Barber, D.C. 2011. *On Diaspora: Christianity, Religion, And Secularity*. Eugene, OR: Cascade Books.

Barker, P., and S. Boadi-Siaw. 2003. *Changed by the Word: The Story of Scripture Union Ghana*. Accra: Scripture Union Ghana, Africa Christian Press, and Asempa Publishers, Christian Council of Ghana.

Basch, L., N.G. Schiller, and C.S. Blanc. 1994. *Nations Unbound: Transnational Projects, Postcolonial Predicaments, and Deterritorialized Nation-States*. Langhorne, PA: Gordon and Breach.

Beidelman, T.O. 1982. *Colonial Evangelism: A Socio-Historical Study of an East African Mission at the Grassroots*. Bloomington: Indiana University Press.

Bell, C. 1992. *Ritual Theory, Ritual Practice*. Oxford: Oxford University Press.

Benjamin, W. 1968. "Theses on the Philosophy of History." In *Illuminations: Essays and Reflections*, edited by Hannah Arendt and translated by Harry Zohn, 255–66. New York: Harcourt, Brace & World.

Berlant, L. 2011. *Cruel Optimism*. Durham, NC: Duke University Press. http://dx.doi.org/10.1215/9780822394716.

Bialecki, J., N. Haynes, and J. Robbins. 2008. "The Anthropology of Christianity." *Religion Compass* 2 (6): 1139–58. http://dx.doi.org/10.1111/j.1749-8171.2008.00116.x.

Bloch, M. 1973. "The Long Term and the Short Term: The Economic and Political Significance of the Morality of Kinship." In *The Character of Kinship*, edited by J. Goody, 75–87. Cambridge: Cambridge University Press.

– 1998. *How We Think They Think: Anthropological Approaches to Cognition, Memory and Literacy*. Boulder, CO: Westview Press.

Boddy, J. 1989. *Wombs and Alien Spirits: Women, Men and the Zar Cult in Northern Sudan*. Madison: University of Wisconsin Press.

– 1998. "Afterword: Embodying Ethnography." In *Bodies and Persons: Comparative Perspectives from Africa and Melanesia*, edited by M. Lambek and A. Strathern, 252–73. Cambridge: Cambridge University Press. http://dx.doi.org/10.1017/CBO9780511802782.012.

Brah, A. 1996. *Cartographies of Diaspora: Contesting Identities*. London: Routledge.

Breidenbach, P.S. 1979. "*Sunsum Edwuma*: The Limits of Classification and the Significance of Events." *Social Research* 46 (1): 63–87.

Bynum, C. 2011. *Christian Materiality: An Essay on Religion in Late Medieval Europe*. New York: Zone Books.

Cannell, F. 2006a. "Introduction: The Anthropology of Christianity." In *The Anthropology of Christianity*, edited by F. Cannell, 1–50. Durham, NC: Duke University Press. http://dx.doi.org/10.1215/9780822388159-001.

– 2006b. "Reading as Gift and Writing as Theft." In *The Anthropology of Christianity*, edited by F. Cannell, 134–62. Durham, NC: Duke University Press.

Caplan, P. 2010. "'Child Sacrifice' in Uganda? The BBC, 'Witch Doctors' and Anthropologists." *Anthropology Today* 26 (2): 4–7. http://dx.doi.org/10.1111/j.1467-8322.2010.00720.x.

Carsten, J. 2000. *Cultures of Relatedness: New Approaches to the Study of Kinship*. Cambridge: Cambridge University Press.

Chigbundu, A. 1991. *Loose Him & Let Him Go!* Benin City, NG: Voice of Freedom Publications.

Church of Pentecost, The (CoP). 2000. *The Church of Pentecost Songs. Compiled for Council Meetings, Retreats, Conferences, Conventions, etc.* English and Twi. Addendum: "God's First Covenant and Promises with The Church of Pentecost (Revealed)." Accra: Pentecost Press.
– 2008. *37th Session of the General Council Meetings.* Accra: Pentecost Press.
– n.d. *The Church of Pentecost International Missions: Know Your Mission Areas.* Accra: Pentecost Press.
Clark, G. 1994. *Onions Are My Husband: Survival and Accumulation by West African Market Women.* Chicago: University of Chicago Press. http://dx.doi.org/10.7208/chicago/9780226107769.001.0001.
Clarke, K.M. 2004. *Mapping Yoruba Networks: Power and Agency in the Making of Transnational Communities.* Durham, NC: Duke University Press. http://dx.doi.org/10.1215/9780822385417.
Clifford, J. 1994. "Diasporas." *Cultural Anthropology* 9 (3): 302–38. http://dx.doi.org/10.1525/can.1994.9.3.02a00040.
Coleman, S. 2000. *The Globalisation of Charismatic Christianity: Spreading the Gospel of Prosperity.* Cambridge: Cambridge University Press. http://dx.doi.org/10.1017/CBO9780511488221.
– 2004. "The Charismatic Gift." *Journal of the Royal Anthropological Institute* 10 (2): 421–42. http://dx.doi.org/10.1111/j.1467-9655.2004.00196.x.
– 2010a. "An Anthropological Apologetics." *South Atlantic Quarterly* 109 (4): 791–810. http://dx.doi.org/10.1215/00382876-2010-017.
– 2010b. "Constructing the Globe: A Charismatic Sublime." In *Traveling Spirits. Migrants, Markets, and Moralities,* edited by K. Krause and G. Huewelmeier, 186–202. New York: Routledge.
– 2011a. "Introduction: Negotiating Personhood in African Christianities." *Journal of Religion in Africa. Religion en Afrique* 41 (3): 243–55. http://dx.doi.org/10.1163/157006611X592296.
– 2011b. "Prosperity Unbound? Debating the 'Sacrificial Economy.'" In *The Economics of Religion: Anthropological Approaches,* edited by L. Obadia, and D.C. Wood, 23–45. Research in Economic Anthropology 31. Bingley, UK: Emerald Group Publishing.
Comaroff, J., and J.L. Comaroff. 1991. *Of Revelation and Revolution: Christianity, Colonialism, and Consciousness in South Africa,* Vol. 1. Chicago: University Chicago Press. http://dx.doi.org/10.7208/chicago/9780226114477.001.0001.
– 1997. *Of Revelation and Revolution: The Dialectics of Modernity on a South African Frontier,* Vol. 2. Chicago: University of Chicago Press. http://dx.doi.org/10.7208/chicago/9780226114675.001.0001.
– 1999. "Occult Economies and the Violence of Abstraction: Notes from the South African Postcolony." *American Ethnologist* 26 (2): 279–303.

- 2000. "Millennial Capitalism: First Thoughts on a Second Coming." *Public Culture* 12 (2): 291–343.
Cooper, F. 2005. *Colonialism in Question: Theory, Knowledge, History*. Berkeley: University of California Press.
Corten, A., and R. Marshall-Fratani, eds. 2001. *Between Babel and Pentecost: Transnational Pentecostalism in Africa and Latin America*. Bloomington: Indiana University Press.
Csordas, T.J. 2007. "Introduction: Modalities of Transnational Transcendence." *Anthropological Theory* 7 (3): 259–72. http://dx.doi.org/10.1177/1463499607080188.
Cunningham, H. 1999. "The Ethnography of Transnational Social Activism: Understanding the Global as Local Practice." *American Ethnologist* 26 (3): 583–604. http://dx.doi.org/10.1525/ae.1999.26.3.583.
Daneel, M.L. 1974. *Church Growth: Causative Factors and Recruitment Techniques*. Vol. II of *Old and New in Southern Shona Independent Churches*. The Hague: Mouton de Gruyter.
Dave, N. 2012. *Queer Activism in India: A Story in the Anthropology of Ethics*. Durham, NC: Duke University Press. http://dx.doi.org/10.1215/9780822395683.
Debrunner, H.W. 1959. *Witchcraft in Ghana: A Study on the Belief in Destructive Witches and Its Effects on the Akan Tribes*. Kumasi, GH: Presbyterian Book Depot.
- 1967. *A History of Christianity in Ghana*. Accra: Waterville Publishing House.
Delanty, G. 2009. *The Cosmopolitan Imagination: The Renewal of Critical Social Theory*. Cambridge: Cambridge University Press.
Derrida, J. 2000. "Hostipitality." Translated by B. Stocker and F. Morlock. *Angelaki: Journal of the Theoretical Humanities* 5 (3): 3–18. http://dx.doi.org/10.1080/09697250020034706.
de Witte, M. 2012. "Television and the Gospel of Entertainment in Ghana." *Exchange* 41 (2): 144–64. http://dx.doi.org/10.1163/157254312X633233.
Dick, H.P. 2010. "Imagined Lives and Modernist Chronotopes in Mexican Nonmigrant Discourse." *American Ethnologist* 37 (2): 275–90. http://dx.doi.org/10.1111/j.1548-1425.2010.01255.x.
Dombrowski, K. 2001. *Against Culture: Development, Politics and Religion in Indian Alaska*. Lincoln: University of Nebraska Press.
Dumont, L. 1985. "A Modified View of Our Origins: The Christian Beginnings of Modern Individualism." In *The Category of the Person: Anthropology, Philosophy, History*, edited by M. Carrithers, S. Collins, and S. Lukes, 93–122. Cambridge: Cambridge University Press.
Durkheim, E. (1912) 1995. *The Elementary Forms of Religious Life*. New York: The Free Press.

Eisenlohr, P. 2006. *Little India: Diaspora, Time and Ethnolinguistic Belonging in Hindu Mauritius*. Berkeley: University of California Press.

Elisha, O. 2011. *Moral Ambition: Mobilization and Social Outreach in Evangelical Megachurches*. Berkeley: University of California Press.

Engelke, M. 2002. "The Problem of Belief: Evans-Pritchard and Victor Turner on 'The Inner Life.'" *Anthropology Today* 18 (6): 3–8. http://dx.doi.org/10.1111/1467-8322.00146.

– 2004. "Discontinuity and the Discourse of Conversion." *Journal of Religion in Africa. Religion en Afrique* 34 (1): 82–109. http://dx.doi.org/10.1163/157006604323056732.

– 2007. *A Problem of Presence: Beyond Scripture in an African Church*. Berkeley: University of California Press.

Englund, H. 2002a. "Ethnography after Globalism: Migration and Emplacement in Malawi." *American Ethnologist* 29 (2): 261–86. http://dx.doi.org/10.1525/ae.2002.29.2.261.

– 2002b. "The Village in the City, the City in the Village: Migrants in Lilongwe." *Journal of Southern African Studies* 28 (1), Special Issue: Malawi, 137–154.

– 2004. "Cosmopolitanism and the Devil in Malawi." *Ethnos* 69 (3): 293–316. http://dx.doi.org/10.1080/0014184042000260008.

– 2007a. "Pentecostalism beyond Belief: Trust and Democracy in a Malawian Township." *Africa: Journal of the International African Institute* 77 (04): 477–99. http://dx.doi.org/10.3366/afr.2007.77.4.477.

– 2007b. "Witchcraft and the Limits of Mass Mediation in Malawi." *Journal of the Royal Anthropological Institute* 13 (2): 295–311. http://dx.doi.org/10.1111/j.1467-9655.2007.00429.x.

Eni, E. 1987. *Delivered from the Powers of Darkness*. Ibadan, NG: Scripture Union Press.

Eto, V. 1981. *How I Served Satan until Jesus Christ Delivered Me: A True Account of My Twenty-One Years Experience as an Agent of Darkness and of My Deliverance by the Power Arm of God in Jesus Christ*. Warri, NG: Christian Shalom Mission.

Evans-Pritchard, E.E. 1937. *Witchcraft, Oracles and Magic among the Azande*. Oxford: Clarendon Press.

Evens, T.M.S. 2005. "Some Ontological Implications of Situational Analysis." *Social Analysis* 49 (3): 46–60. http://dx.doi.org/10.3167/015597705780275066.

Fanon, F. (1952) 1967. *Black Skin, White Masks*. New York: Grove Press.

Faubion, J.D. 2001. "Toward an Anthropology of Ethics: Foucault and the Pedagogies of Autopoiesis." *Representations (Berkeley, Calif.)* 74 (1): 83–104. http://dx.doi.org/10.1525/rep.2001.74.1.83.

Fortes, M. 1950. "Kinship and Marriage among the Ashanti." In *African Systems of Kinship and Marriage*, edited by A.R. Radcliffe-Brown and D. Forde, 252–284. London: Oxford University Press.

Foucault, M. 1993. "About the Beginning of the Hermeneutics of the Self: Two Lectures at Dartmouth." Transcribed and edited by M. Blasius and T. Keenan. Introductory note by M. Blasius. *Political Theory* 21 (2): 198–227.

– 1997a. "The Ethics of the Concern of the Self as a Practice of Freedom." In *Ethics: Subjectivity and Truth*, edited by P. Rabinow, 281–301. New York: The New York Press.

– 1997b. "Friendship as a Way of Life." In *Ethics: Subjectivity and Truth*, edited by P. Rabinow, 135–40. New York: The New York Press.

– 1997c. "Technologies of the Self." In *Ethics: Subjectivity and Truth*, edited by P. Rabinow, 223–52. New York: The New York Press.

Fumanti, M. 2010. "'Virtuous Citizenship': Ethnicity and Encapsulation among Akan-Speaking Ghanaian Methodists in London." *African Diaspora* 3 (1): 12–41. http://dx.doi.org/10.1163/187254610X505655.

Fumanti, M., and P. Werbner. 2010. "The Moral Economy of the African Diaspora: Citizenship, Networking and Permeable Ethnicity." *African Diaspora* 3 (1): 2–11. http://dx.doi.org/10.1163/187254610X508454.

Geschiere, P. 1997. *The Modernity of Witchcraft: Politics and the Occult in Postcolonial Africa*. Charlottesville: University Press of Virginia.

Ghana Evangelism Committee. 1993. *National Church Survey: Facing the Unfinished Task of the Church in Ghana*. 1993 update. Accra: Ghana Evangelism Committee.

Ghana Pentecostal Council (GPC). 2000. "Editorial: Duty to God and Man." *Pentecostal Voice* 1 (2): 4.

Gifford, P. 2004. *Ghana's New Christianity: Pentecostalism in a Globalising African Economy*. London: Hurst & Co.

Gordon, A. 1997. *Ghostly Matters: Haunting and the Sociological Imagination*. Minneapolis: University of Minnesota Press.

Gow, P. 2006. "Forgetting Conversion: The Summer Institute of Linguistics Mission in the Piro Lived World." In *The Anthropology of Christianity*, edited by F. Cannell, 211–39. Durham, NC: Duke University Press. http://dx.doi.org/10.1215/9780822388159-008.

Graveling, E. 2010. "'That Is Not Religion, That Is the Gods': Ways of Conceiving Religious Practices in Rural Ghana." *Culture and Religion* 11 (1): 31–50. http://dx.doi.org/10.1080/14755610903528838.

Guyer, J. 2007. "Prophecy and the Near Future: Thoughts on Macroeconomic, Evangelical, and Punctuated Time." *American Ethnologist* 34 (3): 409–21. http://dx.doi.org/10.1525/ae.2007.34.3.409.

Gyekye, K. (1987) 1995. *An Essay on African Philosophical Thought: The Akan Conceptual Scheme*. Revised Edition. Philadelphia, PA: Temple University Press.

– 1992. "Person and Community in African Thought." In *Person and Community: Ghanaian Philosophical Studies I*, edited by K. Wiredu and K. Gyekye, 101–22. Washington, DC: CIPSH/UNESCO, The Council for Research in Values and Philosophy.

Hackett, R.I.J. 1998. "Charismatic/Pentecostal Appropriation of Media Technologies in Nigeria and Ghana." *Journal of Religion in Africa. Religion en Afrique* 28 (3): 258–77. http://dx.doi.org/10.1163/157006698X00026.

Hagan, G.P. 2000. "Modern Technology, Traditional Mysticism and Ethics in Akan Culture." In *Ghana: Changing Values/Changing Technologies. Ghanaian Philosophical Studies, II*, edited by H. Lauer, 31–52. Washington, DC: CIPSH/UNESCO, The Council for Research on Values and Philosophy.

Hann, C. 2007. "The Anthropology of Christianity Per Se." *European Journal of Sociology* 48 (3): 383–410. http://dx.doi.org/10.1017/S0003975607000410.

Hanson, S. 2002. *A History of Pentecostalism in Ghana (1900–2002)*. Accra: Heritage Graphix.

Harding, S.F. 2000. *The Book of Jerry Falwell: Fundamentalist Language and Politics*. Princeton, NJ: Princeton University Press.

Hardt, M., and A. Negri. 2001. *Empire*. Cambridge, MA: Harvard University Press.

Harris, H. 2006. *Yoruba in Diaspora: An African Church in London*. New York: Pelgrave Macmillan. http://dx.doi.org/10.1057/9780230601048.

Harris, O. 2006. "The Eternal Return of Conversion: Christianity as Contested Domain in Highland Bolivia." In *The Anthropology of Christianity*, edited by F. Cannell, 51–76. Durham, NC: Duke University Press.

Hastings, A. 1979. *A History of African Christianity 1950–1975*. Cambridge: Cambridge University Press.

Heidegger, M. 1977. *The Question Concerning Technology and Other Essays*. Translated and with an Introduction by William Lovitt. New York: Harper Perennial.

Heyman, J.M., and H. Campbell. 2009. "The Anthropology of Global Flows: A Critical Reading of Appadurai's 'Disjuncture and Difference in the Global Cultural Economy.'" *Anthropological Theory* 9 (2): 131–48. http://dx.doi.org/10.1177/1463499609105474.

Hirschkind, C. 2006. *The Ethical Soundscape: Cassette Sermons and Islamic Counterpublics*. New York: Columbia University Press.

Hollenweger, W.J. 1972. *The Pentecostals: The Charismatic Movement in the Churches*. London: SCM Press.

Horst, H. 2007. "'You Can't Be in Two Places at Once': Rethinking Transnationalism through Jamaican Return Migration." *Identities: Global Studies in Culture and Power* 14 (1–2): 63–83.

Horton, R. 1960. "A Definition of Religion and Its Uses." *Journal of the Royal Anthropological Institute of Great Britain and Ireland* 90 (2): 201–26.

Humphrey, C., and J. Laidlaw. 1994. *The Archetypal Actions of Ritual: A Theory of Ritual Illustrated by the Jain Rite of Worship*. Oxford: Clarendon Press.

Hunt, S., and N. Lightly. 2001. "The British Black Pentecostal 'Revival': Identity and Belief in the 'New' Nigerian Churches." *Ethnic and Racial Studies* 24 (1): 104–24. http://dx.doi.org/10.1080/014198701750052523.

Hüwelmeier, G., and K. Krause, eds. 2010. *Travelling Spirits. Migrants, Markets, and Moralities*. New York: Routledge.

James, W., and D.H. Johnson. 1988. *Vernacular Christianity: Essays in the Social Anthropology of Religion Presented to Godfrey Lienhardt*. JASO Occasional Papers No. 7. Oxford: JASO.

Jenkins, P. 2007. *The Next Christendom: The Coming of Global Christianity*. Oxford: Oxford University Press.

Kalilombe, P. 1997. "Black Christianity in Britain." *Ethnic and Racial Studies* 20 (2): 306–24. http://dx.doi.org/10.1080/01419870.1997.9993963.

Kapferer, B. 2005. "Situations, Crisis, and the Anthropology of the Concrete: The Contribution of Max Gluckman." *Social Analysis* 49 (3): 85–122. http://dx.doi.org/10.3167/015597705780275110.

– 2010. "Introduction: In the Event – Toward an Anthropology of Generic Moments." *Social Analysis* 54 (3): 1–27. http://dx.doi.org/10.3167/sa.2010.540301.

Keane, W. 1998. "Calvin in the Tropics: Objects and Subjects in the Religious Frontier." In *Border Fetishism: Material Objects in Unstable Spaces*, edited by P. Spyer, 13–34. London: Routledge.

– 2003. "Semiotics and the Social Analysis of Material Things." *Language and Communication* 23 (2–3): 409–23.

– 2007. *Christian Moderns: Freedom and Fetish in the Mission Encounter*. Berkeley: University of California Press.

Kirsch, T.G. 2008. *Spirits and Letters: Reading, Writing and Charisma in African Christianity*. New York: Berghahn.

Klaits, F. 2010. *Death in a Church of Life: Moral Passion during Botswana's Time of AIDS*. Berkeley: University of California Press.

– 2011. "Introduction: Self, Other and God in African Christianities." *Journal of Religion in Africa. Religion en Afrique* 41 (2): 143–53. http://dx.doi.org/10.1163/157006611X569210.

Koser, K. 2003. "New African Diasporas: An Introduction." In *New African Diasporas*, edited by K. Koser, 1–16. London: Routledge.

Kumah, D.P. 2000. *Is Ghana under a Curse?* Accra: SonLife Books.

Laidlaw, J. 2002. "For an Anthropology of Ethics and Freedom." *Journal of the Royal Anthropological Institute* 8 (2): 311–32. http://dx.doi.org/10.1111/1467-9655.00110.

Lambek, M. 1981. *Human Spirits: A Cultural Account of Trance in Mayotte*. Cambridge: Cambridge University Press.

– 1992. "Taboo as Cultural Practice among Malagasy Speakers." *Man* (New Series) 27 (2): 245–66. http://dx.doi.org/10.2307/2804053.

– 2000. "The Anthropology of Religion and the Quarrel between Poetry and Philosophy." *Current Anthropology* 41 (3): 309–20. http://dx.doi.org/10.1086/300143.

– 2007. "Sacrifice and the Problem of Beginning: Mediations from Sakalava Mythopraxis." *Journal of the Royal Anthropological Institute* 13 (1): 19–38. http://dx.doi.org/10.1111/j.1467-9655.2007.00411.x.

– 2008. "Value and Virtue." *Anthropological Theory* 8 (2): 133–57. http://dx.doi.org/10.1177/1463499608090788.

– 2010. "Introduction." In *Ordinary Ethics: Anthropology, Language, and Action*, edited by M. Lambek, 1–36. New York: Fordham University Press.

Larbi, E.K. 2001. *Pentecostalism: The Eddies of Ghanaian Christianity*. Accra: Centre Pentecostal Charismatic and Studies.

Leonard, C. 1989. *A Giant in Ghana*. Chichester, UK: New Wine Press.

Levitt, P. 2003. "'You Know, Abraham Was Really the First Immigrant': Religion and Transnational Migration." *International Migration Review* 37 (3): 847–73. http://dx.doi.org/10.1111/j.1747-7379.2003.tb00160.x.

Lindhardt, M. 2010. "'If You Are Saved You Cannot Forget Your Parents': Agency, Power, and Social Repositioning in Tanzanian Born-Again Christianity." *Journal of Religion in Africa. Religion en Afrique* 40 (3): 240–72. http://dx.doi.org/10.1163/157006610X530330.

LiPuma, E. 1998. "Modernity and Forms of Personhood in Melanesia." In *Bodies and Persons: Comparative Perspectives from Africa and Melanesia*, edited by M. Lambek and A. Strathern, 53–79. Cambridge: Cambridge University Press.

Long, N. 1968. *Social Change and the Individual: A Study of the Social and Religious Responses to Innovation in a Zambian Rural Community*. Manchester, UK: Manchester University Press.

Luhrmann, T. 2004. "Metakinesis: How God Becomes Intimate in Contemporary U.S. Christianity." *American Anthropologist* 106 (3): 518–28. http://dx.doi.org/10.1525/aa.2004.106.3.518.

MacIntyre, A. 2007. *After Virtue: A Study in Moral Theory.* London: Duckworth.

Mahmood, S. 2005. *Politics of Piety: The Islamic Revival and the Feminist Subject.* Princeton, NJ: Princeton University Press.

Marriot, M. 1976. "Hindu Transactions: Diversity without Dualism." In *Transaction and Meaning: Directions in the Anthropology of Exchange and Symbolic Behavior,* edited by B. Kapferer, 109–37. Philadelphia, PA: Institute for the Study of Human Issues.

Marshall, R. 2009. *Political Spiritualities: The Pentecostal Revolution in Nigeria.* Chicago: University of Chicago Press. http://dx.doi.org/10.7208/chicago/9780226507149.001.0001.

– 2010. "The Sovereignty of Miracles: Pentecostal Political Theology in Nigeria." *Constellations (Oxford, England)* 17 (2): 197–223. http://dx.doi.org/10.1111/j.1467-8675.2010.00585.x.

Massumi, B. 2002. *Parables for the Virtual: Movement, Affect, Sensation.* Durham, NC: Duke University Press. http://dx.doi.org/10.1215/9780822383574.

Mattingly, C. 2012. "Two Virtue Ethics and the Anthropology of Morality." *Anthropological Theory* 12 (2): 161–84. http://dx.doi.org/10.1177/1463499612455284.

Mauss, M. 1985. "A Category of the Human Mind: The Notion of Self." In *The Category of the Person: Anthropology, Philosophy, History,* edited by M. Carrithers, S. Collins, and S. Lukes, translated by W.D. Halls, 1–25. Cambridge: Cambridge University Press.

– 1990. *The Gift: The Form and Reason for Exchange in Archaic Societies.* London, New York: W.W. Norton Publishing.

– 2008. *On Prayer.* Translated by Susan Leslie. Edited and with an Introduction by W.S.F. Pickering. New York: Berghahn Books.

Maxwell, D. 1998. "'Delivered from the Spirit of Poverty?' Pentecostalism, Prosperity, and Modernity in Zimbabwe." *Journal of Religion in Africa. Religion en Afrique* 28 (3): 350–73.

– 1999. "Historicizing Christian Independency: The Southern African Pentecostal Movement ca 1908–1960." *Journal of African History* 39 (2): 243–64.

– 2006. *African Gifts of the Spirit: Pentecostalism and the Rise of a Zimbabwean Transnational Religious Movement.* Oxford: James Currey Press.

Mbembe, A. 2002. "On the Power of the False." *Public Culture* 14 (3): 629–41.

McCaskie, T.C. 2000. *Asante Identities: History and Modernity in an African Village, 1850–1950.* London: Edinburgh University Press; Bloomington: Indiana University Press.

McGregor, J. 2007. "'Joining the BBC (British Bottom Cleaners)': Zimbabwean Migrants and the UK Care Industry." *Journal of Ethnic and Migration Studies* 33 (5): 801–24. http://dx.doi.org/10.1080/13691830701359249.

Mercer, C. B. Page, and M. Evans. 2008. *Development and the African Diaspora: Place and the Politics of Home*. London: Zed Books.

Meyer, B. 1995. "Delivered from the Powers of Darkness: Confessions of Satanic Riches in Christian Ghana." *Africa: Journal of the International African Institute* 65 (2): 236–55. http://dx.doi.org/10.2307/1161192.

– 1998a. "Commodities and the Power of Prayer: Pentecostalist Attitudes towards Consumption in Contemporary Ghana." *Development and Change* 29 (4): 751–76. http://dx.doi.org/10.1111/1467-7660.00098.

– 1998b. "Make a Complete Break with the Past: Memory and Postcolonial Modernity in Ghanaian Pentecostalist Discourse." *Journal of Religion in Africa. Religion en Afrique* 28 (3): 316–49.

– 1999. *Translating the Devil: Religion and Modernity among the Ewe in Ghana*. International African Library 21. Edinburgh: Edinburgh University Press.

– 2004a. "Christianity in Africa: From African Independent to Pentecostal-Charismatic Churches." *Annual Review of Anthropology* 33 (1): 447–74. http://dx.doi.org/10.1146/annurev.anthro.33.070203.143835.

– 2004b. "'Praise the Lord': Popular Cinema and Pentecostalite Style in Ghana's New Public Sphere." *American Ethnologist* 31 (1): 92–110. http://dx.doi.org/10.1525/ae.2004.31.1.92.

– 2006. "Religious Revelation, Secrecy, and the Limits of Visual Representation." *Anthropological Theory* 6: 431–53.

– 2009. "Response to ter Haar and Ellis." *Africa: Journal of the International African Institute* 79 (03): 413–15. http://dx.doi.org/10.3366/E0001972009000886.

– 2010. "Pentecostalism and Globalization." In *Studying Global Pentecostalism: Theories and Methods*, edited by A. Anderson, M. Bergunder, A. Droogers, and C. van der Laan, 113–30. Berkeley: University of California Press.

– 2011. "Mediation and Immediacy: Sensational Forms, Semiotic Ideologies and the Question of the Medium." *Social Anthropology* 19 (1): 23–39.

Miller, J. 2003. *Missionary Zeal and Institutional Control: Organizational Contradictions in the Basel Mission on the Gold Coast, 1828–1917*. London: Routledge.

Mitchell, J.C. 1956. *The Kalela Dance: Aspects of Social Relationships among Urban Africans in Northern Rhodesia*. Rhodes-Livingstone Paper No. 27. Manchester, UK: Manchester University Press.

Moore, H.L. 2004. "Global Anxieties: Concept-Metaphors and Pre-Theoretical Commitments in Anthropology." *Anthropological Theory* 4 (1): 71–88. http://dx.doi.org/10.1177/1463499604040848.

Moore, S.F. 1975. "Epilogue." In *Symbol and Politics in Communal Ideology: Cases and Questions*, edited by S. Falk Moore and B.G. Myerhoff, 210–40. Ithaca, NY: Cornell University Press.

– 1999. "Reflections on the Comaroff Lecture." *American Ethnologist* 26 (2): 304–6.

Mosko, M. 2010. "Partible Penitents: Dividual Personhood and Christian Practice in Melanesia and the West." *Journal of the Royal Anthropological Institute* 16 (2): 215–40. http://dx.doi.org/10.1111/j.1467-9655.2010.01618.x.

Napolitano, V., and K. Norget. 2009. "Economies of Sanctity." *Postscripts: The Journal of Sacred Texts and Contemporary Worlds* 5 (3): 251–64.

Newell, S. 2007. "Pentecostal Witchcraft: Neoliberal Possession and Demonic Discourse in Ivoirian Pentecostal Churches." *Journal of Religion in Africa. Religion en Afrique* 37 (4): 461–90. http://dx.doi.org/10.1163/157006 607X230517.

Nieswand, B. 2005. "Charismatic Christianity in the Context of Migration: Social Status, the Experience of Migration and the Construction of Selves among Ghanaian Migrants in Berlin." In *Religion in the Context of African Migration*, edited by A. Adogame and C. Weissköppel, 243–265. Bayreuth African Studies Series 75. Bayreuth, DE: Eckhard Breitinger.

Olupona, J.K. and R. Gemignani. 2007. *African Immigrant Religions in America*. New York: New York University Press.

Omenyo, C. 2002. *Pentecost Outside Pentecostalism: A Study of the Development of Charismatic Renewal in the Mainline Churches in Ghana*. Zoetemeer, NL: Boekencentrum.

– 2005. "From the Fringes to the Centre: Pentecostalization of the Mainline Churches in Ghana." *Exchange* 34 (1): 39–60. http://dx.doi.org/10.1163/ 1572543053506338.

O'Neill, K.L. 2009. "But Our Citizenship Is in Heaven: A Proposal for the Future Study of Christian Citizenship in the Global South." *Citizenship Studies* 13 (4): 333–48. http://dx.doi.org/10.1080/13621020903011047.

– 2010. *City of God: Christian Citizenship in Postwar Guatemala*. Berkeley: University of California Press.

Ong, A. 1996. "Cultural Citizenship as Subject-Making: Immigrants Negotiate Racial and Cultural Boundaries in the United States." *Current Anthropology* 37 (5): 737–62. http://dx.doi.org/10.1086/204560.

Onyinah, O. 1994. *Ancestral Curses*. Accra: Pentecost Press.

– 1995. *Overcoming Demons*. Accra: Pentecost Press.

– 2002. "Akan Witchcraft and the Concept of Exorcism in the Church of Pentecost." PhD diss., University of Birmingham.

Opoku, K.A. 1978. *West African Traditional Religion*. Accra: FEP International Private Ltd.

Pandolfo, S. 2007. "'The Burning': Finitude and the Politico-Theological Imagination of Illegal Immigration." *Anthropological Theory* 7 (3): 329–63. http:// dx.doi.org/10.1177/1463499607080194.

Parish, J. 2000. "From the Body to the Wallet: Conceptualizing Akan Witch-craft at Home and Abroad." (New Series) *Journal of the Royal Anthropological Institute* 6 (3): 487–500. http://dx.doi.org/10.1111/1467-9655.00028.

– 2001. "Black Market, Free Market: Anti-Witchcraft Shrines and Fetishes among the Akan." In *Magical Interpretations, Material Realities: Modernity, Witchcraft, and the Occult in Postcolonial Africa*, edited by H.L. Moore and T. Sanders, 118–35. London, New York: Routledge.

Parry, J. 1986. "The Gift, the Indian Gift and the 'Indian Gift.'" Malinowski Lecture, 1985. *Journal of the Royal Anthropological Institute* 21: 453–73.

Peel, J.D.Y. 1968. *Aladura: A Religious Movement among the Yoruba*. London: Oxford University Press.

– 1989. "Review of 'Vernacular Christianity: Essays in the Social Anthro-pology of Religion Presented to Godfrey Lienhardt' by W. James and D.H. Johnson." *Africa: Journal of the International African Institute* 59 (3), 422–4. http://www.jstor.org/stable/1160256.

– 1995. "For Who Hath Despised the Day of Small Things? Missionary Narratives and Historical Anthropology." *Comparative Studies in Society and History* 37 (3): 581–607. http://dx.doi.org/10.1017/S0010417500019824.

– 2003. *Religious Encounter and the Making of the Yoruba*. Bloomington: Indiana University Press.

– 2004. "Divergent Modes of Religiosity in Africa." In *Ritual and Memory: Toward a Comparative Anthropology of Religion*, edited by H. Whitehouse and J. Laidlaw, 11–30. Walnut Creek, CA: AltaMira Press.

Peil, M. 1995. "Ghanaians Abroad." *African Affairs* 94: 345–67.

Pobee, J.S. 1991. *Religion and Politics in Ghana*. Accra: Asempa Publishers.

Pouillon, J. 1982. "Remark on the Verb 'To Believe.'" In *Between Belief and Transgression*, edited by M. Izard and P. Smith, 1–8. Chicago: University of Chicago Press.

Povinelli, E. 2011. *Economies of Abandonment: Social Belonging and Endurance in Late Liberalism*. Durham, NC: Duke University Press. http://dx.doi.org/10.1215/9780822394570.

Prince, D. 1986. *From Curse to Blessing: A Transcription of the Radio Program Today with Derek Prince*. Lauderdale: Derek Prince Ministries.

Quayson, A. 2002. "Obverse Denominations?" *Public Culture* 14 (3): 585–8.

Ramji, H. 2006. "British Indians 'Returning Home': An Exploration of Transna-tional Belonging." *Sociology* 40 (4): 645–62. http://dx.doi.org/10.1177/0038038506065152.

Ranger, T.O. 2007. "Scotland Yard in the Bush: Medicine Murders, Child Witches and the Construction of the Occult: A Literature Review." *Africa:*

Journal of the International African Institute 77 (02): 272–83. http://dx.doi.org/
10.3366/afr.2007.77.2.272.

Rappaport, R. 1999. *Ritual and Religion in the Making of Humanity*. Cambridge:
Cambridge University Press. http://dx.doi.org/10.1017/
CBO9780511814686.

Rattray, R.S. 1927. *Religion and Art in Ashanti*. Oxford: Clarendon Press.

Robbins, J. 2003a. "On the Paradoxes of Global Pentecostalism and the Perils
of Continuity Thinking." *Religion* 33 (3): 221–31. http://dx.doi.org/10.1016/
S0048-721X(03)00055-1.

– 2003b. "What Is a Christian? Notes toward an Anthropology of Christianity." *Religion* 33 (3): 191–9.

– 2004a. *Becoming Sinners: Christianity and Moral Torment in a Papua New
Guinea Society*. Berkeley: University of California Press.

– 2004b. "The Globalization of Pentecostal and Charismatic Christianity."
Annual Review of Anthropology 33 (1): 117–43. http://dx.doi.org/10.1146/
annurev.anthro.32.061002.093421.

– 2007a. "Between Reproduction and Freedom: Morality, Value, and Radical
Cultural Change." *Ethnos* 72 (3): 293–314. http://dx.doi.org/10.1080/
00141840701576919.

– 2007b. "Continuity Thinking and the Problem of Christian Culture: Belief,
Time and the Anthropology of Christianity." *Current Anthropology* 48 (1):
5–38. http://dx.doi.org/10.1086/508690.

– 2009a. "Pentecostal Networks and the Spirit of Globalization: On the Social
Productivity of Ritual Forms." *Social Analysis* 53 (1): 55–66. http://dx.doi
.org/10.3167/sa.2009.530104.

– 2009b. "Value, Structure, and the Range of Possibilities: A Response to
Zigon." *Ethnos* 74 (2): 277–85. http://dx.doi.org/10.1080/
00141840902940500.

– 2010a. "Anthropology, Pentecostalism, and the New Paul: Conversion,
Event, and Social Transformation." *South Atlantic Quarterly* 109 (4): 633–52.
http://dx.doi.org/10.1215/00382876-2010-010.

– 2010b. "Is the *Trans-* in *Transnational* the *Trans-* in *Transcendental*? On Alterity
and the Sacred in the Age of Globalization." In *Transnational Transcendence:
Essays on Religion and Globalization*, edited by T.J. Csordas, 55–72. Berkeley:
University of California Press.

Rothchild, D., ed. 1991. *Ghana: The Political Economy of Recovery*. Boulder, CO:
L. Rienner Publishers.

Sanders, T. 2003a. "Imagining the Dark Continent: The Met, the Media and the
Thames Torso." *Cambridge Anthropology* 23 (3): 53–66.

2003b. "Invisible Hands and Visible Goods: Revealed and Concealed Economies in Millennial Tanzania." In *Transparency and Conspiracy: Ethnographies
of Suspicion in the New World Order*, edited by H.G. West and T. Sanders,
148–74. Durham, NC: Duke University Press. http://dx.doi.org/10.1215/
9780822384854-005.

Sanders, T., and H.G. West. 2003. "Revealed and Concealed in the New World
Order." In *Transparency and Conspiracy: Ethnographies of Suspicion in the New
World Order*, edited by H.G. West and T. Sanders, 1–37. Durham, NC: Duke
University Press.

Schiller, N.G., and G.E. Fouron. 2001. *Georges Woke Up Laughing: Long-Distance
Nationalism and the Search for Home*. Durham, NC: Duke University Press.
http://dx.doi.org/10.1215/9780822383239.

Shaw, R. 2007. "Displacing Violence: Making Pentecostal Memory in Postwar
Sierra Leone." *Cultural Anthropology* 22 (1): 66–93. http://dx.doi.org/
10.1525/can.2007.22.1.66.

Shaw, R., and C. Stewart. 1994. *Syncretism/Anti-Syncretism: The Politics of Religious Synthesis*. London: Routledge.

Shipley, J.W. 2009. "Comedians, Pastors, and the Miraculous Agency of
Charisma in Ghana." *Cultural Anthropology* 24 (3): 523–52. http://dx.doi.
org/10.1111/j.1548-1360.2009.01039.x.

Shoaps, R. 2002. "'Pray Earnestly': The Textual Construction of Personal
Involvement in Pentecostal Prayer and Song." *Journal of Linguistic Anthropology* 12 (1): 34–71. http://dx.doi.org/10.1525/jlin.2002.12.1.34.

Smith, M.P., and L.E. Guarnizo, eds. 1998. *Transnationalism from Below*. New
Brunswick, NJ: Transaction.

Strathern, M. 1988. *The Gender of the Gift*. Berkeley: University of California
Press.

Street, A. 2010. "Belief as Relational Action: Christianity and Cultural Change
in Papua New Guinea." *Journal of the Royal Anthropological Institute* 16 (2):
260–78. http://dx.doi.org/10.1111/j.1467-9655.2010.01624.x.

Stromberg, P.G. 1993. *Language and Self-Transformation: A Study of the Christian
Conversion Narrative*. Cambridge: Cambridge University Press.

Synan, V. 1997. *The Holiness-Pentecostal Tradition: Charismatic Movements in the
Twentieth Century*. Grand Rapids, MI: Eerdmans.

ter Haar, G. 1998. *Halfway to Paradise: African Christians in Europe*. Cardiff:
Cardiff Academic Press.

ter Haar, G., and S. Ellis. 2009. "The Occult Does Not Exist: A Response to
Terence Ranger." *Africa: Journal of the International African Institute* 79 (03):
399–412. http://dx.doi.org/10.3366/E0001972009000874.

Tomlinson, M., and M. Engelke. 2006. "Meaning, Anthropology, Christianity." In *The Limits of Meaning: Case Studies in the Anthropology of Christianity*, edited by M. Engelke and M. Tomlinson, 1–38. New York: Berghahn.

Turner, V.W. 1957. *Schism and Continuity in an African Society: A Study of Ndembu Social Life*. Manchester, UK: Manchester University Press.

– 1967. "Betwixt and Between: The Liminal Period in 'Rites de Passage.'" In *The Forest of Symbols: Aspects of Ndembu Ritual*. Ithaca, NY: Cornell University Press.

– 1968. *The Drums of Affliction: A Study of Religious Processes among the Ndembu of Zambia*. Oxford: Clarendon Press.

– 1979. *Religious Innovation in Africa: Collected Essays on New Religious Movements*. Boston, MA: G.K. Hall.

– 1985. *On the Edge of the Bush: Anthropology as Experience*. Tuscon: University of Arizona Press.

van Dijk, R.A. 1997. "From Camp to Encompassment: Discourses of Transsubjectivity in the Ghanaian Pentecostal Diaspora." *Journal of Religion in Africa. Religion en Afrique* 27 (2): 135–59. http://dx.doi.org/10.2307/1581683.

– 2001. "Time and Transcultural Technologies of the Self in the Ghanaian Pentecostal Diaspora." In *Between Babel and Pentecost: Transnational Pentecostalism in Africa and Latin America*, edited by A. Corten and R. Marchall-Fratani, 216–34. Bloomington: Indiana University Press.

– 2002a. "Ghanaian Churches in the Netherlands: Religion Mediating a Tense Relationship." In *Merchants, Missionaries and Migrants: 300 Years of Dutch-Ghanaian Relations*, edited by I. van Kessel, 89–97. Amsterdam: KIT Publisher.

– 2002b. "Religion, Reciprocity and Restructuring Family Responsibility in the Ghanaian Pentecostal Diaspora." In *The Transnational Family*, edited by D. Bryceson and U. Vuorela, 173–96. Oxford: Berg.

– 2002c. "The Soul Is the Stranger: Ghanaian Pentecostalism and the Diasporic Contestation of 'Flow' and 'Individuality.'" Special Issue: The Faith Movement: A Global Religious Culture? *Culture and Religion* 3 (1): 49–65. http://dx.doi.org/10.1080/01438300208567182.

– 2004. "Negotiating Marriage: Questions of Morality and Legitimacy in the Ghanaian Pentecostal Diaspora." *Journal of Religion in Africa* 34 (4): 438–67.

van Hear, N. 1998. *New Diasporas: The Mass Exodus, Dispersal and Regrouping of Migrant Communities*. London: UCL Press.

Van Velsen, J. 1967. "The Extended-Case Method and Situational Analysis." In *The Craft of Social Anthropology*, edited by A.L. Epstein, 129–49. London: Tavistock.

Weber, M. (1922) 1963. *The Sociology of Religion*. Boston: Beacon Press.
- 1958. "The Social Psychology of the World Religions." In *From Max Weber: Essays in Sociology*, edited by H.H. Gerth and C. Wright Mills, 267–301. Oxford: Oxford University Press.
Weiss, B. 1998. "Electric Vampires: Haya Rumours of the Commodified Body." In *Bodies and Persons: Comparative Perspectives from Africa and Melanesia*, edited by M. Lambek and A. Strathern, 172–94. Cambridge: Cambridge University Press. http://dx.doi.org/10.1017/CBO9780511802782.008.
Werbner, R. 2011. *Holy Hustler, Schism, and Prophecy: Apostolic Reformation in Botswana*. Berkeley: University of California Press. http://dx.doi.org/10.1525/california/9780520268531.001.0001.
Wilding, R. 2007. "Transnational Ethnographies and Anthropological Imaginings of Migrancy." *Journal of Ethnic and Migration Studies* 33 (2): 331–48. http://dx.doi.org/10.1080/13691830601154310.
Wiredu, K. 1980. *Philosophy and an African Culture*. Cambridge: Cambridge University Press.
- 1996. *Cultural Universals and Particulars: An African Perspective*. Bloomington: Indiana University Press.
Wyllie, R.W. 1980. *The Spirit-Seekers: New Religious Movements in Southern Ghana*. Missoula, MT: Scholars Press.
Zigon, J. 2009. "Within a Range of Possibilities: Morality and Ethics in Social Life." *Ethnos* 74 (2): 251–76. http://dx.doi.org/10.1080/00141840902940492.
- 2011. *"HIV Is God's Blessing": Rehabilitating Morality in Neoliberal Russia*. Berkeley: University of California Press.

Index

ANTHROPOLOGICAL HORIZONS

Editor: Michael Lambek, University of Toronto

Published to date:

An Irish Working Class: Explorations in Political Economy and Hegemony, 1800–1950 / Marilyn Silverman (2001)

The Double Twist: From Ethnography to Morphodynamics / Edited by Pierre Maranda (2001)

The House of Difference: Cultural Politics and National Identity in Canada / Eva Mackey (2002)

Writing and Colonialism in Northern Ghana: The Encounter between the LoDagaa and the 'World on Paper,' 1892–1991 / Sean Hawkins (2002)

Guardians of the Transcendent: An Ethnography of a Jain Ascetic Community / Anne Vallely (2002)

The Hot and the Cold: Ills of Humans and Maize in Native Mexico / Jacques M. Chevalier and Andrés Sánchez Bain (2003)

Figured Worlds: Ontological Obstacles in Intercultural Relations / Edited by John Clammer, Sylvie Poirier, and Eric Schwimmer (2004)

Revenge of the Windigo: The Construction of the Mind and Mental Health of North American Aboriginal Peoples / James B. Waldram (2004)

The Cultural Politics of Markets: Economic Liberalization and Social Change in Nepal / Katherine Neilson Rankin (2004)

A World of Relationships: Itineraries, Dreams, and Events in the Australian Western Desert / Sylvie Poirier (2005)

The Politics of the Past in an Argentine Working-Class Neighbourhood / Lindsay DuBois (2005)

Youth and Identity Politics in South Africa, 1990–1994 / Sibusisiwe Nombuso Dlamini (2005)

Maps of Experience: The Anchoring of Land to Story in Secwepemc Discourse / Andie Diane Palmer (2005)

Beyond Bodies: Rain-Making and Sense-Making in Tanzania / Todd Sanders (2008)

We Are Now a Nation: Croats between 'Home' and 'Homeland' / Daphne N. Winland (2008)

Kaleidoscopic Odessa: History and Place in Post-Soviet Ukraine / Tanya Richardson (2008)

Invaders as Ancestors: On the Intercultural Making and Unmaking of Spanish Colonialism in the Andes / Peter Gose (2008)

From Equality to Inequality: Social Change among Newly Sedentary Lanoh Hunter-Gatherer Traders of Peninsular Malaysia / Csilla Dallos (2011)

Rural Nostalgias and Transnational Dreams: Identity and Modernity among Jat Sikhs / Nicola Mooney (2011)

Dimensions of Development: History, Community, and Change in Allpachico, Peru / Susan Vincent (2012)